ENGLISH LITERATURE

OF THE

EIGHTEENTH CENTURY

*With a Preface on the Relations Between
Literary History and Literary Criticism*

BY

R. C. CHURCHILL, M.A.

AUTHOR OF "ENGLISH LITERATURE OF THE NINETEENTH
CENTURY", ETC.

LONDON

UNIVERSITY TUTORIAL PRESS LTD

CLIFTON HOUSE, EUSTON ROAD, N.W. 1

To
R. E. KELLETT

Published 1953

PRINTED IN GREAT BRITAIN BY UNIVERSITY TUTORIAL PRESS LTD, FOXTON
NEAR CAMBRIDGE

PREFACE

THE hitherto calm relations between literary history and literary criticism have been disturbed in recent years by the efforts of some influential critics to deny to literary history any importance at all. These attempts proceed from a combination of amnesia and illogicality that is itself one of the most interesting features of literary history in our time.

Fortunately for our good humour, it is also one of the most entertaining. There is amusement as well as instruction in the spectacle of an army dancing in imagination on the bodies of their adversaries, while being totally unaware that their own retreat has been cut off. When Sir Herbert Read, for instance, reviewed my *English Literature of the Nineteenth Century*, he evidently thought himself in an impregnable position. He made, as he thought, a complete dismissal of literary history in my person—unfortunately showing himself sorely in need of just such literary history as I had provided.

One of his points was that I had been unjust to Landor; and he quoted against me the astonishing observation of Mr Ezra Pound, that Landor had "very possibly the best mind in England of his day, save for those months that Voltaire spent in London"! This is a remarkable statement. It was bad enough for Mr Pound to have made such an error in the first place, but for Sir Herbert to seize upon the blunderbuss as a weapon to use against literary history!— that is truly a fine instance of a critic hoisted with his own petard. Voltaire came to England in 1726, nearly fifty years before Landor was born. The Frenchman was the elder contemporary of Johnson, the Englishman the younger contemporary of Wordsworth. Literary history, according to Sir Herbert, is "the method that kills", but it is not responsible for the death of the author of *Candide* before he had a chance to become a contemporary mind of the author of the *Imaginary Conversations*. Born as he was in the seventeenth century, Voltaire would have been a hundred and thirty years old had he lived to the date of the first volume

of Landor's *Conversations*, and over a hundred and fifty had
he seen fit to linger till the last. Whether Sir Herbert
approves of it or not, the fact remains that the two authors
belong to entirely different periods.

Sir Herbert may say that this error of a hundred years—
taking the time between Voltaire's visit to England and
Landor's principal works—is of no great importance, compared
with the relation that might be established of Landor's
mind with Voltaire's. But how would he like it himself if
he were treated in so cavalier a fashion, if he were described,
for example, as "very possibly the best of our aesthetic
critics, with the exception of his contemporary Walter
Pater"? He reminds me in his review that "a book is a
concrete object, a piece of a man's life", but he will not find
any case in history of a writer who did not live at one time
rather than another.

Nevertheless, there is something to be said for Sir Herbert's
argument, if little for his expression of it. Ideally, one would
imagine, one should be able to consider literature entirely by
itself, without need of knowing when the writers lived or
who were their contemporaries. But it is remarkable how
seldom, in practice, we do consider a literary work in this
virgin state, how often we find ourselves using historical
expressions like "Elizabethan" or "Victorian". In Sir Herbert
Read's and Professor Dobrée's introduction to *The London
Book of English Verse*, for example, occur such unaesthetic
phrases as "the social consciousness of eighteenth-century
England" and "the pathological condition of sentimentality
which set in about 1810" (or, to be more accurate, about
1750). Not that this excellent anthology is arranged on any
historical plan: its only failing is that it is not. The arrangement is not chronological, but according to the editors' whim.
I would rather be guided by Sir Herbert Read and Professor
Dobrée than by most contemporary critics, but inevitably
the cases where a reader agrees with an editor's particular
juxtaposition are bound to be fewer than the cases where he
disagrees. Where the arrangement is chronological, or roughly
so, such differences of individual interpretation disappear.

They should also disappear, as far as humanly possible, in the writing of literary history. Sir Herbert Read evidently thinks me very human in this respect, for what principally annoyed him in my *Nineteenth Century* volume was that my opinion on some writers disagreed with his own. But, when we look into the matter, what do we find? That it is Sir Herbert who is eccentric in his judgments, while those of my book were mostly in accordance with the most widely-accepted opinion. In regard to Landor, for instance, I find myself supported by the latest edition of *Chambers's Biographical Dictionary*— hardly a prejudiced source—which writes: "By a narrow circle of admirers Landor is ranked with the great names of English literature. But most readers find his work artificial".

Sir Herbert Read criticised the relative space given by me to individual authors. Such criticism is certainly relevant to the consideration of a literary history, but it should bear some relation to the facts. It will scarcely be credited in a writer of Sir Herbert's usual perspicacity, but he actually criticised me for giving twelve pages " and numerous incidental references" to an author called Charles Dickens and only nineteen lines to Borrow! I freely admit that I should have liked, if room had allowed, to have given more space to minor novelists like Borrow and Collins; but Dickens, I had always supposed, is one of the greatest writers who have ever lived, and to dismiss him in a mere twelve pages, out of some 250, is not by any means excessive. Had I given twelve pages to Borrow, and nineteen lines to Dickens, I should have expected some criticism of my partiality; but to be criticised, in Johnson's phrase, for "concurring with the common reader" is a stab in the back hardly to be anticipated even from a philosophical anarchist. I am afraid Sir Herbert will find the present book as sadly lacking in what he conceives to be proportion. He will find that I have given more space to Pope than to Prior, to Fielding than to Walpole, to Burns than to Smart. And the reason is the same as with Dickens and Borrow: that among the facts of literary history is the fact that Pope, Fielding, and Burns have been more widely read and more generally admired than Prior, Walpole, and

Smart. This enduring popularity, "by the common sense of readers uncorrupted with literary prejudices", as Johnson put it, is the final proof of a writer's excellence.

It is literary prejudice, of course, that Sir Herbert Read endeavours to convict me of. Fortunately, there is no need for me to challenge him to a duel, in the eighteenth-century manner, for his chief critical weapon appears to be the boomerang. Among the literary prejudice he sees in my *Nineteenth Century* volume is my dismissing Chatterton, a "perverted genius", in a footnote. He implies: first, that Chatterton belongs to the nineteenth century; second, that to call him a "perverted genius"—my actual phrase was "a somewhat similar perverted genius" (to Macpherson)—is a breach of taste. Chatterton, however, died in 1770, and I rightly mentioned him only in passing, in my discussion of the influence of the ballads on Wordsworth and Coleridge. I made a point of quoting Wordsworth's far more favourable opinion of Chatterton than of Macpherson, but it is impossible to deny that the *Rowley* poems are evidence of perverted genius. The word "perverted", as applied to Chatterton, Sir Herbert Read will find has been used by scores of writers before—including Sir Herbert Read. On p. 845 of the latest edition of *The London Book of English Verse* occurs the note: "Whether it is legitimate to modernise Chatterton's false antique English may be doubted, but certainly to do so offers less impediment to the real poetry underlying the perverse original". What the difference is between my use of the word "perverse", and Sir Herbert Read's and Professor Dobrée's use of it, is not clear to me and I doubt whether it is clear to Sir Herbert. However, he succeeded in his object: which was to pretend to the readers of his review that I had dismissed an interesting minor poet of the century—who had actually died thirty years before the century opened—in a mere footnote, and had further displayed my literary prejudice by referring to this poet in the unheard-of phrase, "perverted genius". One hardly knows which to wonder at more: the innocence of Sir Herbert in literary history or his amnesia in literary criticism.

But I would not thus introduce the preface to the present volume were I not certain that Sir Herbert's review of the previous work was directed not to a particular literary historian but to literary history in general. When a critic so usually distinguished can make so many elementary blunders, both of fact and analysis, it is evident that something more than a particular book must have been the object of his irritation. Indeed, he opens his review by remarking: "Criticism of this book must be directed to its conception, which is the publisher's, rather than to its execution, which is the author's"; though he allows that I have a "moral responsibility" for accepting a commission that requires me "to prolong a tradition of teaching English literature which is dull and pernicious".

We have now found the source of Sir Herbert's irritation: he believes that the tradition of literary history, particularly it seems in the educational field, is a dull and pernicious one, and that we should concentrate on literary criticism and the actual works of literature. "Not the textbook, but the text," is his final flourish.

That *Gulliver's Travels* is more important than any writing about *Gulliver's Travels* can be granted. (Another truism is that, if the skies fell, we should all catch larks.) But mixed up with that evident truth in Sir Herbert's mind is the much more questionable assumption that literary criticism has necessarily a relevance to the study of Swift that literary history has not. Literary criticism is conceived to be a valuable adjunct to literature; literary history to be the method that kills. Such a misconception is, I believe, fairly widespread to-day, and it deserves a careful examination.

My own view, as a writer of both literary criticism and literary history—and I have written much more of the former than the latter—is that each is valuable in its own sphere. Sir Herbert Read says that I "distinguish sharply" the method of the one from the method of the other. What I actually wrote, in my preface to the previous volume, was that "no absolute division" exists between them. I went on to point out that the difference is partly one of stress or

interest, partly one of tone: "To take an easy example: it is
literary criticism that remarks on the relation of Pre-
Raphaelite poetry to the poetry of Keats, but it is literary
history that points out the fact that it was in one of Keats's
letters first printed in Lord Houghton's collection of 1848
that the Pre-Raphaelite Movement found both its name and
inspiration. In the matter of tone, it is mainly a difference
between the historical 'we' and the critical 'I'—the 'we'
trying to keep in mind, as much as possible, that there are
varying opinions on most works of literature, the 'I' expressing
the writer's personal opinion alone".

The "we" is justified in another sense, I would add, where
there is so common an assent among readers as to the merits
of a work that it becomes virtually a "fact" in literary history.
Such a "fact" is the superiority of Gray's *Elegy* to his other
poems—because few readers, if any, have ever denied it.
Where there is a genuine difference of opinion, with about
equal weight on either side, then it is the responsibility of the
literary historian to give both views as impartially as humanly
possible. In the present book, I have endeavoured to meet
that obligation in regard to Richardson and Fielding.* A
literary critic may feel inclined to give an equally balanced
view, but if he holds strong opinions on one side he will
express them as forcibly as he can, without bothering about
what could be said on the other. It is the critic's purpose to
convert the reader to his own view—not out of conceit, but
because he feels, often with justification, that he has studied the
work or the writer more closely, that by the analysis he provides
and the enthusiasm he imparts he can take the reader along
with him, at least part of the way. Such persuasive analysis
we find in the writings of such excellent critics as Mr Eliot
and Mr Murry, as the late George Orwell and Dr Leavis. The
literary historian's purpose is to give the facts about a writer
or an age, to try to provide, from his study of the evidence, a
balanced survey, a more easily grasped view of what actually
occurred, with the various influences and movements—and
usually also the various connections of literature with the

* See below, pp. 111-13, 129-30, 170.

life of the time—more clearly seen.   Such balanced surveys
are Stephen's *English Literature and Society in the Eighteenth
Century*, Coulton's *Chaucer and his England*, Brailsford's
Shelley, Godwin, and their Circle, the Oxford symposia
Shakespeare's England and *Johnson's England*, Mr Somervell's
English Thought in the Nineteenth Century, Mr Muir's *The
Present Age from 1914*, and Professor Willey's *The Seventeenth
Century Background*.   Reading such books gives us an insight
into the circumstances of a period that is surely as valuable
to the re-reading of a poem or a novel or a play or a philosophical work as any critical analysis or display of enthusiasm
can be.   The best biographies, such as Boswell's, are also
very useful to the study of a particular writer and his social
environment, besides being sometimes works of literature in
their own right.

A literary history, then, should be criticised from much
the same point of view as a history of any other subject.
The balance, the proportion, the continued interest, the skill
in presentment of the facts: these should be the critic's
concern to find—as criticism of criticism will concern itself
with the skill in analysis shown, the quality of the enthusiasm,
and the degree of relevance to the text.   If we come away
from a reading of a literary history without a clearer picture
of the period (and/or particular subject) dealt with, then
the historian has failed; if we come away from a reading of a
work of literary criticism without more consciousness of the
features of the text discussed, then the critic has failed.   Such
elementary observations would not be worth making if there
were not to-day so great a misconception about these matters.

I will not pretend that all the reviews of my *Nineteenth
Century* volume were as frivolous as Sir Herbert Read's.   I had
several which reviewed my literary history as literary histories
should be reviewed.   But there were several, too—and I
have noticed similar instances among reviews of other literary
histories—that did not make the slightest attempt to judge
the work by literary historical standards.   The chief criticism
of one reviewer was that I had not mentioned the minor
Victorian poet Frederick Locker-Lampson.   "Alas, poor

Locker!'' he continued. Alas, poor reviewer! who could
waste his very limited space on so paltry an objection. Locker
may be, as the critic observed, an "accomplished poet", but
in a volume of 250 pages, covering a century's work in all
branches of literature, and indicating their relation to contemporary thought, the poetry of Locker is not a very
important matter. This critic will search in vain in the
present volume for any discussion of the poetry of those
accomplished figures John Armstrong and Christopher
Anstey.*

Such objections to a particular literary history proceed,
of course, from objections to literary history in general. This
reviewer, like Sir Herbert Read, started from the assumption
that literary histories serve no useful purpose. "Nobody
denies that Wordsworth died in 1850." I will not match
this reviewer's frivolity by reminding the reader that both
Mr Pound and Sir Herbert Read stoutly deny that Voltaire
died in 1778; for I am more interested to find that, while
literary histories are conceived to have no value in themselves,
they are allowed to be incidentally valuable to "send the
reader on to more profitable studies". The position, then,
is the same as with Sir Herbert Read: the "more profitable
studies" are works of criticism, to which a literary history
bears the role of poor relation.

We have only to take examples of each, to expose the
absurdity of this opinion. Is Stephen's *Literature and
Society in the Eighteenth Century* chiefly valuable because it
sends the reader to the "more profitable study" of Arnold's
essay on Gray? Is Brailsford's *Shelley, Godwin, and their
Circle* chiefly of interest because it leads to Hazlitt's *Spirit*

---

* Another school of critics condemns literary history because it
contains too *many* minor writers. Some literary historians have
apparently accepted this criticism in advance, for a recent book on
the Augustan Age was condemned in some quarters, and praised in
others, for managing to omit all reference to John Gay. This is
certainly a remarkable achievement, for if Gay's poetry and his *Beggar's
Opera* are considered unworthy of attention, I fail to see how any
historian can discuss the *Tatler* and the *Spectator* without a reference
to the chief contemporary witness to their popularity and influence—
Gay's pamphlet *The Present State of Wit*.

of the Age? Few readers would claim so; or would claim that Coulton's *Chaucer and his England* is a poor relation of Mr Speirs's recent excellent study *Chaucer the Maker*, or that Professor Willey's *Seventeenth Century Background* is incidentally worth reading because it leads to Dr Tillyard's *Milton*, or that Dr Collins's *Authorship in the Days of Johnson*, Mr Thomas's *William Cowper and the Eighteenth Century*, and Mr Somervell's *English Thought in the Nineteenth Century* are mere textbooks to carry the reader forth to Dr Leavis's *Revaluation* and his introduction to Coleridge's essays on Mill and Bentham. Certainly not all literary histories are so valuable as those named; but this applies also to literary criticism, where the mediocre studies equally outnumber the valuable.

If I were to give an example from my own work, assuring the reader that my *English Literature of the Nineteenth Century* is not intended to lead up to my essay on Dickens, I should have to add that the former contains some extracts from the latter. This is common. Few literary histories contain no literary criticism, as few works of criticism contain no literary history. The chief objection of contemporary critics to most literary histories is that the criticism contained in them is inadequate—or, as Dr Leavis puts it, mere "quasi-critical" comment. What these critics conveniently forget is that their own criticism, where it contains either social or literary history, is often woefully inadequate from that point of view—is, in fact, to emulate their bluntness, mere "quasi-historical" comment. I see nothing surprising in this: it seems to me to be expected that the best works of criticism should be superior, as criticism, to the criticism contained in literary history; as the best literary and social histories should be superior, as history, to the history contained in literary criticism. The pot can, of course, call the kettle black, as Sir Herbert Read can criticise me for using a phrase about Chatterton which he himself has used before, but such dubious proceedings cannot expect to escape criticism themselves.

I will illustrate the adage in the fairest manner possible, not by taking inferior critics and exposing their historical weaknesses, but by considering the two contemporary critics whom I personally admire the most and who have had, as I conceive, the most influence upon my own writing. I refer to the late George Orwell and Dr F. R. Leavis. They have not much in common, are indeed excellent examples of two of the main strands in literary criticism, which we can call for brevity the "journalistic" and the "academic" (though not all of the former have been professional journalists and not all of the latter dons). The characteristic of the journalist-critic, seen in its most impressive form in Johnson, is the common-sense approach. In the present book, the virtues and the limitations of that approach, as exemplified in Johnson, are summarised.* Johnson is the mightiest specimen of the race, but some of his virtues, if more of his limitations, are found in such twentieth-century critics as Arnold Bennett, G. K. Chesterton, D. H. Lawrence, George Orwell, and Mr Wyndham Lewis. The academic approach is rather different: as its title indicates, it is particularly concerned with education, with the maintenance of what it conceives to be the true literary tradition. Its characteristic approach is circuitous: instead of giving straight away the personal opinion of the critic, based on his own common-sense reading of the work or author in question, without bothering much, if at all, about what previous critical opinion may have said, the academic critic is first of all very much concerned with previous critical opinion, which he proceeds to chew over and modify or reject. It will be found that many of the essays of Mr T. S. Eliot and Dr Leavis, two of the most eminent contemporary practitioners of the academic approach, do in fact begin with a discussion of previous critical opinion and only then proceed to give their own opinion in relation to that. Whereas the characteristic procedure of the Bennetts and the Lawrences and the Orwells is to put no previous critical barrier between themselves and the text.

Which approach is the more valuable? Surely each is equally valuable. The common-sense approach can give us superb instances of critical penetration, such as Johnson's

* See below, pp. 168-71.

words about dramatic realism or Orwell's parallel between Tolstoy and Lear (or Johnson's criticism of "the sonorous magnificence" of Addison's Latin poems and Orwell's criticism of "the inflated style" of contemporary political literature, where "a mass of Latin words falls upon the facts like soft snow, blurring the outlines and covering up all the details"). As a journalist-critic myself, I can see equal critical penetration in the academics; fine examples, to my mind, are Mr Eliot's essay on Dryden and Dr Leavis's on Keats. It is surely equally valuable to have the direct common-sense opinion of a critic upon an author, such as Orwell's upon Swift, as to have previous critical opinion reviewed and modified by a more learned and analytical approach, such as Dr Leavis's upon George Eliot. It is not a question whether we happen to agree with either judgment; the value occurs, if it does occur, when we find ourselves able, through the penetration of the critic, to re-read these authors with greater discernment.

The circuitous approach of the academic mind, and its concern for what it conceives to be the true literary tradition, have naturally led to a number of revolutions in literary criticism. These have been mostly the work of dons, from the revolution of the later eighteenth century, in which the Wartons played the leading part, to the revolution of more recent years, propagated, among others, by Mr Eliot, Mr Murry, Professor Richards, Dr Leavis, Mr Rickword, Mr Empson, and Professor Knights. It is not surprising that academics should be revolutionaries,* for their concern for the correct placing of authors in a literary hierarchy has naturally led some of them—and will lead some of them again—to question and then to overthrow their predecessors' opinions. We find this in political criticism, too: it was not

* The reason for the customary equating of "academic" with "conservative" means no more than that, at a given time, the majority of dons are strongly in favour of the *last* revolution, so are likely to condemn the current one. A political analogy is provided by the case of Burke, a strong supporter of the 1688 Revolution, who opposed with all his strength the agitation for reform influenced by the French Revolution of 1789.

Cobbett, the practical journalist, the man of common sense, who propagated a political revolution, but the academic mind of Karl Marx, who had spent much of his life in the British Museum.

The distinctive feature of Orwell's literary criticism is its relation to social and political history. The criticism, at its best, such as the essays on Dickens, on Swift, on Tolstoy, on Kipling, on Koestler, is very fine indeed; but is the history reliable? Sometimes it is, sometimes it is not. To give just one small instance of its inadequacy: Orwell—in one of his few "academic" moments—criticises Chesterton for claiming Sam Weller as a typical member of the English lower classes: "and Sam Weller is a valet!" But at the time Dickens wrote *Pickwick*, if not for very long afterwards, there were actually many more domestic servants in England than, for example, workers in the cotton industry. (Trevelyan, *English Social History*, p. 478.) So Chesterton was more correct than Orwell over the typical quality of Weller.

This is a very small point; but my contention is that even a large number of such very small points, if they incline us to take Orwell's history with a pinch of salt, do not really affect the excellence of his criticism. A similar observation can be made of Dr Leavis's introduction to Coleridge's essays upon Mill and Bentham. Here we have more careful, if sometimes equally brilliant, literary criticism; but is the history adequate? One of the points made by Dr Leavis concerns the relation of Beatrice Webb to anti-Benthamite ideas. This is a subtle observation, backed up by the relevant texts. But the reader knowing only Dr Leavis's essay would come away with the false historical impression that the philosophy of Bentham and that of the Webbs were fundamentally different, whereas there is a strong connection— often noticed—between the two, and between the reforms based on the one and those based on the other. Dr Leavis has made a valuable point, which probably no one else would have made, but in his subtlety he has forgotten the more elementary observation which makes that point just an exception.

We find a similar thing in Dr Leavis's relation to more literary history. He once wrote in *Scrutiny*, in the course of an exchange with Mr F. W. Bateson on Criticism and Literary History, that he knew of no literary history "that doesn't make a show of criticism". I know of few pieces of criticism which do not make a show of literary history —and a very poor show it often is. We need look no further than Dr Leavis himself for an example. The second paragraph of his essay on *English Poetry in the Eighteenth Century* (later incorporated in his principal critical work: *Revaluation: Tradition and Development in English Poetry*) runs as follows:

> Mr Edgell Rickword, reviewing *The Oxford Book of Eighteenth Century Verse*, sees the bad turn as coming at about 1720, the period "which no anthological charity can do much to rehabilitate", running from then to 1780. "The vulgar prejudice against the minor poetry of the eighteenth century", he reports, "may be defended so long as it does not attempt to include the period that may properly be called Augustan." And certainly, wherever we place the turn, the contrast between the two centuries, taken each in the lump, in their showing of minor talent is an extreme one. A tradition that does not enlist, or make good use of, minor talent may be suspected of having also confined major talent to minor performance. This distinction between "major" and "minor" incites to questions, of course; but everyone will agree that the seventeenth century is extraordinarily rich in good poetry by writers of distinctively minor gift; on the other hand, hardly any taste could find a great deal of major poetry in the period stigmatised by Mr Rickword.

My questioning of this paragraph is only concerned with its show of literary history. Both Mr Rickword and Dr Leavis evidently believe that—wherever exactly "we place the turn"—the greatest period of Augustan poetry was before 1720, and that "hardly any taste" can find much poetry worth attention in the period from about 1720 onwards. The truth is almost the exact opposite, the greatest period of Augustan poetry, by common consent, being from about the mid-'twenties to the early 'forties, the period *c.* 1700-20 being

comparatively barren. The majority of the greatest works
of Pope were published well within "the period stigmatised
by Mr Rickword", in fact from 1728 to 1743: this period
saw the *Dunciad*, the *Moral Essays*, the *Essay on Man*, the
Imitations of Horace, the dialogues entitled *1738*, and the
Epistle to Arbuthnot. Probably the poem of Swift's which
most readers would place first among his poetry—the *Verses
on the Death of Dr Swift, written by himself*—was written
in 1731 and published in 1739. Gay's most attractive
works, in common acceptance, are his *Fables* (1727) and his
ballads in *The Beggar's Opera* (1728). Dyer's *Grongar Hill*
(1726) and Matthew Green's *The Spleen* (1737) are perhaps
the best of the other minor verse of the period. While
Thomson, who admittedly looks forward to the succeeding
age of Gray and Collins, produced his chief work, *The Seasons*,
between 1726 and 1730.

The period from the death of Dryden in 1700 to about
1720 is comparatively empty. There is, indeed, the early
Pope, including such excellent things as the *Essay on Criticism*,
The Rape of the Lock, the *Elegy to the Memory of an Unfortunate Lady*, and *Eloisa to Abelard*. But "hardly any taste"—
certainly not Dr Leavis's—would prefer this early Pope to
the Pope of the later works. There is also the early Gay,
including some excellent light pieces such as *Trivia*; but the
same observation applies. There are the poems of Prior;
the hymns of Isaac Watts and Addison and Nahum Tate;
Addison's *Cato*; and poems by Diaper, Lady Winchilsea, and
others. But most readers would agree that, in both major
and minor verse, the period is inferior to its successor of the
'twenties, the 'thirties, and the early 'forties.

Inferior, of course, in *poetry*. For the common estimation
of the central Augustan Age as being roughly in the reign of
Queen Anne (1702-14) is justified by the prose of that period
and by the existence of the coffee-house society addressed by
Steele and Addison. My criticism of Dr Leavis and Mr
Rickword is directed only to their false historical assumption
that the principal works of Augustan poetry were produced
during that central Augustan Age and that there is little of

interest in either major or minor poetry in the 'twenties and 'thirties.

But the historical inadequacy of that paragraph having been noticed, we must ask ourselves whether the literary criticism is at all affected. In my opinion, not in the slightest degree. The chief literary criticism in the paragraph, that the minor poetry of the eighteenth century is inferior to that of the seventeenth, is not affected by the disregard for literary history shown by Mr Rickword and which seems to have gone uncorrected by Dr Leavis—as Sir Herbert Read took over the greater blunder of Mr Pound. It would have been gratifying to find Mr Rickword and Dr Leavis, and Mr Pound and Sir Herbert Read, equally at home in history as in criticism, as it would have been gratifying to Dr Leavis to find the literary historians he has condemned equally at home in criticism as in history. But in my opinion such gratifications are not to be expected, and it is surely more reasonable to regard literary history from the literary historical angle, and literary criticism from the critical, and not to expect the one to be always distinguished in the province of the other.

If I read Dr Leavis aright, he will have no truck with any such compromise. He has, indeed, suggested that the only literary history which would be valuable (or valuable to him) would be one written by a literary critic, and then, of course, as he says, it would be essentially literary criticism and not literary history. But if literary history, "as a matter of 'facts about' and accepted critical (or quasi-critical) description" is "a worthless acquisition", is it necessarily worth while to possess criticism combined with quasi-historical description, with the facts sometimes wrong? Dr Leavis's *Revaluation* is certainly one of the most valuable works of literary criticism that have appeared during the last quarter of a century— I personally consider Dr Leavis as superior to his master Eliot in criticism as Mr Eliot in poetry to his master Pound— but would even *Revaluation* be fitted to become the kind of critical substitute for literary history that its author seems to envisage? And when we turn to his criticism of the novel, represented by his chief work on the subject, *The Great*

Tradition, is his exaltation of literary criticism over literary history seen to be any more logical?

Much of the criticism in this book is extremely penetrating, particularly perhaps the essay on George Eliot and that, in the appendix, on Dickens. But, in making this brief acknowledgment of Dr Leavis's critical powers, I have already made one criticism of his inadequacy as a literary historian—for what is Dickens doing in an *appendix* when the theme of the book is the great tradition in the English novel? For Dr Leavis, this tradition seems to be extremely exclusive: Jane Austen, part of George Eliot, Henry James, part of Conrad, and D. H. Lawrence. It is evidently a most uncommon reader whom Dr Leavis concurs with, if indeed he seriously thinks that a standard of greatness can be found in the English novel to exclude, to name no more, both Scott and Dickens.

His essay on *Hard Times*, in the appendix, is, in my opinion, one of the best that has ever been written on Dickens. (Chesterton and the Marxist critic Mr Jackson had already noted some of the points Dr Leavis makes, but he is much more subtle—and in my judgment much sounder—than his predecessors here.) But, in his subtle analysis, he has completely forgotten the entirely elementary, common-sense observation that a Dickens who had only written *Hard Times* would have been a very minor writer indeed. In a sentence that is as finely expressed as it is true, Dr Leavis seems to acknowledge this: "The final stress," he writes, "may fall on Dickens's command of word, phrase, rhythm, and image: in ease and range there is surely no greater master of English except Shakespeare". And this great master—whose greatness, Dr Leavis would probably agree, is found as much in the other novels as in *Hard Times*—is relegated to an appendix in a book whose theme is the great tradition in the English novel!

What is the reason for this discrepancy? The probable reason we shall be discussing in a moment, but first we must observe that it is only a part of the great tradition—or, to put it perhaps more accurately, only one of the great traditions

—that the critic is interested in. This is quite proper in a
literary critic—if not in a literary critic who believes that only
a critic can write literary history; there is no reason, in
literary criticism, why a book should not be written, called
The Great Tradition in Poetry, dealing exclusively with Colley
Cibber, part of Laurence Eusden, Samuel Rogers, part of
Locker-Lampson, and Alfred Austin (with perhaps Shakespeare in an appendix).   The critic can, in fact, find his Great
Traditions anywhere he pleases, even in such extremely
unlikely examples as those given. But a literary historian
has to take a great deal of notice of that "accepted" criticism
which Dr Leavis condemns; he cannot agree that the latest
revolution or revaluation is necessarily final, nor that it is
the regiment which is always out of step.   The revaluation of
the Restoration period, after all, was inclined to censure
Shakespeare himself—but the man recovered of the bite;
the dog it was that died.

There are at least three great traditions in the English
novel, and that running from Richardson to Henry James is
only one of them.   In the fourth and fifth chapters of the
present book—and in a recent article on Scott—I give the
main lines which can be said to exist, though they cross one
another so much that the true picture may be more like the
railway lines at Clapham Junction than the rough sketch
I have indicated. One exclusion from Dr Leavis's *Great
Tradition* is particularly noticeable: he says nothing about
the humorous tradition in English fiction, which bears such
a strong relation to dramatic comedy. In his concern for the
subtle psychological novel, he thinks it necessary to disparage
Defoe, Fielding, and Sterne, to pass (respectfully enough)
over Scott, and to consider Dickens by only one of his works.
But this has not been considered necessary before: George
Eliot, who conceived herself in the tradition of *Tom Jones*,
would have disagreed with Dr Leavis over Fielding; Lawrence
would have disagreed with him over Sterne; while the critic
who first observed that *Middlemarch* "is the greatest novel of
the Victorian Age" was Scott's great admirer and biographer
John Buchan. Why, then, should Dr Leavis believe that

his own opinions—persuasively expressed as they are—could
be adequate for the writing of a work of literary criticism
that would take the place of literary history? Clearly a
history of the English novel, on Leavisian lines, would be
like a history of the English people from the Marxist point of
view: that is, a history written on abstract principles.

In a series of articles in *Scrutiny* in recent years, Dr Leavis
has acknowledged his abstract principle by the general title
of the series: "The Novel as Dramatic Poem". Now, novels
are not dramatic poems, and nothing is gained by considering
them as such; the chief relation between fiction and the
drama is in that tradition of comedy which Dr Leavis dis-
counts. A Shakespearian play is, in book form, about the
length of a short story; since it can be acted in about three
hours, it can be read silently in much less. Looking for a
similar concentration in fiction, with every phrase bearing a
significant relation to the whole, Dr Leavis naturally finds
few examples. *Hard Times* is, as he says, the only example
in Dickens; in George Eliot, he admits *Middlemarch* with
some reservations, but has to dismember both *Felix Holt* and
Daniel Deronda. Only the Transome portions of *Felix Holt*
he deems truly significant, and only the non-Deronda parts
of *Deronda*. We can imagine what George Eliot's opinion
of these amputations would have been, as we can imagine
Dickens's astonishment at Mr Robert Graves's "bowdlerised"
version of *David Copperfield*.

It would be foolish to deny the grain of common sense in
the arguments of both Mr Graves and Dr Leavis. The
sentimentality of Dickens at its lowest depth is as irritating
to most modern readers as to Mr Graves, and, superficially,
there seems a lot to be said for an edition of *Copperfield* or
Chuzzlewit with the tearful passages ruthlessly censored.
Dr Leavis is probably equally right in stressing the artistic
superiority of the non-Deronda half of *Daniel Deronda* and
the non-Felix half of *Felix Holt* to what George Eliot herself
conceived to be the main idea of those novels. But the
example of Bowdler should give us pause. Victorian sentimentality is as noxious to the modern world as Elizabethan

bawdiness was to the Victorians; but perhaps the opinion of the twenty-first century would be as astonishing to us as our opinion would have been to Bowdler. There is no harm in our deciding what are the best parts of a literary work, so long as we do not attempt to impose upon posterity the parts we like in place of the original. Mr Graves's *Copperfield* is no longer read, and Dr Leavis has, I believe, given up his intention to edit an edition of *Deronda* with Deronda cut out.

A more serious criticism is not so much that Mr Graves and Dr Leavis have taken it for granted that they know better than their author what their author had in mind, as that they have not fully realised that a literary work can only be judged as a whole. Neither critic would think of denying this in the case, for example, of *King Lear*, and both probably regard with suitable contempt Tate's "happy-ending" version which held the stage for more than a century. The novel, like the poetic drama, has its own characteristics. It is a looser form of literature, and often contains, in fact, whole chapters which can be skipped. While the very few novels which partake of the concentration of dramatic poetry—or, more accurately, of half a dozen plays by Shakespeare—are among the best, they are not exclusively the best. The mastery of Dickens, for instance, which Dr Leavis recognises so well, is not confined to the short concentrated novel of *Hard Times*; it is equally evident in long loose novels such as *Chuzzlewit* and *Little Dorrit*. Only if we take as our abstract standard an artistic concentration suitable to a three hours' performance in a theatre—and totally irrelevant to a novel that might take a week to read aloud— can we put *Hard Times* on a higher level than *Chuzzlewit* or Scott's *Wandering Willie's Tale* (which Dr Leavis singles out for praise) on a higher level than *Old Mortality*.

The humorous novel, in particular, has always been as loose-bellied as Falstaff—and not only in England; consider Rabelais and Cervantes and Gogol. Dickens seldom knew, when he had reached the middle of a novel, what the end was going to be; Fielding's *Joseph Andrews* alters its mind about fifty pages on; while *Tristram Shandy* is deliberately spun out by diversions.

By totally condemning Sterne, Dr Leavis seems to give proof of his own condemnation of literary history—or of any kind of literary criticism that might be envisaged as taking the place of literary history. For what may be regarded as a virtue in a critic—the refusal to perceive the merit of any view not his own—is a vice in an historian, whose duty it is to check his personal opinion by the light of such common agreement as may be available. It is easily available in the case of Sterne. The indecency which Dr Leavis censures has been censured by every previous critic, but no previous critic has condemned Sterne wholly. The fact that D. H. Lawrence admired *Tristram Shandy* is significant, for no two novelists could be more unlike. It was evidently not Sterne's indecency which appealed to Lawrence, or to Dickens, so there must be something more in him than Dr Leavis recognises. And this something more is what has been recognised by all previous critics: namely, his humorous characterisation. He is not as eminent in this field as Fielding or Scott or Dickens, but My Uncle Toby is a genuine creation, one of the comic masterpieces of the eighteenth century.

I hope my general point will not be lost sight of, among these critical details. I greatly admire the literary criticism of Dr Leavis, as I do some of Sir Herbert Read's; but I regard their opinions on literary history as most uncritical. This would not matter if they were not such influential persons; the admiration aroused by their literary criticism has given them a hearing on literary history—so that the whole species is frequently prejudged as "a kind of writing about literature that one would imagine had been completely discredited". Some such phrase was used of another volume in this series, by a different author, and is typical of the misapprehension that this preface has sought to reveal.

R. C. C.

CONTENTS

ENGLISH LITERATURE OF THE EIGHTEENTH CENTURY

CHAPTER I

STEELE, ADDISON, AND THE AUGUSTAN AGE
1688-1729

"As for my labours, if they wear but one impertinence out of human life, destroy a single vice, or give a morning's cheerfulness to an honest mind; in short, if the world can be but one virtue the better, or in any degree less vicious, or receive from them the smallest addition to their innocent diversions; I shall not think my pains, or indeed my life, to have been spent in vain."

STEELE: in the *Tatler*.

"It was said of Socrates that he brought philosophy down from heaven to inhabit among men; and I shall be ambitious to have it said of me, that I have brought philosophy out of closets and libraries, schools and colleges, to dwell in clubs and assemblies, at tea-tables and in coffee-houses."

ADDISON: in the *Spectator*.

Period of the Augustans

It was the poet Goldsmith who first called the early eighteenth century, the time of his immediate predecessors, "the Augustan Age", though the epithet "Augustan" had been used originally by Pope's friend Atterbury to describe the classicism of the poetry influenced by Waller. Wherever we exactly place the period, the title is evidently just; for the literary men of the age were trying to emulate the achievements of Latin literature under the Emperor Augustus; and the French critic Boileau, who had a great influence in England and who had praised the Latin verses of the young Addison, was advising writers to find models in poets like Virgil and Horace, who, it was thought, had brought natural speech to its perfection. But in England the conscious classicism of the age had political and religious implications, too, and we do well to remember these when we attempt to fix a more definite period to the new Augustans than just "the early eighteenth century". Centuries themselves, we know, are not usually dividing lines of any great significance, nor are events in politics necessarily of any significance at all in literary or cultural history. But occasionally a political event, especially one which has a religious interest, has enough literary and social importance to justify a more than political division. Such an event was the "glorious revolution", as Burke called it, of 1688, when the Catholic James II was considered by his actions to have abdicated the throne, the Tory party reluctantly joining with the Whigs in welcoming his Protestant son-in-law, Prince William of Orange.

This was the start of a new political and religious era in England, the final defeat of the doctrine of the Divine Right of Kings. The complete victory of Parliament and the Church of England decided at last the long and confused struggles of the past hundred years. Up to the reform of Church and Parliament in the early nineteenth century, no other fundamental change was made—though the revolutions in America and France in the 'seventies and 'eighties had political and literary repercussions on the England whose liberty of 1688 they had sought to emulate.* It was the opening, too, of a period of comparative rationality and tolerance, when ordinary Englishmen, grown weary of the dogmatic miseries they had known for nearly half a century, were only too willing to listen to poets and philosophers who condemned "enthusiasm" and advocated classical decorum. When typical Augustans like Steele and Addison prided themselves on the classical impulse of their age, they had in mind,

* In France, the nobleman Montesquieu was to discuss, in his *De l'Esprit des Lois*, a free constitution on the English model. Gibbon in his *Autobiography* refers to Montesquieu's "energy of style and boldness of hypothesis" which "were powerful to awaken and stimulate the genius of the age". Voltaire, too, who was in England 1726-9, was much influenced by English thought and political practice, his panegyric on English ways, *Lettres sur les Anglais*, forcing him to flee from Paris. Though we can understand this attraction of England for liberal Frenchmen, both Voltaire and Montesquieu were inclined to misjudge the extent of English liberty in the eighteenth century, as liberal Englishmen like Godwin were later to misinterpret some of the facts of the French Revolution.

not only the literary achievements of Swift and Pope, but the dominant political and religious philosophy, which, summed up in the writings of John Locke, had substituted for the zeal of their fathers the more classical virtues of Reason and Proportion. The triumph of Parliament and the Church of England in 1688 is as accurate a starting-point as any for what we know in literary history as the Augustan Age.

The year 1688 saw also the death of Bunyan, the last and greatest of the Puritan writers of the popular school, and the birth of Pope, who was to become the greatest poet of the new age. In the present chapter we shall be concerned mainly with the background of the Augustans, and with their periodical literature to the death of Steele in 1729; the next chapter treats of Swift and the Tory Opposition; and the third of Augustan poetry from the death of Dryden in 1700 to the death of Thomson in 1748.

Characteristics of the Age

It had points in common with its predecessor, the Restoration Age, but also some significant points of difference. Each period in history reacts to some extent against the prevailing philosophy of the previous period; though it is equally true to say that history is continuous, not only in the sense that each age is an age of transition, but in the fact that there always exist varying groups in society, some of which incline more to the past than the present. As the "Restoration", we say—meaning certain dominant groups of the period from the Restoration of Charles II—reacted violently against the enforced strictness of Puritanism, so the Augustan Age, or the dominant group, reacted against the cynicism and debauchery of the Restoration Court. It was natural that when the officious prudery of the Cromwellian Protectorate was overthrown, England—or a certain section of London—should go to the other extreme and witty rakes like the Earl of Rochester be tolerated in high society. But not only were men like Wren and the pious Newton as typical of the Restoration period as aristocrats like Rochester or actresses like Nell Gwyn, beneath the extravagance of the Court and upper classes there existed the more sober middle class and that part of the lower classes whose spokesman was Bunyan. The literature of Puritanism in defeat, particularly, of course, *Paradise Lost* and the *Pilgrim's Progress*, affected many who were not Puritans themselves and had a great influence on the country as a whole. Dryden and the Court wits read Milton;* Swift later expressed his admiration for Bunyan; Addison contributed a series of papers on *Paradise Lost* to the *Spectator*; and behind Defoe—though perhaps too far behind—stands the general influence of popular Puritanism. Even more significant is the fact that Collier and Law, two of the chief writers who attacked the debauchery of the Restoration stage, the tradition of which extended to Congreve, were Tories and High Churchmen, men who could not be accused of "nonconformity" in other matters. The dislike of "enthusiasm" became separated from a leaning towards cynicism, and the virtues of defeated Puritanism did much to modify the reaction against the vices of the Puritan in power.

There was a social change, too: Puritanism had been connected with capitalism, and the inevitable result was for the Restoration dramatists to make the tradesman, the unfashionable citizen, the butt of their comedies, the hero, of course, being the young buck who seduces the tradesman's wife. The tradition is seen, on its last legs, as late as Congreve's *Old Bachelor* (1693), where the banker Fondlewife is deceived by the pleasure-loving aristocrat Bellmour. But the tradition was weakening now, as the state of society was changing. The public that Swift and Addison addressed was by no means exclusively aristocratic, and Pope, the son of a prosperous linen-draper, could pride himself on the fact that, by the wide sale of his Homer, he could manage to exist for the rest of his life without patronage:

> (thanks to Homer) since I live and thrive,
> Indebted to no Prince or Peer alive . . .

* In the dedication to his translation of Juvenal (1692), Dryden refers to "Mr Milton, whom we all admire with so much justice", though he adds that "'tis true he runs into a flat of thought, sometimes for a hundred lines together, but 'tis when he is got into a track of scripture".

Patronage of literature and the arts by the aristocracy remained, of course, very great by modern standards; but the tendency, nevertheless, was for courtly patronage to be gradually superseded, first by parliamentary patronage—as the new kind of statesman became dependent on parliamentary influence instead of court favour—and then by the patronage of the general literate public, expressed through the book-sellers and publishers (who were, at that date, the same people). The influence of Puritanism, seemingly defeated on all sides, was seen again here, for one of the characteristics of the Puritans had been their love of reading, and the Noncon-formist public of the early eighteenth century was large enough to enter into the calculation of booksellers and the interest of authors. Defoe, who was himself a Nonconformist, wrote the most widely-read literary work of the whole century.

Part of the reason for this social change was, of course, the decline in power of the King, and therefore of his court. Charles II's was the last "Renaissance" Court that we have had in England: a Court, that is to say, interested in literature and the arts as well as in politics and fashion. But Charles's Court, consciously modelled as it was on the Court of the Sun-King at Versailles, was rather frivolous compared with his father's, to say nothing of the Elizabethan. It had an enforced gaiety, as unnatural as the enforced gravity of the Cromwellian period; a gaiety typified in the self-conscious bawdiness of many Restoration comedies, with one eye of the dramatist and the actor turned on the public *outside* the theatre, a public that was conceived of as being easily shocked. With the continued rise in power of Parliament and the trading classes, the Court lost its central position, till the advent of the Hanoverians in 1714 left it a mere appendage of parliamentary government. The more lasting developments of the Restoration period were in the classical propaganda of such writers as Dryden, who saw London as the new Rome, and in the growing interest in "natural philosophy", based on the scientific investigations of Newton, Boyle, Ray, and lesser members of the Royal Society of London for Improving

Natural Knowledge. Charles's patronage of science was to prove more valuable to the eighteenth century than any other of his activities.

Classicism and the Language of Science

In the twentieth century, we are inclined to treat the study of the classics and the study of science as poles apart, though it was, of course, the Greeks who laid the foundations of European science. To the scholarly Augustan they seemed parts of the same philosophy, the same use of Reason, as contrasted with the prejudice and pedantry of the barbarous ages between the old Rome and the new. We can so far agree with them as to admire the toleration of the Augustans, compared with the bigotry of Cromwell or Laud, and to praise that clear urbane style of writing, seen at its best in Addison and Swift. But there were disadvantages in the current attitude, prejudice even among the apparent lack of prejudice. The limitations of the Augustans are as clear to us as the limitations of "enthusiasm" were to them—and as our own limitations will be strikingly clear to our descendants. It is not an accident that neither the Restoration nor the Augustan period could produce any poetic drama remotely approaching the level of the Elizabethan-Jacobean. Nor is it an accident that, though the *Pilgrim's Progress* was even more popular in the new century than in the old, no Nonconformist could be found to write an allegory of anything like the same power. With the accent on Reason and Proportion, some of the poetic qualities of the English language disappeared, the wealth of natural imagery and idiom that can be seen as much in Bunyan as in Shakespeare seeming a little barbarous to Dryden and his successors.* "It must be allowed to the present age," Dryden had written, "that the tongue in general is so much refined since Shakespeare's time that many of his words, and more of his phrases, are scarce intelligible. And

* In one of his essays on *Paradise Lost* in the *Spectator*, Addison says that "a poet should take particular care to guard himself against idiomatic ways of speaking", though he admits that "Milton has but few failings in this kind".

of those which we understand, some are ungrammatical, others coarse; and his whole style is so pestered with figurative expressions that it is as affected as it is obscure." Shakespeare's plays, "improved" for the stage, were still performed, but to a rather patronising audience. Both Pepys and Evelyn record in their diaries their own reactions: "To the Duke's house," writes Pepys, "and there saw *Twelfth Night* acted well, though it be but a silly play"; "I saw *Hamlet Prince of Denmark* played," writes Evelyn, "but now the old plays begin to disgust this refined age." In 1694, when the young Addison wrote a verse *Account of the Greatest English Poets,* he omitted Shakespeare altogether; and the critic Rymer, who thought "the tragical part" of *Othello* "none other than a bloody farce", wrote that "in the neighing of a horse, or in the growling of a mastiff, there is a meaning, there is as lively expression, and, may I say, more humanity than many times in the tragical flights of Shakespeare".

The accounting of the barbarous age of Shakespeare was not all on the debit side, however. Dryden himself had too much natural English taste to comply altogether with the critical rules of French classicism; and, in general, as the Restoration period gave way to the Augustan, and the Augustan to the mid-eighteenth century, we witness a remarkable change—from Pope's comparison of Shakespeare ("with all his faults") to "an ancient, majestic piece of Gothic architecture", which is still more or less the Dryden view, to Fielding's description of him as "the greatest genius the world has ever produced" and Gibbon explaining that his taste for the French theatre "has perhaps abated my idolatry for the gigantic genius of Shakespeare, which is inculcated from our infancy as the first duty of an Englishman". There are several favourable references to Shakespeare in the *Spectator,* and in one of them Addison makes the sensible remark that "*King Lear* is an admirable tragedy, as Shakespeare wrote it; but as it is reformed according to the chimerical notion of Poetical Justice, in my humble opinion it has lost half its beauty". This "improvement" of *Lear* was the work of

Nahum Tate, Poet Laureate 1692-1715, who provided the play with a happy ending.*

The Augustans, then, like their predecessors, could sometimes reluctantly admire such language as the Elizabethan, and could see some of its "Gothic" virtues; but they conceived their own idiom to be altogether superior, whereas it was only superior for some purposes, not others. The non-Augustan or Elizabethan virtues seem to be necessary for English poetic drama, as for mysticism and most kinds of imaginative writing. The Augustans were superior in other ways, notably in satire and journalism, in the technical language of philosophy and science, and in that great branch of modern literature, the novel, of which they were among the English pioneers.

The Augustan Attitude to Religion

The Revolution of 1688 was a triumph for the moderate party within the Church of England, those who stood between the Puritan faction on the one side and the High Church on the other. Though prominent Augustans included the Catholic poet Pope, the Deist philosopher Bolingbroke, and the Nonconformist novelist Defoe, the typical Augustan religion was that of Steele and Addison, who spoke for the majority of their coffee-house public in London and possibly also for the majority of country squires and their tenants. It was natural that a reaction from religious zeal should be favourable to the "middle" people, who wanted neither Popery nor Puritanism, but who had learnt by past experience that nothing is so conducive to the spreading of heretical enthusiasm as persecution of its adherents. So Catholics and Dissenters were not persecuted in the old sense, but they were deprived of certain benefits available to others. Thus Pope was not eligible for a university education, Oxford and Cambridge being wholly in the hands of the Anglican Church. Dissenters were also barred, from the time of Defoe to the time

* This version, published in 1681, held the stage until early Victorian times, being adopted in succession by Booth, Barry, Garrick, Kemble, and Kean. Critics from Fielding and Gibbon to Coleridge and Hazlitt might laud the genius of Shakespeare, but on the stage he continued to be presented under truly "Restoration" auspices.

of Browning; but being far more numerous than their fellow-sufferers and having more enlightened ideas of education than either they or the Anglicans, their deprivation acted as a spur to their own conceptions, the Dissenting schools and academies, which soon sprang up all over England, giving a better education than most of the grammar schools.

That is one aspect of the Augustan religious attitude: the central party in power but having learnt by past experience that nothing was to be gained by persecuting nonconformists on either side. But such an attitude of compromise and comparative tolerance evidently meant much more than just sober knowledge gained from past bigotry; the central doctrine itself must have had certain principles which cannot be summed up entirely in negative terms. In his three *Letters on Toleration* (1690-2) Locke had attacked the idea that the unity of the Church was to consist in everybody thinking alike. The unity was to be the binding of all in love, but not in opinion; a Church could make laws which should exclude certain people from it, but these people should not suffer in their natural rights. No Church, wrote Locke, had power from Christ to persecute any individual by withholding from him the right to worship God as he thought best.

This principle of toleration was evidently based upon a different conception of the Church from that obtaining in the earlier seventeenth century. Locke was a sincere Christian, but he reduced the dogmatic element in Christianity to a minimum, so that some of his followers became Deists or free-thinkers.* For dogma, to be accepted blindly, the Augustans

* Deism is, literally, a belief in one Supreme Being; but the term is used particularly to characterise a movement of religious thought in the seventeenth and eighteenth centuries which opposed a "religion of nature" to the revealed religion of Christianity. The father of English Deism was Lord Herbert of Cherbury, who died in 1648. Among his Augustan successors were Anthony Collins, Matthew Tindal, Thomas Chubb, and Lord Bolingbroke. Collins's best-known work was *A Discourse of Free-thinking* (1713). Locke's influence meant that the line between Deists and Churchmen was not always clearly drawn; for instance, Conyers Middleton, a clergyman contemporary with Pope, came to deny verbal inspiration and miracles in his last work *A Free Inquiry into the Miraculous Powers which are supposed to have existed in the Christian Church* (1748).

substituted the right of every educated man to think for himself; faith, they held, should be founded on reason, and reason could bring men to religion without help from professional theology.   Dryden's contemporary, Archbishop Tillotson, whose collected sermons, published in 1717, had a great influence, was the first master of the new pulpit style, easy and unrhetorical, appealing to the common sense of the congregation.   The same reasonable lucidity is seen later in the philosophy of Bishop Berkeley, who was able to confute some of the ideas of Locke and the Deists in their own language.

The religious struggles of the seventeenth century had had one prevailing characteristic, that there was no common ground between the various disputants, Laud and Cromwell being united only in their zeal.   The most important characteristic of the Augustan religious attitude was precisely the extent of the ground common to all parties.   Pope, the greatest poet of the age, is a good example of this tendency. A Roman Catholic, refusing all his life to abjure his religion for personal benefit, he yet wrote his *Essay on Man* on the deistical principles of his friend Bolingbroke.   And his *Universal Prayer*, beginning

> Father of All! in ev'ry Age,
>   In ev'ry Clime ador'd,
> By Saint, by Savage, and by Sage,
>   Jehovah, Jove, or Lord . . .

was considered by the orthodox "the Deist's Prayer".   Even stranger was his attitude in his last illness: he had to be reminded by a Catholic friend of the need to see a priest— "Thank you very much," he said, "for putting me in mind of it."   He died a good Catholic in the end—much to Bolingbroke's indignation—but his attitude must seem as strange to a modern Catholic or High-Churchman as it would have done to the seventeenth century.   We can feel sure that Mr T. S. Eliot, for example, will approach his dissolution in a much more orthodox manner.

The explanation is evidently that the general belief in Reason and Proportion meant more to the men of the age than the particular beliefs of their own religion.   This is illustrated by the development of Dissent. We search in vain in the writings of Augustan Nonconformists for any of the theological niceties that troubled the minds of the Puritans during the Commonwealth. Calvinism had given place to Conduct, and Dissenters could co-operate with Churchmen in the support of such ventures as the Society for the Propagation of the Gospel in Foreign Parts. Defoe wrote *Robinson Crusoe* to show how a man who has started his life on wrong principles may yet learn the truth through the sufferings he has brought upon himself. This is a moral, didactic theme; but the only theology in the book is a repeated assertion of the necessity to read the Bible, Crusoe's attitude to the conversion of Friday being remarkably similar to the religious attitude of Addison and Steele:

> The conversation which employed the hours between Friday and me was such as made the three years which we lived together perfectly and completely happy. This savage was now a good Christian, a much better than I; though I have reason to hope, and bless God for it, that we were equally penitent, and comforted, restored penitents. The same plain instruction sufficiently served to the enlightening this savage creature, and bringing him to be such a Christian as I have known few equal to him in my life. As to all the disputes, wrangling, strife, and contention, which have happened in the world about religion, whether niceties in doctrine or schemes of Church government, they were all perfectly useless to us, and for aught I can yet see, they have been so to the rest of the world.

When we remember that *Crusoe* was read by nearly everybody, including those untouched by the more learned writings of Pope and Addison, we can gauge something of the influence of such a passage as this.

Some of the lower classes, of course, particularly in the villages, were illiterate—though the efforts of the Dissenting schools and the rival Anglican Charity Schools were rapidly reducing illiteracy. The villagers must have depended for some of their religious ideas on the sermons of the parish priest. We know little about such sermons, but if Addison's Sir Roger de Coverley can be said to be in any way typical of

the country squire of the time, his giving the parson a collection
of the best English sermons, and requesting him to read one
every Sunday, is significant of the easy religious manners that
may have led to a degree of "Augustan tolerance" even among
the poor.   Addison tells us that the Coverley collection
included sermons by such different divines as the high-church
Sanderson, the middle-of-the-road Tillotson, and the nonconformist Calamy; so the villagers must have received a much
greater variety of religious experience than if the parson had
composed his sermons for himself.

But Addison and Steele were pre-eminently the voices of
the town, of that coffee-house public in London to which the
Tatler and the *Spectator* were principally addressed.   In this
society, the religious zeal of the seventeenth century was condemned partly because it led to melancholy and unsociability,
Addison in the *Spectator* giving a portrait of one of those
religious enthusiasts whose "superstitious fears and groundless
scruples cut them off from the pleasures of conversation" and
other innocent pursuits:

> Sombrius is one of these Sons of Sorrow.   He thinks
> himself obliged in duty to be sad and disconsolate.   He
> looks on a sudden fit of laughter as a breach of his
> baptismal vow.   An innocent jest startles him like
> blasphemy . . . He is a religious man, and would have
> behaved himself very properly had he lived when
> Christianity was under a general persecution.

The kind of Christianity that was admired can be seen
from the *Tatler's* review of Swift's *Project for the Advancement
of Religion*:

> It is written with the spirit of one who has seen the
> world enough to undervalue it with good breeding.   The
> author must certainly be a man of wisdom as well as piety,
> and have spent much time in the exercise of both.   The
> real causes of the decay of the interest in religion are set
> forth in a clear and lively manner, without unseasonable
> passions; and the whole air of the book, as to the
> language, the sentiments and the reasonings, shows it was
> written by one whose virtue sits easy about him and to

whom vice is thoroughly contemptible. It was said by one of this company, alluding to that knowledge of the world the author seems to have, that the man writes much like a gentleman and goes to Heaven with a very good mien.*

This comfortable "gentlemanly" religion had its obvious limitations, leading by too easy a path to the sort of wine-bibbing parson we often find in eighteenth-century novels and who was one of the causes of the Methodist mission. But it was preferable to the religion of Sombrius, which it largely displaced, as well as superior to the fashionable cynicism of such Restoration courtiers as Rochester. Though Voltaire could remark with sardonic surprise that the English people had a hundred religions but only one sauce, our variety of religious experience had nevertheless an extent of common ground that we see as much in Dissenters like Defoe and Catholics like Pope as in the triumphant Anglicanism of Addison and Swift.

Literature and Politics

The relation between politics and literature was closer in the Augustan Age than it had ever been before or was ever to be again. One reason for this was the decline in court patronage that we have noted. In this transition time between the decay of court power and the rise of strict party organisation under Walpole, individual aristocratic statesmen like Halifax or Somers wielded enormous influence and were in the temporary position of being able to dispose of public appointments among their friends and dependants, as the king had formerly rewarded his courtiers and their dependants. It was the one period in our history when poets and pamphleteers could rise to high positions in the state, not so much by their ability in political affairs as by their actual literary merit. Prior, the son of an artisan, became Ambassador to France; he started on his climb to fame by collaborating with

* What intrigued Voltaire, of course, was the number of routes open. "An Englishman," he wrote in his *Lettres sur les Anglais*, "goes to Heaven by the road he pleases."

Charles Montague, later Earl of Halifax, in a burlesque poem called *The Town and Country Mouse.* Addison held several important positions, including one of the Secretaries of State; he first won the Government's notice by composing a poem in honour of Marlborough's victory at Blenheim. Congreve was given the sinecure post of Commissioner for licensing Hackney Coaches on the strength of his first comedy, *The Old Bachelor*; he later became Secretary for Jamaica. Steele became Surveyor of the Royal Stables and, after the failure of the Jacobite Rebellion of 1715, a Commissioner of Forfeited Estates in Scotland. Gay became Secretary to the Earl of Clarendon, while the Earl was Ambassador to Hanover. Even such lesser lights as Tickell and Dennis, mainly known to-day because they figure in Pope's satires, obtained public employment and were able to "touch the King's coin" through the influence of the statesmen who had gained the distribution of it.

The two greatest writers of the age, Swift and Pope, were a partial exception. Undoubtedly Swift expected a greater reward for his political services than the Deanery of St Patrick's, Dublin; disappointment at his lack of advancement is probably part of the background of *Gulliver's Travels.* Pope as a Catholic was, of course, ineligible for public employment, and the state of his health was a further bar. He prided himself, as we have observed, on his independence of patronage; but the main cause of his independent position was the overwhelming success of his Homer translation, a success which he owed in great part to the influence of Swift among those aristocratic politicians whom he himself in later life was inclined to despise. We owe to Pope, though, an insight into the disadvantages of this close connection between politics and literature, one of which was the fulsome adulation of poets for their aristocratic patrons, whose own amateur verses were insincerely compared with Virgil or Horace. (As Dryden, addressing the Earl of Dorset on the subject of modern writers comparable to the ancients, had written: "I would instance your lordship in satire, and Shakespeare in tragedy".)

These lines from the *Epistle to Arbuthnot* probably refer to the Earl of Halifax:

> Proud as Apollo on his forked hill,
> Sat full-blown Bufo, puff'd by ev'ry quill;
> Fed with soft Dedication all day long,
> Horace and he went hand in hand in song.
> His Library (where busts of Poets dead
> And a true Pindar stood without a head,)
> Receiv'd of wits an undistinguish'd race,
> Who first his judgment ask'd, and then a place:
> Much they extoll'd his pictures, much his seat,
> And flatter'd ev'ry day, and some days eat:
> Till grown more frugal in his riper days,
> He paid some bards with port, and some with praise;
> To some a dry rehearsal was assign'd,
> And others (harder still) he paid in kind.

But it was not altogether a disadvantage that so many aristocratic statesmen prided themselves on their own poetry—however hard it might have been for a poet, just delivered of an ode, to be paid not by a sinecure but by another ode. For part of the reason of this close relation between literature and politics was the fact that writers could mix freely with aristocratic politicians in the London coffee-houses. In 1708 there were no less than three thousand coffee-houses in London. Some of these were frequented mainly by traders and stock-brokers, others by gamblers and men of fashion. But there were a good many houses where "wits" and politicians used to meet, where the talk would be alternately of affairs of state and the latest book or play. These were rigidly divided into Whig and Tory: "A Whig," wrote Defoe "will no more go to the Cocoa Tree or Ozindas's than a Tory will be seen at the coffee-house of St James." The most famous literary house had been Will's, much frequented by Dryden; but its popularity declined as other houses sprang up in the same district. Addison, who formerly went to Will's, removed in 1712 to the Whig stronghold of Button's, where he used to spend five or six hours a day and, according to Pope,

> Like Cato, give his little Senate laws,
> And sit attentive to his own applause.

The popularity of the coffee-house, and other places of social refreshment, naturally gave rise to the club, some of which became so important in later years that they took over the ownership of the house. The most famous was the Kit-cat Club, which used to meet at a mutton-pie house near Temple Bar, kept by a man named Christopher Cat, after whom the pies were called Kit-cats; the publisher Tonson was secretary, and among the members were not only writers like Addison and Congreve, and painters like Kneller, but most of the Whig aristocracy. During the short period when Swift was a political power in the land, he helped to found the Brothers' Club, which was intended to act as a meeting-place between Tory statesmen and those writers who were willing, for the usual favour, to support the Tory cause.*

London was even more important then than it is to-day, for the big towns of the Midlands and the North—places like Birmingham and Sheffield—were then in their infancy, only becoming centres of wealth and influence during the later eighteenth century. There were no bookshops in Birmingham, for example, at this date; Johnson's father, who had a small bookshop at Lichfield, used to go regularly to Birmingham on market-days to open a stall. Apart from such small ventures, the literary world of England was almost exclusively in the hands of the capital and the university towns of Oxford and Cambridge. An author born in the provinces, like Johnson, would as inevitably come up to London to seek his fortune, as a London publisher would ride to Oxford or Cambridge with a commission in his pocket for a promising poet or translator. In this powerful literary world of London, the most powerful element was in the coffee-houses and it was to this public that the two most representative writers of the age came to address themselves.

* A popular joke in the *Spectator* was the description of a number of fictitious clubs: including the Ugly Club, addressed by Steele "May it please your Deformities"; the Everlasting Club, whose "senior member," wrote Addison, "has outlived the whole club twice over and has been drunk with the grandfathers of some of the present sitting members"; and the Corpulent Club, which "though it consisted but of fifteen persons, weighed above three ton".

Steele and the " Tatler "

Sir Richard Steele (1672-1729) was typical of the transition in life and literature from the Restoration period to the Augustan. He had much of Restoration wit and gallantry in his composition—Johnson called him "the most agreeable rake that ever trod the rounds of indulgence "—but his easy wit was tempered by an Augustan conscience, his first published work bearing the pious title *The Christian Hero : an Argument proving that no Principles but those of Religion are sufficient to make a great man*. It was written, said the author with characteristic candour, "principally to fix upon his own mind a strong impression of virtue and religion in opposition to a stronger propensity towards unwarrantable pleasure ".

Steele had been born in Dublin, of English parents* and had been educated at the Charterhouse, where one of his fellow-pupils was his future collaborator Addison. They were later at Oxford together, but in 1696 Steele left the University without taking a degree and joined those undergraduates who had enlisted as privates in the Chancellor's regiment of the Coldstream Guards when the King was in danger from a rising of the Jacobites. The colonel of the regiment made him his secretary and got him an ensign's commission, whence he rose to be captain. It was as Captain Steele that he wrote *The Christian Hero*, which ends with a patriotic sketch of the King.

In the same year that *The Christian Hero* was published, 1701, he saw his first play, *The Funeral ; or Grief à la Mode*, acted with success at Drury Lane. This was the first of four comedies in which he determined to amuse his audience in the Restoration manner but also to edify them by painting virtue

* Irishmen by birth or race played an astonishingly large part in English literature during the eighteenth century. Farquhar, Steele, Berkeley, and Swift were followed by Goldsmith, Sterne, Burke, and Sheridan, besides lesser figures like Parnell, Brooke, Murphy, and Kelly. With the immense Scottish contribution—Burnet, Arbuthnot, Thomson, Blair, Ramsay, Hume, Robertson, Smollett, Boswell, Macpherson, Mackenzie, Burns, Adam Smith, Beattie, Reid, Stewart, etc., etc.—English literature became for the first time the centre of talent drawn from the whole of the British people.

and vice in less ambiguous colours. This was a favourite
theme of his, to which he returned in the *Spectator* ten years
later, when he subjected Etherege's *Man of Mode; or Sir
Fopling Flutter* to a severe moral criticism, concluding that
"This whole celebrated piece is a perfect contradiction to
good manners, good sense, and common honesty".*

There is much truth in Steele's criticism, but his own plays
cannot be said to be very lively. They point forward to the
sentimental drama of Cumberland and Kelly rather than to
Goldsmith and Sheridan. The last comedy of the four,
indeed, *The Conscious Lovers* (1722), is mainly known to-day
by the remark of Parson Adams in Fielding's *Joseph Andrews*:
that *Cato* and *The Conscious Lovers* were the only plays he
ever heard of that were fit for a Christian to read, "and I must
own, in the latter there are some things almost solemn enough
for a sermon".

Steele had meanwhile found his true genius in the periodical
essay and his true public in the London coffee-houses. Defoe
had issued in 1704 the first number of the *Weekly Review*, to
which he had added a supplement called *Advice from the
Scandal Club*: "After our serious matters are over," he wrote,
"we shall at the end of every paper present you with a little
diversion, as anything occurs to make the world merry; and
whether friend or foe, one party or another, if anything happens
so scandalous as to require an open reproof, the world may meet
with it there." This supplement, with the idea of a club to
which letters were supposed to be addressed asking for advice,
quickly proved popular, and Steele saw in it the crude begin-
nings of a form of literature in which he thought, with justice,
he could excel. In 1708 Swift, under the name of Isaac
Bickerstaff, Esq., had attacked the astrologer Partridge, "to
prevent the people of England from being further imposed on
by vulgar almanack makers". The success of this joke had
made the name of Bickerstaff "famous through all parts of
Europe". Other coffee-house wits kept up the jest, and
Londoners, Steele thought, would be keen to read anything

* For the Augustan attack on the Restoration drama, see further
below, pp. 114-17.

professing to come from the same person. So he borrowed the name of this fictitious astrologer from Swift (who at that date was a fellow-Whig) and on the 12th of April, 1709, appeared the first number of *The Tatler; By Isaac Bickerstaff, Esq.*, "published for the use of the good people of England . . . wherein [continued Steele] I shall from time to time report and consider all matters of what kind soever that shall occur to me, and publish such my advices and reflections every Tuesday, Thursday, and Saturday in the week for the convenience of the post". This last reference gives us an idea of the extent of the *Tatler's* circulation, for it must have served not only London itself but the outer region covered by the new penny-post. The paper cost a penny in London, but was issued also for another halfpenny for transmission by post, with a blank half-sheet on which could be written a personal message.

But it was meant mainly, of course, for the coffee-houses of London, and was supposed to be written from there, in a style reminiscent of coffee-house conversation:

> We shall not upon a dearth of news [wrote Steele] present you with musty foreign edicts, or dull proclamations, but shall divide our relation of the passages which occur in action or discourse throughout this town, as well as elsewhere, under such dates or places as may prepare you for the matter you are to expect, in the following manner:
>
> All accounts of gallantry, pleasure and entertainment, shall be under the article of White's Chocolate-house; poetry, under that of Will's Coffee-house; learning, under the title of Grecian;* foreign and domestic news you will have from St James's Coffee-house; and what else I shall on any other subject offer shall be dated from my own apartment.

---

* That is, the Grecian Coffee-house, off the Strand, started by a Greek servant named Constantine. This was much patronised by Greek scholars and members of the Royal Society. It was in this house that two gentlemen are said to have quarrelled over the correct placing of a Greek accent, whence they resorted to a duel in which one of them was killed.

Thus, after this preliminary notice, we have in the first number a mock-sorrowful account of a young lover, dated White's Chocolate-house, April 7th; an account of the acting of Congreve's *Love for Love*, for the benefit of the veteran actor Betterton, dated Will's Coffee-house, April 8th; some news from the Allied front in Holland, dated St James's Coffee-house, April 11th; and "from my own apartment" a further baiting of the unfortunate Partridge, possibly written by Swift. Steele was in a fortunate position as regards political news, for Harley (later Lord Oxford) had appointed him writer of the official *Gazette* some months before; it may have been because of some political indiscretion that he had to bring the *Tatler* to an end, after 271 numbers, on the 1st of January, 1711.

Popularity of the "Tatler"

Steele himself wrote most of the *Tatler*, the only other frequent contributor being his friend Addison, who wrote about forty essays. (Congreve wrote one, Swift two or three.) It is characteristic of Steele that, though he founded the *Tatler* and wrote the major part of it, he afterwards, when the papers were reprinted in four volumes, attributed most of their success to Addison. "I fared," he wrote, "like a distressed prince who calls in a powerful neighbour to his aid. I was undone by my auxiliary. When I had once called him in, I could not subsist without dependence on him." This is generous acknowledgment, recalling Defoe's public greeting of the *Tatler* in the *Review*, but it has been well said that Addison owes more to Steele than Steele to Addison. Steele not only edited in succession the *Tatler*, the *Spectator*, and the *Guardian*, contributing about 500 articles to Addison's 350, his reputation was merely enhanced by Addison's collaboration, whereas Addison might not have written any of the essays by which he is mainly remembered if Steele had not begun the work. The two men were, of course, complementary, Steele being more a man of the world, Addison more scholarly, the one deeply read in life, the other in literature. Steele's flair was for the topical, the witty treatment of contemporary foibles; while Addison, though he could deal with such matters with equal lightness, had also a vein of more profundity, suiting his famous definition: "A philosopher, which is what I mean by a gentleman". It was Steele who promised to "have something which may be of entertainment to the fair sex, in honour of whom I have taken the title of this paper"; and its appeal to the home as well as to the coffee-house must have been one of the reasons for the *Tatler's* success.

How much it was missed, and how great was the enthusiasm when it was found that the same writers were starting the *Spectator*, can be seen from a pamphlet by John Gay, *The Present State of Wit, in a Letter to a Friend in the Country*, which came out in May, 1711. Part of this can be quoted, as showing the opinion of Steele's work by one of the ablest of his younger contemporaries:

> Before I proceed further in the account of our weekly papers, it will be necessary to inform you that at the beginning of the winter, to the infinite surprise of all the town, Mr Steele flung up his *Tatler*, and instead of Isaac Bickerstaff, Esquire, subscribed himself Richard Steele to the last of those papers, after a handsome compliment to the town for their kind acceptance of his endeavours to divert them . . .
>
> His disappearance seemed to be bewailed as some general calamity. Everyone wanted so agreeable an amusement, and the coffee-houses began to be sensible that the Esquire's *Lucubrations* alone had brought them more customers than all their other newspapers put together.
>
> It must indeed be confessed that never man threw up his pen under stronger temptations to have employed it longer. His reputation was at a greater height than I believe ever any living author's was before him. It is reasonable to suppose that his gains were proportionately considerable. Everyone read him with pleasure and good-will; and the Tories, in respect to his other good qualities, had almost forgiven his unaccountable imprudence in declaring against them . . .
>
> To give you my own thoughts of this gentleman's writings, I shall, in the first place, observe that there is a

noble difference between him and all the rest of our
gallant and polite authors. The latter have endeavoured
to please the age by falling in with them, and encouraging
them in their fashionable vices and false notions of things.
It would have been a jest, some time since, for a man to
have asserted that anything witty could be said in praise
of a married state, or that devotion and virtue were any
way necessary to the character of a fine gentleman.
Bickerstaff ventured to tell the town that they were a
parcel of fops, fools and coquettes; but in such a manner
as even pleased them and made them more than half
inclined to believe that he spoke truth . . .

It is incredible to conceive the effect his writings
have had on the town; how many thousand follies they
have either quite banished or given a very great check to;
how much countenance they have added to virtue and
religion . . . how entirely they have convinced our young
fops and young fellows of the value and advantages of
learning.

He has indeed rescued it out of the hands of pedants
and fools, and discovered the true method of making it
amiable and lovely to all mankind. In the dress he gives
it, it is a most welcome guest at tea-tables and assemblies,
and is relished and caressed by the merchants on the
Change. Accordingly there is not a lady at court, nor a
banker in Lombard Street, who is not verily persuaded
that Captain Steele is the greatest scholar and best casuist
of any man in England . . .

The vast variety of subjects which Mr Steele has
treated of, in so different manners, and yet all so perfectly
well, made the world believe that it was impossible they
should all come from the same hand. This set everyone
guessing who was the Esquire's friend? and most people
at first fancied it must be Doctor Swift; but it is now no
longer a secret that his only great and constant assistant
was Mr Addison.

This is that excellent friend to whom Mr Steele owes so
much; and who refuses to have his name set before those
pieces which the greatest pens in England would be
proud to own. Indeed, they could hardly add to this
gentleman's reputation: whose works in Latin and
English poetry long since convinced the world that he was
the greatest master in Europe in those two languages.

Addison and the "Spectator"

There is no doubt that Gay's opinion of Addison's work was the common one at the time and was probably shared, in all modesty, by Addison himself. He would have been rather taken aback had he known that he would live, not by *Cato* or his Latin and English poems, but by his contributions to the *Tatler* and *Spectator*. He would have expected that these essays, though valuable enough as a corrective to the age and a commentary upon it, would pass with the age, or at most be sometimes consulted by historians and scholars; but that his poetry, not being so topical, would survive. But it is hardly even a question of topicality, for few poets have been more topical than Pope, and he survives in poetry as Addison in essay-writing. It is rather a question of pure literary merit, for most of Addison's English poems seem as dead to us now as his Latin,* whereas some of the *Spectator* essays—particularly, of course, the Coverley series—are as alive now as when they were written. The only two poems by Addison which are still widely known—the hymns *The spacious firmament on high* and *When all thy mercies, O my God*—were themselves originally contributed to the *Spectator*.

We should not forget, however, that part of the cause of his influence as a journalist was the previous reputation he had won as poet, scholar, and politician. The *Spectator* comes roughly half-way through his career, and we must glance first of all at his earlier work.

Joseph Addison (1672-1719) was the son of a Wiltshire parson who afterwards became Dean of Lichfield. His schoolboy friendship with Steele was continued at Oxford, but while Steele enlisted in the army he remained at the University to become Fellow of Magdalen. There he obtained, by dedication of some poems, the patronage of both Sir John Somers and the future Earl of Halifax. He was intended for the Church, but these two powerful politicians saw in him a useful recruit

* They were not very much favoured by the opinion of the Augustans' immediate successors. Gray, for instance, referred in 1748 to Addison's "three or four notes in poetry, sweet enough indeed, like those of a German flute, but such as soon tire and satiate the ear with their frequent return".

for the state and in 1699 procured for him a government
pension of £300 a year, to enable him to study on the Continent and so qualify for the diplomatic service.   In France
he met the critic Boileau, who, it is said, first became aware by
Addison's poetry and conversation that England was not
altogether a barbarous nation.   On his return he resumed his
intimacy with Steele, who was able to introduce him to the
rising wits of the London coffee-houses.

Meanwhile, things were not going too favourably for him
in the financial sense; his pension had ceased on the King's
death in 1702 and his patrons were temporarily out of office.
But Halifax had not forgotten his protégé, and when the
Government wanted a poem upon Marlborough's victory at
Blenheim he recommended Addison to the Lord Treasurer
Godolphin.   Addison accepted the commission and published
The Campaign in 1705.   It is said that the first part of the
poem was presented to Godolphin for his approval and that,
by a lucky chance, Addison had left off writing at the afterwards famous comparison of Marlborough and the battle with
the angel and the storm:

> So when an Angel by divine command
> With rising tempests shakes a guilty land
> (Such as of late o'er pale Britannia pass'd),
> Calm and serene he drives the furious blast;
> And, pleas'd the Almighty's orders to perform,
> Rides in the whirlwind and directs the storm.

The figure was judged to be among the greatest produced in
either ancient or modern verse, and the promised reward of
the Government's—a post in the office of the Commissioner
of Appeals worth £200 a year—was virtually in Addison's
possession by the time Godolphin had read to the end of this
first instalment.

The poet quickly rose in the government service.   He was
soon appointed Under-Secretary of State, accompanied
Halifax on a diplomatic mission to Hanover, and in 1709
became Chief Secretary to the Lord-Lieutenant of Ireland.
While in Dublin, he sent some pieces to the *Tatler*, and when
the Whig ministry fell from power, and he was out of office, he

joined Steele in London and began to contribute more regularly.

Though already famous as a poet, he had not really written much of value: a few Latin poems; a book of travels; *Dialogues upon the Usefulness of Ancient Medals*; the "prize poem" *The Campaign*; some contributions to the *Tatler*; four acts of *Cato*, which he had begun at Oxford; and a few other pieces in poetry and prose. Whatever view we now take of the Augustan relation between politics and literature, we can be grateful that the coming of the Tories set Addison free to write the Coverley papers, as later the return of the Whigs set Swift free to write *Gulliver's Travels*.

Though under the same editorship of Steele, the *Spectator* was not simply the *Tatler* revived: it differed in several ways from its predecessor. For one thing, political affairs were not among the subjects discussed in the new paper; for another, it consisted of a single long essay or pamphlet, whereas the *Tatler* had contained several short articles on different subjects; thirdly, the *Spectator* came out daily, from the 1st of March, 1711, to the 6th of December, 1712; and lastly, the fictitious astrologer Isaac Bickerstaff perished with the *Tatler*, as the real astrologer Partridge was supposed to have done before.*

The supposed editor of the new paper was called simply "Mr Spectator". He was a member of an imaginary club, described by Steele in the second number, his own character having been sketched by Addison in the first. The other members were a witty lawyer "of the Inner Temple"; Sir Andrew Freeport, "a merchant of great eminence in the City of London"; Will Honeycomb, an elderly gallant, who "where women are not concerned, is an honest worthy man"; a rare visitor, a clergyman, "a very philosophic man, of

---

* The cream of the original Bickerstaff jest was contained in Swift's *Predictions for the Year 1708*, in which Bickerstaff prophesied the death of Partridge the almanack-maker "upon the 29th of March next, about eleven at night, of a raging fever". When that date had passed, Partridge added to the town's mirth by protesting publicly that he was still alive; and the first number of the *Tatler* included a solemn note reproving him for this exaggeration.

general learning, great sanctity of life, and the most exact good breeding"; and, most famous of the members, "a gentleman of Worcestershire", Sir Roger de Coverley, and his "next heir" Captain Sentry, "a gentleman of great courage, good understanding, but invincible modesty".

This method of having a club as a centre, round which the various essays could be constructed, was ideal for the purpose, as Defoe had realised in the supplement to his *Review*. The various members were typical of the upper-middle classes of the day, and their various pursuits could lead naturally—like those of Chaucer's pilgrims—to an interesting variety of topics. The *Tatler* had kept almost exclusively to the town, but by following Sir Roger home to Worcestershire the *Spectator* was able to strike a better balance between urban and country life.

The part which most continued the work of the *Tatler* was the good-humoured criticism of contemporary fashion and "French fopperies". Addison could turn from reflections on the exercise of virtue to comment wittily on such French importations as the habit of ladies of receiving visitors in their bedrooms:

> As I love to see everything that is new, I once prevailed upon my friend Will Honeycomb to carry me along with him to one of these travelled ladies . . . The lady, though willing to appear undressed, had put on her best looks and painted herself for our reception. Her hair appeared in a very nice disorder, as the night-gown which was thrown upon her shoulders was ruffled with great care.

The fashion of patching came in for some lively criticism, Addison imagining that part of the face was patched by Tory ladies, another part by Whig:

> I must here take notice that Rosalinda, a famous Whig partisan, has most unfortunately a very beautiful mole on the Tory part of her forehead; which being very conspicuous has occasioned many mistakes and given a handle to her enemies to misrepresent her face, as though it had revolted from the Whig interest.

In a letter which Mr Spectator is supposed to receive while

staying at Sir Roger's, he is urged to return to London as the petticoats in fashion are growing wider and wider:

> You have diverted the town almost a whole month at the expense of the country; it is now high time that you should give the country their revenge. Since your withdrawing from this place, the fair sex are run into great extravagancies. Their petticoats, which began to heave and swell before you left us, are now blown up into a most enormous concave . . . What they have lost in height they make up in breadth, and contrary to all rules of architecture widen the foundations at the same time that they shorten the superstructure.

Coverley Papers and Saturday Sermons

Though they do not take up more than about thirty papers out of a total of over 500, the Coverley series were among the most popular at the time and are almost the only ones which have retained their popularity. This is largely explained by our taste for novels, the Coverley *Spectators* being among the pioneers of modern fiction, about half-way between the old periodical essay and the new novel of Richardson and Fielding. Addison wrote the majority of the series, including the famous pieces about Sir Roger and Will Wimble and Sir Roger at church:

> As Sir Roger is landlord to the whole congregation, he keeps them in very good order and will suffer nobody to sleep in it besides himself; for if by chance he has been surprised into a short nap at sermon, upon recovering out of it he stands up and looks about him, and if he sees anybody else nodding, either wakes them himself or sends his servants to them. Several others of the old knight's particularities break out upon these occasions: sometimes he will be lengthening out a verse in the singing-psalms half a minute after the rest of the congregation have done with it; sometimes, when he is pleased with the matter of his devotion, he pronounces Amen three or four times to the prayer; and sometimes stands up when everybody else is upon their knees, to count the congregation or see if any of his tenants are missing.

Pieces like this are where the *Spectator* comes at once nearest the novel and nearest the realities of life at the time.

Though the Augustan Age is pre-eminently in literature the age of the town, most of the inhabitants of England lived in isolated villages, where the character of the local squire and parson was a very important matter. Such benevolent despots as Addison's Sir Roger or Fielding's Squire Allworthy undoubtedly existed, as did clergymen of the type of Sir Roger's chaplain or Parson Adams. Fielding knew the darker side, and even Addison, though a mere spectator from the town, is careful to distinguish between Sir Roger's benevolent rule and the situation in the next village, where the squire and the parson "live in a perpetual state of war". The squire "has not said his prayers either in public or private this half-year" and the parson "threatens him, if he does not mend his manners, to pray for him in the face of the whole congregation". Addison reflects that

> feuds of this nature, though too frequent in the country, are very fatal to the ordinary people; who are so used to be dazzled with riches that they pay as much deference to the understanding of a man of an estate as of a man of learning, and are very hardly brought to regard any truth, how important soever it may be, that is preached to them, when they know there are several men of five hundred a year who do not believe it.

This observation was to be frequently made during the eighteenth century, even sceptics like Hume being anxious to preserve the "pious ignorance" of the Lower Orders. It was not till the end of the century that conscious free-thought, though comparatively common among the upper and middle classes, made any great impression upon the poor.*

* There were naturally exceptions, such as the chandler-Deist Thomas Chubb and his friends at Salisbury. Chubb, the contemporary of Addison, wrote many tracts on theological subjects, taking a freer view of Christianity than was usual except in a few literary circles. Hazlitt observes in his essay *On Reading Old Books*: "Much about the same time . . . I took a particular satisfaction in reading Chubb's Tracts, and I often think I will get them again to wade through. There is a high gusto of polemical divinity in them; and you fancy that you hear a club of shoemakers at Salisbury, debating a disputable text from one of St Paul's Epistles in a workmanlike style, with equal shrewdness and pertinacity".

But everyone knows the part of the *Spectator* taken up by the Coverley papers. It is more important perhaps to turn to Addison's other contributions. Some of these were the Saturday "lay-sermons", intended for Sunday reading. The "text" is as often from classical writers as from the Bible, a variation which was characteristic of the Augustan mind. A typical sermon of this sort begins thus:

> We all of us complain of the shortness of time, saith Seneca, and yet have much more than we know what to do with. Our lives, says he, are spent either in doing nothing at all, or in doing nothing to the purpose, or in doing nothing that we ought to do: we are always complaining our days are few, and acting as though there would be no end of them. That noble philosopher has described our inconsistency with ourselves in this particular, by all those various turns of expression and thought which are peculiar to his writings.
>
> I often consider mankind as wholly inconsistent with itself in a point that bears some affinity to the former. Though we seem grieved at the shortness of life in general, we are wishing every period of it at an end. The minor longs to be at age, then to be a man of business, then to make up an estate, then to arrive at honours, then to retire. Thus although the whole of life is allowed by everyone to be short, the several divisions of it appear long and tedious. We are for lengthening our span in general, but would fain contract the parts of which it is composed.

Had Addison gone into the Church, no doubt he would have written his sermons in a similar cool and reasonable style. Compared with the fervour of a Donne or a Bunyan, the style may seem truly as suited to Saturday as to Sunday, but it was part of the philosophy of the age that "the exercise of virtue" was as necessary to the ordinary business of the world as the use of reason and proportion in religion.

The most interesting of the Saturday *Spectators* was Addison's series of essays on *Paradise Lost*, which appeared during the winter and spring of 1712. There were eighteen of these essays, forming Addison's most extensive piece of literary criticism. It is Augustan criticism at its best, but

also—to a modern eye—with its most serious limitations.
Addison tries bravely to break out of the prison of classical
"rules", yet begins his examination with Aristotle's handcuffs
only partially loosed:

> There is nothing in nature more irksome than general
> discourses, especially when they turn chiefly upon words.
> For this reason I shall waive the discussion . . . whether
> Milton's *Paradise Lost* may be called an Heroic Poem . . .
> It will be sufficient to its perfection if it has in it all the
> beauties of the highest kind of poetry . . .
>
> I shall therefore examine it by the rules of epic poetry,
> and see whether it falls short of the *Iliad* or *Aeneid* in the
> beauties which are essential to that kind of writing. The
> first thing to be considered in an epic poem is the fable,
> which is perfect or imperfect, according as the action
> which it relates is more or less so. This action should
> have three qualifications in it. First, it should be but
> one action. Secondly, it should be an entire action; and,
> thirdly, it should be a great action . . . (etc.)

Fortunately for Addison, Milton could come out of this
examination room with a higher mark than was possible for
Shakespeare. There was little the Augustans could do about
Shakespeare: either the rules were wrong or he was wrong.
But Milton had been a classical scholar himself and had
endeavoured with remarkable success to justify the ways of
Aristotle to the Puritans. Though it may seem strange that
Addison, the voice of Augustan decorum, should call a poem
by a Puritan enthusiast "an honour to the English nation",
yet if we remember the continuity of classical education from
Jonson's time to Johnson's, and also how little else in English
poetry could satisfy the rules of Athens and the French critics,
the triumph of Milton in the eighteenth century is not so
remarkable.

The triumph, if it did not begin with Addison, nevertheless
found its first full expression in these *Spectator* essays.* The

* It was helped, of course, by the reaction from the more rigid
of Augustan ideas that began early in the Augustan Age itself. John
Dennis, for instance, in *The Advancement and Reformation of Modern
Poetry* (1701) and *The Grounds of Criticism in Poetry* (1704) had
realised the inadequacy of the classical rules and had seen the virtue

kind of criticism employed seems largely irrelevant to us, but it seemed highly relevant to its original readers. The series proved very popular and undoubtedly contributed both to the growing toleration for Nonconformity and to that combination of Christian and classical ideals which the Augustans, like Milton himself, were seeking.

Other criticism in the *Spectator* included Steele on Restoration and contemporary drama, and Addison on some of the old ballads—to which, as to *Paradise Lost*, he was able to show classical parallels, to silence all objectors. Steele wrote much upon the stage and also gave some glimpses of the London underworld, rather in the spirit of his younger contemporary Hogarth. He contributed 236 papers altogether, to Addison's 274, the remaining numbers being the work of occasional contributors like Pope and Parnell, Philips and Tickell. The popularity of the *Spectator* can best be judged by the fact that Steele found it safe to double the price, after the government tax on periodicals had destroyed a number of his rivals.

"Cato" and the "Guardian"

In that pamphlet by Gay which we quoted earlier, there is an amusing description of the scene in the London literary world after Steele had closed the *Tatler* and not yet started the *Spectator*. The death of the real *Tatler* gave birth to a succession of false *Tatlers*, "each of which", says Gay, "with equal truth and wit, assured us he was the genuine Isaac Bickerstaff"; and also to other papers of the same kind, with names like the *Growler*, the *Whisperer*, the *Tell-tale*, etc. Most of these lesser stars were extinguished in the blaze of glory that attended the new venture of Steele and Addison.

The successors of the *Spectator* were even more numerous. Steele himself was responsible for the *Guardian* (1713), the *Englishman*, the *Lover*, and the *Reader*, followed by *Town Talk*, the *Tea-Table*, *Chit-chat*, the *Plebeian*, and the *Theatre*

of enthusiasm both in the composition of poetry and in the appreciation of it. He was followed by Isaac Watts, who in the preface (1709) to *Horae Lyricae* had stressed the imaginative quality of the literature of the Bible.

(1720). Rather like Dickens in Victorian journalism, Steele seems to have been always in a hurry to break new ground and was continually starting new projects, each of which he thought would make his fortune. The *Guardian* was the most distinguished of these later papers, none of which lasted very long. Steele assumed for it the role of "Nestor Ironside", an elderly man who, having got his wards safely off his hands, wishes to act the "guardian" to the whole town, "to make the pulpit, the bar, and the stage all act in concert in the care of piety, justice, and virtue". The contributors included Addison, Berkeley, and Pope, but the paper was not of the same kind as the *Spectator*, being even more political than the *Tatler*. In its successor, the *Englishman*, Steele—now M.P. for Stockbridge—fought vigorously for Whig principles against Swift's Tory *Examiner*. In 1710 Addison had started a *Whig Examiner* for the same purpose, but this, though it contained some of his wittiest work, had proved unsuccessful.

One of the most interesting pieces in the *Guardian* was Steele's description of the overwhelming success of his friend's *Cato*. Addison had at last finished this poetic drama, but had come to agree with Dryden that it was poetry for reading rather than a drama for the stage.* But he consented to its production at Drury Lane, when it was urged that the time was ripe for animating the public with the sentiments of liberty that he had put into Cato's mouth. The political atmosphere was stormy: the Tories, though in office, felt very insecure, two of their senior statesmen, Harley (Lord Oxford) and Bolingbroke, being, it was suspected, in league with the Jacobites. The Queen was ill, and the Hanoverian succession—and therefore the Protestant cause—seemed more in danger than at any time since the Revolution. *Cato* was therefore received almost as a contemporary political manifesto,

* "When Addison was a student at Oxford," records Edward Young, "he sent up this play [or the first three or four acts] to his friend Dryden, as a proper person to recommend it to the theatre, if it deserved it; who returned it, with very great commendation; but with his opinion that, on the stage, it could not meet with its deserved success."

the Tories, anxious to prove themselves staunch friends to liberty, applauding it as warmly as the Whigs. Pope, who wrote the prologue, says in a letter to a friend: "The numerous and violent claps of the Whig party on the one side of the theatre were echoed back by the Tories on the other; while the author sweated behind the scenes with concern to find their applause proceeding more from the hand than the head".

There seems little in the play itself to cause so much enthusiasm. The characters are mere mouth-pieces for fine sentiments, expressed in the dullest of Augustan verse. As Dennis pointed out at the time, the play is full of absurd situations, owing to Addison's concern for the classic rule of Unity of Place; conspiracy against Cato, and love-making to his daughter, all take place in Cato's own hall. But Dennis's opinion was not shared by most contemporary critics. More typical was the opinion of Voltaire, who called the play a masterpiece, praising Addison as "the first English writer who composed a regular tragedy "—that is, a tragedy composed by the classical rules. It is significant that Voltaire's opinion of Shakespeare was nearly as disparaging as Rymer's.

The later career of Steele and Addison in journalism and politics is not of much literary importance. In 1714 Addison revived the *Spectator* for six months, with the assistance of Tickell and John Byrom. Some of Byrom's pieces are well worth reading, but the death of the Queen that year, and Addison's political preoccupations, soon brought the revival to a close. On the return of the Whigs to office, Addison took up again his old post in Ireland and was later employed in writing a Government paper called the *Freeholder*. He was rewarded with the post of Commissioner for Trade, afterwards becoming for a short time a Secretary of State. But in 1718 he had to resign for reasons of health, and he died the year after at the age of forty-seven.

Steele survived his friend ten years. He had been knighted in 1714 and had held various official positions. His only literary success during the years after Addison's death was his last comedy, *The Conscious Lovers*, which was acted in 1722.

Other men attempted to repeat the popularity of the *Spectator*, with no more success than the original collaborators. A partial exception was the *Freethinker* (1718-21), edited by Ambrose Philips; this ran to 350 numbers and ranked high in contemporary estimation. The title was rather misleading, for the kind of free-thinking advocated was not in religion but in politics, and even there it was only a cover for orthodox Whig principles.

Gentlemen-Philosophers

We have observed that the Augustans had a suspicion of pedantry, that their ambition was to bring philosophy out of colleges to dwell at coffee-tables. Addison equated the twin ideals of the age when he remarked that a *philosopher* was what he meant by a *gentleman*.

This notion of every gentleman his own philosopher seems an attractive one, but in point of fact, of course, there were "professional" philosophers in the Augustan Age as in any other, though they might not have regarded themselves as such. Before we go on to treat of Swift and the Tory Opposition, we can glance at some of the more professional purveyors of the dominant philosophy who were behind the accepted ideas of the *Spectator*.

John Locke (1632-1704) was the leading theorist of the Revolution. We have observed his influence on religious toleration. His chief work, *An Essay concerning Human Understanding*, was published in 1690 and had a great influence in France as well as in England. It helped to correct established errors and to get rid of prejudice, and if Locke's thought had some striking limitations, particularly over the place of imagination in human life, it was his own pupil, the third Earl of Shaftesbury (1671-1713), who came to amend him, without losing his master's sense of proportion.

Shaftesbury, though often called a Deist, was in truth opposed to religious controversy of any kind. His writings, collected under the title *Characteristics of Men, Manners, Opinions and Times* (1711), deal with moral and aesthetic topics in a way that recalls the Cambridge Platonists of the seventeenth century—those philosophers who were the only neutral element during the Civil War—and anticipates to some degree the philosophy of Coleridge. His influence is seen on the poetry of Pope, Thomson, and Akenside, and on the criticism of Addison, Francis Hutcheson, and the Scottish philosophers of the later eighteenth century. His *Characteristics* were attacked by the Dutch physician Bernard Mandeville in the elaborated version (1723) of *The Fable of the Bees*. The most distinguished Christian philosopher of the age, George Berkeley (1685-1753), later Bishop of Cloyne, replied to both Shaftesbury and Mandeville in his *Alciphron* (1732).

The work of Berkeley takes us a little out of our period and is, in any case, too large and technical a subject for literary history. But his *Essay on Vision* (1709) and *Principles of Human Knowledge* (1710) come within the period of the *Tatler* and *Spectator*, and after he came to England in 1712 he gained the friendship of both Swift and Steele and wrote papers in the *Guardian* against the freethinkers. Part of the argument in his *Essay towards Preventing the Ruin of Great Britain* (1721) would have pleased Addison, for he wrote that national salvation was only to be secured by individual uprightness and deplored such things as "the trifling vanity of apparel" imported from France. All in all, Berkeley was probably the philosopher nearest the ideal of the *Spectator*, the influence of Locke having gone into some directions which Steele and Addison, though tolerant men, could not approve.

CHAPTER II

SWIFT AND THE TORY OPPOSITION

1697-1745

"I have ever hated all nations, professions and com-
munities, and all my love is towards individuals; for
instance, I hate the tribe of lawyers, but I love Counsellor
Such-a-one and Judge Such-a-one; so with physicians—
I will not speak of my own trade—soldiers, English,
Scotch, French, and the rest. But principally I hate and
detest that animal called man, though I heartily love
John, Peter, Thomas, and so forth. This is the system
upon which I have governed myself many years."

SWIFT: writing to Pope about *Gulliver's Travels*.

Whigs and Tories

We have observed the close relation between literature and
politics in the Augustan Age, when even the coffee-houses
were divided into Whig and Tory, where statesmen could mix
with writers willing to support their cause. But inevitably
our first chapter has dealt mainly with Whig writers, for
though there were Tory administrations in 1698 and 1710 it
was the Whig party who were behind the Revolution of 1688
and the basic political assumptions of the Augustan Age.
The Tories were in rather a difficult position at this time, for
traditionally they were the party who supported the rights of
the king, and it was only their fear of a Catholic succession
that made them join the Whigs in welcoming the Prince of
Orange. When they obtained power in 1710, theirs was an
uneasy rule, for several of their ministers were in correspondence with the Pretender and were intriguing for a Stuart
restoration. The Elector of Hanover was in the hands of
the Whigs, and when he eventually succeeded as George I the
main body of the Tories—being anxious, as we have seen in
their reception of Addison's *Cato*, to prove themselves staunch
adherents of Protestantism and Liberty—were forced to further

compromise their old position and acquiesce reluctantly in the rule of a foreign dynasty almost entirely dependent on their rivals.

Curiously enough, though, when we consider the political writers of the age, we find the principal talents on the Tory side rather than the Whig. Steele and Addison, and Burnet and Philips, were able men, but the Tory wits included Swift, Prior, Gay, Bolingbroke, Arbuthnot, Atterbury, Parnell, Dr Sheridan, and to a certain extent Pope.* This apparent paradox is not so remarkable if we remember the genius of the age for satire and how much more potent satire becomes if directed against the party or philosophy in power. After 1714 the Tory satirists did valuable work as a kind of His Majesty's Opposition, showing up the corruption of Whig government, particularly in Ireland; and before that date they were useful critics of some of the political assumptions of the age.

The most important figure, of course, is Swift, who has a depth and bitterness in his writing far removed from the gentle criticism of the *Spectator*. We feel that Steele and Addison, even while mocking the town, were of the town themselves; Swift, in his greatest works, seems to speak from outside and is in a position somewhat parallel to Tory politicians as opposed to the Whigs. The analogy should not be drawn too close, but it is scarcely an accident that the two most representative writers of the age belonged to the generally dominant Whig party, while the satirist most in opposition to the tendencies of contemporary society—in a Newtonian age, for example, he laughed at science in the *Voyage to Laputa*—came to support the losing side. A Tory Spectator and a Whig Gulliver were not persons capable of being produced by the events of the time.

The most public of writers has, however, a private life; and though too much has been made of the personal reasons for Swift's misanthropy, there is no doubt that private bitterness as well as public disappointment formed the mood

* The *Globe* editor of the poet refers to "The opposition, to which Pope was attached by personal friendships rather than by any distinct political creed".

in which *Gulliver* and the Irish pamphlets were written. Swift is not a simple figure to understand, and before we come to the period of his greatest works, when he was, as it were, unofficial leader of His Majesty's Opposition, we must glance at his early career with Sir William Temple and at the subsequent period of the English pamphlets, when he was, for a short time, a real power in the land.

Swift's Early Life

Jonathan Swift (1667-1745) was born, like Steele, of English parents in Dublin, being distantly related on his father's side to the poet Dryden and on his mother's to Dorothy Osborne, wife of the Whig statesman Sir William Temple. He was educated at Trinity College, Dublin, and in 1689 accepted an offer by Dorothy Osborne of a position in Temple's household at Moor Park, Surrey. There he became secretary to the retired statesman and also tutor to Temple's natural daughter Esther Johnson, the "Stella" of the *Journal* and the poems. *

Though he found his position as "poor relation" somewhat irksome, much of his later insight into political affairs must have had its origin in his conversations with Temple and the opportunities he had at Moor Park of meeting the statesmen who were governing the country in the years immediately following the Revolution. He must have discovered early on that "system" he describes in the famous letter to Pope—quoted as epigraph to this chapter—and even at this date must have been able to separate his scorn for politicians as a species from his admiration for certain individuals among them. There is truth, as well as the exaggeration necessary to drive the truth home, in what he was later to write in the person of Surgeon Gulliver. In the island of Glubbdubdrib, where the Governor has the power of calling whom he pleases from the dead,

> Three kings protested to me that in their whole reigns they never did once prefer any person of merit, unless by mistake or treachery of some minister in whom they confided: neither would they do it if they were to live

---

* See further, footnote to p. 61 below.

again. And they showed, with great strength of reason,
that the royal throne could not be supported without
corruption, because that positive, confident, restive
temper, which virtue infused into a man, was a perpetual
clog to public business.

Swift himself was anxious to be preferred, and must have
been exasperated by the compliment Temple paid him of
finding him too useful as secretary to recommend him for a
higher position elsewhere. It has been said that Addison
would have made an excellent Dean of St Patrick's, while
Swift would have been in his right position as Secretary of
State; and the future Dean tells us that he had "a scruple of
entering the Church merely for support". He overcame his
reluctance in 1694, when Temple offered him a small post in
the rolls-office, and, being aggrieved, he went back to Dublin
to seek holy orders.

He was given a small living in a village near Belfast, and
soon found the job even more dispiriting than his life with
Temple. His old master missed his aid and at his request
Swift returned to Moor Park till Temple's death in 1699. He
then returned to Ireland, as chaplain to Lord Berkeley at
Dublin Castle, and in 1700 Berkeley gave him the living of
Laracor in County Meath. But his subsequent career as an
Irish country parson is chiefly remarkable for his long absences
in England and for the beginning of his work as political
pamphleteer.

"A Tale of a Tub"

Though Swift published nothing till after Temple's death,
during his years at Moor Park he had been writing both poems
and prose satires, some of which had been circulated in manuscript among his patron's wide circle of acquaintance. His
poetry was never to become very important, compared with
his prose,* and one of his early Pindaric odes, the feebleness

* Among the few exceptions is the superb *Verses on the Death of
Dr Swift, written by himself*. This must be one of the best pieces of
Augustan verse satire, apart from Pope's, the acknowledged master.
It was written in 1731 and published 1739.

of which has to be read to be believed, led Dryden to say, "Cousin Swift, you will never be a poet". Here we must consider the two principal works in prose satire that preceded his entry into the political field: *The Battle of the Books* and *A Tale of a Tub*, both of which were written in 1697 and published together in 1704.

Compared with *Gulliver*, they are both "dated"; but the argument of the *Tub* is still of considerable interest, whereas the origin of the *Battle*—the controversy between ancient and modern literature—is one of those Augustan quarrels which seem almost incomprehensible to-day. The controversy arose in Paris and spread to England in 1692, when Temple wrote an essay in which he praised ancient literature at the expense of modern, unfortunately citing the *Letters of Phalaris* as an example of ancient superiority. In an appendix to William Wotton's defence of the moderns, Richard Bentley, the most distinguished classical scholar of the age, proved these letters to be spurious, later settling the whole question in a learned *Dissertation upon the Epistles of Phalaris*. Swift sided with Temple, no doubt at his request, but his indifference to the issue, and his contempt for academic controversy, can be seen in the foreword, where after giving a summary of the dispute he tells us that the books in St James's Library (that is, the Royal Library, which Bentley was in charge of) "looking upon themselves as parties principally concerned, took up the controversy, and came to a decisive battle; but the manuscript, by the injury of fortune or weather, being in several places imperfect, we cannot learn to which side the victory fell".

This was a favourite device of Swift's, used again in one of the digressions in *A Tale of a Tub*:

> . . . The present argument is the most abstracted that ever I engaged in; it strains my faculties to their highest stretch; and I desire the reader to attend with the utmost propensity; for I now proceed to unravel this knotty point.
>
> There is in mankind a certain . . . (*Hic multa desiderantur*). And this I take to be a clear solution of the matter.

It is typical of Swift, that last phrase or two, with its contempt for abstract reasoning personified in the shrug of the shoulders by which he leaves the "knotty point" exactly where it was before.

The twin intentions of *A Tale of a Tub*—"written for the universal improvement of mankind"—were to show up "the numerous and gross corruptions in religion and learning". The digressions deal with the corruptions in learning, the central story running through the book being a parable of three brothers, Peter (intended to represent the Church of Rome), Martin (the Lutherans and more especially the Church of England), and Jack (the Calvinists and particularly the Puritans), whose careers show up the corruptions in religion. The brothers are each given a coat by their father, who in his will leaves them directions for their use. The coats represent the outward forms of religion, the will the scriptures. At first the brothers live in harmony together, and travel into various countries, destroying monsters and giants (the heathen religions). But then they come into town and find their coats out of fashion, the will unfortunately forbidding them to embellish the original material. For the moment they are at a loss, but Peter, with an ingenuity that is supposed to satirise the subtle methods of the mediaeval schoolmen, pretends to find permission in the will to adorn their coats, first with shoulder-knots, then with fringes and gold lace. He then persuades his brothers that it would be best to shut the will up out of sight "in a strong box brought out of Greece or Italy . . . and trouble themselves no further to examine it, but only refer to its authority whenever they thought fit".

Peter now becomes very boastful, claiming to be called *lord* Peter and to take precedence over his brothers. He makes a number of inventions, including a pardon for all offences:

> Whenever it happened that any rogue of Newgate was condemned to be hanged, Peter would offer him a pardon for a certain sum of money; which when the poor caitiff had made all shifts to scrape up and send, his lordship would return a piece of paper in this form:
>
> "To all mayors, sheriffs, jailors, constables, bailiffs, hangmen, etc. Whereas we are informed that A.B.

remains in the hands of you, or some of you, under the
sentence of death. We will and command you, upon
sight hereof, to let the said prisoner depart to his own
habitation, whether he stands condemned for murder,
sodomy, rape, sacrilege, incest, treason, blasphemy, etc.,
for which this shall be your sufficient warrant; and if
you fail hereof, G— d—mn you and yours to all eternity.
And so we bid you heartily farewell. Your most humble
man's man, Emperor Peter."

The wretches, trusting to this, lost their lives and
money too.

The contrast between Peter's arrogance and the humility of
his signature—the actual general pardons of the Pope were
signed "*servus servorum*"—is one of Swift's happiest knocks
at the Church of Rome.

It is now, however, the turn of the Puritans. Martin and
Jack, incensed at their brother's insolence, leave him and
resolve to restore their coats to their original condition. But
they find this no easy matter to perform, and while Martin is
careful to take off just those additions that will not injure
the original fabric, the impetuous Jack "stripping down a
parcel of gold lace a little too hastily, rent the main body of
his coat from top to bottom". He endeavours to get Martin
to imitate his rashness, but upon his brother proceeding as
circumspectly as before he flies into a rage and leaves him,
and "in a few days it was for certain reported that he had run
out of his wits". Swift proceeds to give as many examples of
Puritan fanaticism as he had previously given of Roman
corruption; for instance, the Puritan enthusiasm for the
Bible is parodied in Jack's using a copy of the will for every
purpose he can think of:

He had a way of working it into any shape he pleased;
so that it served him for a nightcap when he went to bed
and for an umbrella in rainy weather. He would lap a
piece of it about a sore toe, or, when he had fits, burn two
inches under his nose; or, if anything lay heavy on his
stomach, scrape off and swallow as much of the powder
as would lie on a silver penny . . .

Swift's conclusion, no doubt very gratifying to Anglican readers who recalled the partial alliance between the Dissenting interest and the Catholics during the reign of James II, is that Jack grew so much like his old enemy Peter that

> nothing was more frequent than for a bailiff to seize Jack by the shoulders and cry, "Mr Peter, you are the King's prisoner". Or, at other times, for one of Peter's nearest friends to accost Jack with open arms, "Dear Peter, I am glad to see thee; pray send me one of your best medicines for the worms . . ."

Swift's explanation of this curious mistake is one of the finest instances of his satirical genius:

> For, as it is the nature of rags to bear a kind of mock resemblance to finery, there being a sort of fluttering appearance in both which is not to be distinguished at a distance, in the dark, or by short-sighted eyes, so, in those junctures, it fared with Jack and his tatters, that they offered to the first view a ridiculous flaunting, which, assisting the resemblance in person and air, thwarted all his projects of separation, and left so near a similitude between them as frequently deceived the very disciples and followers of both.

There is no doubt that Swift thought such passages would win him applause from all Anglican readers. But the reception of the book was very mixed, and it is said that Queen Anne (or her ecclesiastical advisers) was eventually to refuse Swift a bishopric because of its authorship.

The reason is not far to seek, for the tone of some of the book must have offended religious people of every denomination. For instance, this passage parodying the sacrament of the eucharist must have annoyed many members of the Church of England who were willing enough to smile with the author over the arrogance of papal pardons:

> "Come, brothers," said Peter, "fall to, and spare not; here is excellent good mutton; or, hold, now my hand is in, I will help you." At which word, in much ceremony, with fork and knife, he carves out two good slices of a loaf, and

presents each on a plate to his brothers. The elder of the
two, not suddenly ent ring into lord Peter's conceit,
began with very civil language to examine the mystery.
"My lord," said he, "I doubt, with great submission,
there may be some mistake . . ." "Pray, sir," says Peter,
"eat your victuals, and leave off your impertinence . . .
I am not a person to refuse you anything that is reasonable: wine, moderately taken, is a cordial; here is a glass
a-piece for you: it is true natural juice from the grape,
none of your damned vintner's brewings." Having spoke
thus, he presented to each of them another large dry
crust, bidding them drink it off, and not be bashful,
for it would do them no hurt.

This is, admittedly, a strange passage to come from a
young clergyman, and the question of Swift's religious opinions
is complicated. But it would appear certain, at any rate, that
he disliked the ceremonies and outward show of Christianity,
admiring the ethical teaching of the New Testament, indicated
in the *Tub* by the "plain, easy directions" of the father's will.
The passage quoted earlier from *Robinson Crusoe* suggests
that this plain religion was by no means unpopular in the
Augustan Age, if something more orthodox was still deemed
necessary for a bishop. In some of his later pamphlets, Swift
strongly supported, for political reasons, "a high and rigid
regard for the church establishment", but there is not much
doubt that his true religious opinions were expressed in
A Tale of a Tub.

The Pamphleteering Years: 1701-14

There is some reason to think that, up to about the year
1710, Swift was trying to form a compromise between the
two political groups.* He came frequently to London from
his "hedge-living", as he called it, at Laracor, and while

* His contempt for mere party differences can be seen in the
Voyage to Lilliput, in the description of the quarrel between those
who wear high heels to their shoes and those who wear low; as his
indifference to religious controversy can be seen in the description of
the quarrel between the Lilliputians and the Blefuscuans, the question
at issue in this case being whether an egg should be broken at the
larger end or the smaller.

interesting himself in political questions, tried as far as possible
to remain a neutral independent figure between Whig and
Tory. The Whigs were grateful for his pamphlet of 1701, about
the impeachment of their ministers; but so far was he, at this
period, from falling in with the wishes of either party that the
three pamphlets on religious matters that he published in
1708—*Argument against abolishing Christianity, Project for the
Advancement of Religion*, and *Sentiments of a Church of England
Man*—had for their political complexion this phrase from the
last: "In order to preserve the constitution entire in Church
and State, whoever has a true value for either would be sure
to avoid the extremes of Whig for the sake of the former and
the extremes of Tory for the sake of the latter". Such a nice
balance was eminently suited to the coffee-house philosophers
(as the *Tatler's* review of the *Project* makes evident), but the
Whig statesmen were more offended than pleased. They
wanted to make concessions to the Dissenters, mainly as a
matter of political expediency, and here was the man they had
expected to be their star pamphleteer recommending "a high
and rigid regard for the church establishment on the one hand
and for the principles of civil liberty on the other". When
he wrote, at the end of this year, his *Letter on the Sacramental
Test*, he insisted that the Test be kept up against the
Dissenters. The Bill for the repeal of the Test Act was
supported by the Whigs, and it was lost mainly, it was believed
at the time, by this pamphlet.

The appeal of these pamphlets for us to-day is largely
historical, but one of them—the *Argument against abolishing
Christianity*—contains some of Swift's most masterly irony.
The writer of this passage is evidently the same man who had,
in the *Tub*, condemned the corruption of the Church from the
"plain, easy directions" of the New Testament:

> I hope no reader imagines me so weak as to stand up in
> the defence of real Christianity, such as used, in primitive
> times, (if we may believe the authors of those ages) to have
> an influence on men's belief and actions: to offer at the
> restoring of that would indeed be a wild project; it would
> be to dig up foundations; to destroy, at one blow, all the

wit, and half the learning, of the kingdom; to break the entire frame and constitution of things; to ruin trade, extinguish arts and sciences, with the professors of them; in short, to turn our courts, exchanges, and shops, into deserts; and would be full as absurd as the proposal of Horace, where he advises the Romans, all in a body, to leave their city, and seek a new seat in some remote part of the world, by way of cure for the corruption of their manners.

This is, admittedly, a gentler sort of irony than much in the *Tub*, and could have appeared in the *Tatler*—as the *Bickerstaff Papers* (1708-9) actually, as we have seen, formed part of the advance publicity for that journal.

Up till now Swift had maintained his independence of party, though he had inclined more to the Whig side than to the Tory; but the Whigs were angered by his writings upon Dissent—which are certainly rather paradoxical—and he was embittered with them because of the failure of his mission to the Government on behalf of the Irish clergy. It was Harley's promise to agree to this request that finally persuaded Swift to throw in his lot with the Tories, and in 1710 he began to contribute to the *Examiner*, a Tory weekly just started by Bolingbroke and Prior. There is no doubt that he was sincere enough in this partial change of allegiance, but once he had definitely taken up the Tory position his pamphleteering became less personal and more unscrupulous. His articles in the *Examiner* had great influence, and his pamphlet *The Conduct of the Allies* (1711) is believed to have made the Peace of Utrecht generally acceptable to the public. "He must be allowed," said Johnson, "for a time to have dictated the political opinions of the English nation."

We know more details of this period of Swift's life than of any other, because while in London he was writing at odd moments those letters to his former pupil, now in Dublin, published posthumously as the *Journal to Stella*. It is evident from this *Journal* that he found his change of circumstances highly agreeable and that he enjoyed the dependence of others upon himself as much as he had hated his earlier dependence upon Sir William Temple. That his mind was not entirely preoccupied with political affairs—even with his party in office and himself the bosom friend of ministers—can be judged by the efforts he made to help as many of his literary brethren as possible.

He had hoped for an appointment in London as a reward for his *Conduct*, but he was offered in 1713 the Deanery of St Patrick's, Dublin, and he accepted it, either for want of a better or because he suspected that the Tory party was nearing the end of its power. Its brief reign, in fact, closed with the death of the Queen a year later, and when the Vicar of Bray

> turned a cat-in-pan once more,
> And so became a Whig, sir,

the Dean of St Patrick's retired to Dublin with dignified haste and took no further part in English politics.

The Scriblerus Club

Shortly before the death of the Queen there was founded by Swift and others an association of Tory wits called the Scriblerus Club. The writings with which this club amused itself were all part of a design intended to parody the weaknesses of contemporary literature in the form of the memoirs of a representative Dunce. The *Memoirs of Scriblerus* contained the original idea of *Gulliver's Travels* and later suggested to Pope his *Treatise on the Bathos*, thus having a hand also in the formation of *The Dunciad*. Though so pregnant of literary masterpieces, the club had, of course, a decided political slant, the writings parodied being mostly those written by Whigs. Before we go on to consider *Gulliver* itself, and the Irish pamphlets, we can glance briefly at the career of two other members of the club—Arbuthnot and Bolingbroke—who were Swift's chief colleagues in the Tory Opposition.

John Arbuthnot (1667-1735) is mainly known to us to-day by Pope's *Epistle* to him and by his connection with Swift. But in his time he was considered the equal in wit of any of the Augustans; and Johnson said, "I think Dr Arbuthnot the first man among them. He was the most universal genius,

being an excellent physician, a man of deep learning, and a
man of much humour". "If there were a dozen Arbuthnots
in the world," said Swift, "I would burn my *Travels*."

He was born in Scotland, studied medicine at Aberdeen,
and came to London about 1700, where he was elected a
Fellow of the Royal Society. In 1709 he became physician
to the Queen, and was soon in close touch with the anti-
Marlborough party at Court, joining with Swift in his efforts
to make the war and the Duke equally unpopular with the
nation. The chief of Arbuthnot's contributions were the
pamphlets later collected under the title of *The History of
John Bull*—in which he popularised the name as a personification of Great Britain—and *The Art of Political Lying*, written
in the same year 1712. His style is so much like Swift's that
several of his works were formerly credited to his friend.
This passage from the introduction to *Political Lying*, where
he is considering "whether a lie is best contradicted by truth
or another lie", is typical:

> The author says that, considering the large extent of
> the cylindrical surface of the soul, and the great propensity
> to believe lies in the generality of mankind of late years,
> he thinks the properest contradiction to a lie is another lie:
> for example, if it should be reported that the Pretender
> was at London, one would not contradict it by saying he
> never was in England, but you must prove by eye-
> witnesses that he came no further than Greenwich, but
> then went back again . . . So there was, not long ago, a
> gentleman who affirmed that the treaty with France, for
> bringing in Popery and slavery into England, was signed
> the 15th of September; to which another answered very
> judiciously, not by opposing truth to his lie, that there
> was no such treaty, but that, to his certain knowledge,
> there were many things in that treaty not yet adjusted.

Arbuthnot seems also to have shared with Swift a certain
innocence about the intrigues of some of their friends. By
the above passage one would not suspect that Prior had been
sent on a secret mission to France to arrange a separate peace,
contrary to the engagements England had made with her
allies; nor that Bolingbroke and Harley, and Pope's friend

Bishop Atterbury, were in secret correspondence with the Pretender and were confidently expecting a Stuart restoration. Part of the reason for Swift's disgusted treatment of politics in *Gulliver* may well have been that he was genuinely disillusioned when the truth came out concerning the extent of Tory intrigues with the Stuarts. (He himself regarded "the coming of the Pretender as a greater evil than we are like to suffer under the worst Whig Ministry that can be found".) It is significant that neither he nor Arbuthnot wrote anything directly about English politics after 1714.

When Atterbury arrived at Calais in 1723, on his journey to exile in France, he learnt that Bolingbroke had just reached there on his way to England, having received a royal pardon through one of the King's mistresses. "Then I am exchanged," the Bishop remarked. It is typical of the corruption of the age that the comparatively harmless Atterbury should have had to die in exile, while the highly dangerous Bolingbroke—"Few people," recorded Lord Hervey, "either believed him without being deceived or trusted him without being betrayed"—should have been allowed to return. Bolingbroke carried on the unofficial Tory battle against the Whig government in a paper called the *Craftsman*, his attack upon Walpole, which appeared there in 1733, failing, however, in its purpose and causing the author to retreat across the Channel again.

We are hardly concerned here with the details of his political career. Like his enemy Marlborough, Henry St John (1678-1751) combined great talent with a complete lack of scruple. He was a Secretary of State at thirty-two, being created Viscount Bolingbroke ten years afterwards. His later writings on patriotism—*Letter on the Spirit of Patriotism* (1736), *Idea of a Patriot King* (1738)—greatly influenced the "King's Friends" of the time of George III and also Disraeli in the "Young England" period. The *Letters on the Study and Use of History* (1735) is his chief historical work.

He comes into Augustan literature mainly as the friend of Swift and Pope. He founded the *Examiner* with Prior, and the Brothers' Club with Prior and Swift. He lived near

Pope for ten years and his deistical philosophy is behind the *Essay on Man*. But he was no more a real philosopher than his friend, his talents in writing being of the rhetorical kind. His oratory was said to be very impressive, Pitt once remarking that his speeches were the most desirable of all the lost items of literature.

Swift's Irish Pamphlets

While his friends Atterbury and Bolingbroke were actually exiled, and Prior and Harley put in prison, Swift merely conceived himself as "banished" from London and the literary world in 1714.* He had never taken much interest in the affairs of his native country, and had always regarded himself as an Englishman, which he undoubtedly was by race. But it would have needed a man of much less imagination than his, not to have been struck by the misery of Ireland at this time, particularly, of course, among the poor. Evidently two motives combined to form his services to Ireland: his natural desire to see some measure of reform in the country of his "exile", and the no less natural, if less honourable, desire to attack the Whigs for their misgovernment of John Bull's Other Island.

The first opportunity came in 1722, when a patent was given by the English Government to a man named Wood, to provide Ireland with a copper coinage. "Wood's ha'pence", as the coins came to be called, were not worth their face value, the margin of profit going chiefly to the King's mistress, the Duchess of Kendal. So much resistance to this dubious transaction was shown in Ireland that the Government in

* He later wrote, in the *Verses on the Death of Dr Swift*:

> With horror, grief, despair the Dean
> Beheld the dire destructive scene:
> His friends in exile, or the Tower,
> Himself within the frown of Power;
> Pursued by base envenom'd pens,
> Far to the land of slaves and fens;
> A servile race in folly nurs'd,
> Who truckle most, when treated worst . . .
> Envy hath own'd it was his doing,
> To save that helpless land from ruin.

1724 was forced to open an enquiry, a Privy Council committee eventually reporting in favour of the patent with some modifications.

It was while this committee was sitting, and the whole country in an uproar, that Swift, who had protested privately, came out into the open. It was a splendid opportunity, and he seized it with as much energy as his earlier opportunities against Marlborough. He came forward in the guise of a simple Dublin draper, asserting in his first *Letter*, addressed to "the tradesmen, shopkeepers, farmers, and country-people in general of the kingdom of Ireland", that the acceptance of the coinage meant the ruin of the land. The second *Drapier's Letter* urged that the coins be refused individually by every patriotic Irishman*; the third *Letter* examined the report of the committee, and found it wanting; while the fourth *Letter* (1725), the most famous, was almost a declaration of Irish independence: "all government, without the consent of the governed, is the very definition of slavery".

It is characteristic of Swift's hold upon the melancholy facts, to see the context in which this famous phrase is couched: "For, in *reason*, all government, without the consent of the governed, is the very definition of slavery; but, in *fact*, eleven men well armed will certainly subdue one single man in his shirt".

From this time forward, Swift busied himself about Irish affairs, as well as about the affairs of Lilliput, Brobdingnag, etc., making two journeys to London between 1726 and 1727, in the first of which he complained personally to Walpole about the misgovernment of Ireland, and in the second, when the death of George I gave him some hope that he might assist

---

* Swift also wrote many ballads on the subject, including *An Excellent New Song*, in which Wood is supposed to cry:

> My dear Irish folks
> Come leave off your jokes
> And buy up my ha'pence so fine;
> So fair and so bright
> They'll give you delight:
> Observe how they glisten and shine . . .

These ballads had an enormous popularity and reached, of course, a public to whom the *Drapier's Letters* were unknown.

Bolingbroke in displacing their Whig enemy from the government, he enjoyed the resounding success of his *Travels*, which he had permitted Pope to dispose of for £200 six months before. But when he returned to Dublin, where he was received with bells and bonfires as the Champion of the Irish—a guard of honour conducted him through the streets—he found Stella on her deathbed; she died in January the following year.

Though the *Drapier's Letters* had been successful in their object, they were written with that unscrupulousness that Swift had earlier displayed in *The Conduct of the Allies* and in the *Examiner* articles. As literature, the *Letters* and the minor Irish pamphlets are inferior, not only to *Gulliver*, but to Swift's last service to Ireland—the famous *Modest Proposal* of 1729—which has a more universal appeal. Its full title is *A Modest Proposal for Preventing the Children of Poor People in Ireland from being a Burden to their Parents or Country, and for making them Beneficial to the Public*, and it is one of the finest pieces of Swift's irony. He apparently recommends the Irish poor to sell their children

> to persons of quality and fortune through the kingdom; always advising the mother to let them suck plentifully in the last month, so as to render them plump and fat for a good table. A child will make two dishes at an entertainment for friends; and when the family dines alone, the fore or hind quarter will make a reasonable dish, and, seasoned with a little pepper or salt, will be very good boiled on the fourth day, especially in winter . . .

The next paragraph but one is among Swift's most excellent effects: "I grant this food will be somewhat dear, and therefore very proper for landlords, who, as they have already devoured most of the parents, seem to have the best title to the children . . .". And a few pages further on: "The poorer tenants will have something of value of their own, which by law may be made liable to distress, and help pay their landlord's rent; their corn and cattle being already seized, and money a thing unknown".

Swift was not content here, as he had been in the *Drapier's Letters*, to be merely a destructive critic; he had his own proposals for Irish reform—first sketched out in his *Proposal for the Universal Use of Irish Manufactures* (1720)—and he puts them forward at the close of his baby-boiling scheme, but so wrapped up in irony that he introduces these perfectly serious proposals only to dismiss them, as being altogether too immodest and extravagant ever to be taken up:

> I desire the reader will observe that I calculate my remedy for this one individual kingdom of Ireland, and for no other that ever was, or I think ever can be, upon earth. Therefore let no man talk to me of other expedients: of taxing our absentees at five shillings a pound: of using neither clothes nor household furniture, except what is our own growth and manufacture . . . of being a little cautious not to sell our country and conscience for nothing: of teaching landlords to have at least one degree of mercy toward their tenants . . . let no man talk to me of these and the like expedients, till he has at least some glimpse of hope that there will be ever some hearty and sincere attempt to put them in practice.

"Gulliver's Travels"

It has often been considered a pity that most people know of Swift only through his authorship of *Travels into several remote Nations of the World : by Lemuel Gulliver, first a surgeon and then a captain of several ships*, which masterpiece first appeared in 1726 and has since been reprinted in numerous editions and translated into most foreign languages. It has, of course, always been a favourite with children, and many critics have claimed that this is the irony of time which has defeated Swift's original ironic intention. Yet we should remember that from the start the book was popular with children as well as their elders—Gay and Pope, in a joint letter to the author, wrote that "from the highest to the lowest it is universally read, from the cabinet council to the nursery . . . the whole town, men, women, and children, are quite full of it"—and, furthermore, that some of the supreme masterpieces of literature (for instance, *Don Quixote* and the *Pilgrim's Progress*) have similarly appealed at various levels and ages, from youth up. Perhaps it is the very definition of a master-piece that it should be universal in this sense as well as in others. *Gulliver* is certainly a fine example of irony, but we should not lose sight of the fact that it is also one of the supreme comic masterpieces of the world, equal to the best work of Chaucer and Dickens, of Rabelais and Molière, of Cervantes and Gogol. We have been so familiar with its comic quality from childhood that in later life we tend to ignore it, concentrating instead on the more brutal satire of the book, particularly in the voyages to Laputa and the Houyhnhnms, which are often missed out in modern editions for children. The first thing to say about *Gulliver* is, then, that as comedy it is not only Swift's masterpiece but one of the masterpieces of all time. The fact that we know it from youth upwards no more detracts from its humorous stature than a similar fact detracts from the height of allegory attained by the *Pilgrim's Progress*.

The second thing to note is that the book is a whole, a clearly-conceived organic unity. The satire deepens, by design, as the adventures proceed; it is almost entirely pleasant in Lilliput, more disturbing in Brobdingnag, sarcastic in Laputa, and "furious, raging, obscene" (or so Thackeray and others have thought it) in the country of the Houyhnhnms and the Yahoos. Thackeray's view here should be taken with a pinch of salt. Satire is satire, and though the *Voyage to the Houyhnhnms* contains the deepest irony of Swift, it also contains that element of humour that runs like a vein of sanity through the book. The Yahoos are dreadful enough, but are clearly intended to depict the *vices* of mankind—or, which was to Swift much the same thing, mankind in the lump rather than the individuals comprising it. They no more represent humanity than Mr Pecksniff represents the Christian spirit; and it is significant that Dickens, too, was saddled with an intention not his own, being forced to put a footnote to a page in *Chuzzlewit* explaining that Mr Pecksniff's views on life were not the author's.

Swift's love of the individual comes out in all four voyages. The Lilliputian court is held up to our derision, but just as

Swift found certain ministers and courtiers in London to be honest and upright men, so Gulliver procures the friendship of Reldresal, principal secretary for private affairs. The Emperor himself is a fairly honest person, besides being taller, by almost the breadth of Gulliver's nail, than any of his court ("which alone is enough to strike an awe into the beholders"); but he is spoilt by the ambition Gulliver arouses in him by the capture of the fleet of Blefescu. In Brobdingnag, we have the varied natures of Glumdalclitch on the one hand and her miserly father on the other. In Laputa, Gulliver conceives the utmost respect for "a great lord at court, nearly related to the King" who is regarded by the nation as "the most ignorant and stupid person among them"; but who is actually one of the few Laputans too intelligent to be taken in by the current academics. Even among the Houyhnhnms, there is the sorrel nag ("who always loved me") neighing on the beach as Gulliver sails away: "Take care of thyself, gentle Yahoo!"

We say "even among the Houyhnhnms", for it has often been noticed, whether by Swift's intention or not,* that these horses, eminent in Reason, have but few natural "human" emotions; their marriages, for instance, are marriages of convenience, or rather of eugenics:

> They are exactly careful to choose such colours as will not make any disagreeable mixture in the breed. Strength is chiefly valued in the male, and comeliness in the female; not upon the account of love [Swift seems hastily to add] but to preserve the race from degenerating ... The young couple meet, and are joined, merely because it is the determination of their parents and friends; it is what they see done every day, and they look upon it as one of the necessary actions of a reasonable being.

Most people would prefer to this near-forecast of a totalitarian-state-incubator—in other passages, it is interesting to observe,

* Probably it was unintentional: it is notoriously more difficult to describe an ideal race than to satirise the vices of actual mankind. Compared with other products of utopia or erewhon, the Houyhnhnms are "reasonably" successful. Whether there was any intention of satirising the Augustan ideal is uncertain, for these are certainly Augustan horses, coffee-house steeds.

Swift has some intentional satire of totalitarian tendencies—even the lust of the young female Yahoo who surprised Gulliver bathing and embraced him "after a most fulsome manner".

Johnson's criticism of *Gulliver*—"When once you have thought of big men and little men, it is very easy to do all the rest"—is as fatuous as his criticism of the *Conduct of the Allies** and only takes into account the first two Voyages. Swift had the more subtle idea, which he puts forward in the early pages of the second Voyage, when Gulliver is in a "terrible agitation of mind" as he expects to be "a morsel in the mouth of the first among these enormous barbarians" who happens to seize him. "Undoubtedly," Gulliver reflects, "philosophers are in the right, when they tell us nothing is great or little otherwise than by comparison." This theme of relativity runs right through the book, and the working-out of it is surely among the finest feats of imaginative genius in the English language.

The Brobdingnagians were not so barbarous as Gulliver had feared. He became aware of a certain respect for their culture and attainments, though he could never get the King—such was the "narrowness" of the nation's education—to appreciate the glory and the art of those wars which he told him were so common an experience in far-off Europe. Indeed, the King was amazed when Gulliver spoke proudly of missiles "which would rip up the pavements, tear the houses to pieces, burst and throw splinters on every side, dashing out the brains of all who came near"; and had the impertinence to be "struck with horror" at the thought that "so impotent and grovelling an insect" as Gulliver "could entertain such inhuman ideas, and

---

* "Swift having been mentioned," records Boswell, "Johnson, as usual, treated him with little respect as an author. Some of us endeavoured to support the Dean of St Patrick's by various arguments. One in particular praised his *Conduct of the Allies*. JOHNSON: 'Sir, his *Conduct of the Allies* is a performance of very little ability.' 'Surely, Sir,' said Dr Douglas, 'you must allow it has strong facts.' JOHNSON: 'Why, yes, Sir; but what is that to the merit of the composition? In the sessions-paper of the Old Bailey there are strong facts. Housebreaking is a strong fact; robbery is a strong fact; and murder is a mighty strong fact . . .'" (etc.)

in so familiar a manner, as to appear wholly unmoved at all the scenes of blood and desolation" he had painted. And the ignorant King ("the learning of this people," says Gulliver, "is very defective") gave it as his opinion—Swift is here paraphrasing Bacon—that "whoever could make two ears of corn, or two blades of grass, to grow upon a spot of ground, where only one grew before, would deserve better of mankind, and do more essential service to his country, than the whole race of politicians put together".

Gulliver has to make two more voyages, and find himself a Yahoo, though a gentle one, before he is able to appreciate the wisdom of the Brobdingnagian king. And then he wishes that the Houyhnhnms could "send a sufficient number of their inhabitants for civilising Europe, by teaching us the first principles of honour, justice, truth, temperance, public spirit, fortitude, chastity, friendship, benevolence, and fidelity". "The names of all which virtues," Swift adds characteristically, "are still retained among us in most languages."*

That "familiarity" which the Brobdingnagian king observed in Gulliver's acquaintance with "the art of war" is only one of several left hooks which Swift deals to the mind of the twentieth century. We, too, have become habituated to warfare and, like Gulliver, can appreciate the finer points of a new missile which will "rip up the pavements" and "tear the houses to pieces". Furthermore, we can easily see from our aeroplanes that the enemy are the most diminutive of Lilliputians, not creatures of flesh and blood like ourselves. If the "Dunces" are more powerful to-day than they were in the Augustan Age, we have suffered even more perhaps from the "polite attentions" of the Yahoos.

One of the earliest and most innocent of Swift's jests had been that parody of Robert Boyle's *Meditations*, *A Meditation upon a Broomstick*, with which he had deceived Lady Berkeley.

* Swift's friend, the poet and critic Edward Young, shrewdly observed that "If his favourite houyhnhnms could write, and Swift had been one of them, every horse with him would have been an ass, and he would have written a panegyric on mankind, saddling with much reproach the present heroes of his pen". (*Conjectures on Original Composition*, 1759.)

It is recorded by Dr Sheridan* that, while reading out this parody, Swift preserved an inflexible gravity of countenance. On a much larger scale, that is the secret behind the comic success of *Gulliver*, the irony owing a great deal to the perfect gravity of the style—for instance, in that passage about the awe of the beholders at the great height of the King of Lilliput or when Gulliver indignantly denies that "an excellent lady" (not six inches high) once came privately to his lodging. But the best example is near the end of the book, when Gulliver assures us that he has not exaggerated the honour he has received from his Houyhnhnm master on leaving:

> I was forced to wait above an hour for the tide, and then observing the wind very fortunately bearing towards the island to which I intended to steer my course, I took a second leave of my master: but as I was going to prostrate myself to kiss his hoof, he did me the honour to raise it gently to my mouth. I am not ignorant how much I have been censured for mentioning this last particular. Detractors are pleased to think it improbable that so illustrious a person should descend to give so great a mark of distinction to a creature so inferior as I. Neither have I forgotten how apt some travellers are to boast of extraordinary favours they have received. But if these censurers were better acquainted with the noble and courteous disposition of the Houyhnhnms, they would soon change their opinion.

We have got so used to seeing the Houyhnhnms through Gulliver's eyes that, by the time we reach this passage, we share some of his feeling of an unmerited honour having been conferred; and it is only after a moment's reflection that the absurdity of the distinction breaks upon us.

But we are still conscious of being sufficiently like the Yahoos—at least, in some of our mass pursuits—that we sympathise with Gulliver's sense of banishment as he leaves this land of horse-sense where wars and theologies are unknown. It is a great feat of ironic genius that we should be compelled to accept Swift's gravity in the *Travels* as Lady

* Grandfather of the dramatist and Swift's collaborator in the *Intelligencer* (1728).

Berkeley accepted the gravity of the *Meditation upon a Broomstick*. Even the passages which have caused some critics the most offence—such as the aversion Gulliver feels for his family and friends after returning to England—are partly the logical outcome of his experiences among the Houyhnhnms. It is characteristic of Swift that he should pursue matters to their logical, if sometimes absurd, conclusions, as in that often-admired episode where Gulliver, drifting from the land of the giants, requests that the crew of the English ship should "take the box out of the sea into the ship and so into the captain's cabin"—the cabin being much smaller than the box. "It is the *veracity* of the blunder which is so admirable," comments Thackeray. "Had a man come from such a country as Brobdingnag he would have blundered so." And if he had had Gulliver's experiences with the Houyhnhnms and the Yahoos, he would have felt some aversion at first from mixing with his wife and family.

There is great variety of humour in the *Travels*, greater than in anything else Swift wrote. Those who dwell on the more brutal satire have forgotten the many occasions on which Swift is struck by a Jonsonian sense of the absurdity and incongruity of things. This is not entirely missing from the earlier work, as can be seen from the passage in the *Tub* where Peter follows a curse—"if you fail hereof, G—— d—mn you and yours to all eternity"—by the greeting, "And so we bid you heartily farewell". But this almost Dickensian comedy is more fully expressed in the *Travels*, where it meets us on nearly every page. To take just one example out of scores: the man who could write of the architect at the Grand Academy of Lagado "who had contrived a new method for building houses, by beginning at the roof, and working downwards to the foundation", was not in a mood of savage irony, any more than the man who could write so logically of the lingering influence of the giants and the horses was a man half-crazed with disappointment. The fact that Swift became insane in 1741 no more entitles us to question the sanity of *Gulliver*, written fifteen years before, than Coleridge's opium can make us suspicious of the wisdom of the Ancient Mariner.

Swift's Character and Genius

The two main charges that have been brought against Swift are characteristically paradoxical: one is that he was needlessly coarse, the other that he was foolishly sentimental.

The coarseness can be admitted; it is in nearly everything he wrote, being particularly nasty in some of his poems—*The Lady's Dressing-Room*, *Strephon and Chloe*, and other things of that kind. The only works reasonably free from it are the *Bickerstaff Papers*, the political pamphlets, the *Verses on the Death of Dr Swift*, and that other minor masterpiece, *A Complete Collection of Genteel and Ingenious Conversation* (1730), whose clichés—"a blind man would be glad to see that", etc.—are chiefly interesting because they have fallen from "the best companies of England" to the stock language of the people. It was, of course, an age of plain speaking, but Swift's preoccupation with the less savoury aspects of life was exceptional and, compared with Rabelais' and Fielding's more genial coarseness, was an unhealthy streak in his character.*

The charge of sentimentality rests mainly on one book which was never intended to be made public: the *Journal to Stella*. In these letters Swift interspersed his comments on public affairs with what he called his "little language", private messages couched in childish jokes and abbreviations. These certainly make tiresome reading for the outsider, but, apart from their originally private nature, their childish sentimentality can be explained perfectly easily. When Swift first met Stella she *was* a child, and it became his habit—possibly foolish, but shared by many adults then and now—to adopt a special "little language" when speaking to her. In later life, they sometimes kept up this language, partly, one presumes, out of affectionate remembrance of their first acquaintance and perhaps of their alliance against the

* Voltaire, however, a good judge in this connection, saw many points of resemblance between Swift and Rabelais: "M. Swift est Rabelais dans son bon sens . . . Il n'a pas, à la verité, la gaîté du premier, mais il a toute la finesse, la raison, le choix, le bon goût qui manquent à notre curé de Meudon. Ses vers sont d'un goût singulier, et presque inimitable . . ." (*Lettres sur les Anglais*.)

pompositees of Moor Park. There is, admittedly, a Victorian flavour about this, a flavour almost of Lewis Carroll—whose own blend of logic and sentimentality has been similarly pounced on by Freudian critics—but the charge of deliberate childishness is only true in the sense that Swift was deliberately going back to the period when he first knew Stella as a child of six.*

These are the two chief charges made against Swift, to which we can add that in his political writings he was sometimes as unscrupulous as any politician of the age. But there is a vigour, a high spirit, a range of invention, about even his most polemical works that clearly show his genius was more than political. He was undoubtedly the chief figure in the Tory Opposition, and he must be regarded, with the possible exception of Cobbett, as the greatest pamphleteer in our history. But his superiority to his colleague Arbuthnot, for example, can best be summed up by paraphrasing his compliment to the Doctor and saying that not a hundred Arbuthnots could have written the *Travels*.

* The fuss that has been made about Swift's apparently strange relations with the adult Stella can be explained even more easily. They are believed to have eventually got married, but they continued to live apart and to see each other only in the presence of a third person. There have been several ingenious psychological explanations of this seemingly strange behaviour; but to get the more probable explanation we have only to remember that there was some doubt about Swift's parentage. His real father may have been Sir John Temple, father in wedlock of Sir William. And Stella was almost certainly Sir William's daughter. So Swift and Stella may have been— or may have thought themselves to be—related by blood, if not formally: a kind of uncle and niece. A mere suspicion of committing incest would have been sufficient for them to resolve never to be intimate, and their problem of how to see each other and yet keep apart was adequately answered by the presence of the seemingly intrusive Mrs Dingley. This simple explanation does away with all the eager attempts that have been made to probe into Swift's private life, and so will never be popular in our time.

CHAPTER III

AUGUSTAN POETRY FROM POPE TO THOMSON
1700-1748

> I love to pour out all my self, as plain
> As downright Shippen, or as old Montaigne:
> In them, as certain to be lov'd as seen,
> The Soul stood forth, nor kept a thought within;
> In me what spots (for spots I have) appear,
> Will prove at least the medium must be clear.
> In this impartial glass, my Muse intends
> Fair to expose myself, my foes, my friends;
> Publish the present age; but where my text
> Is Vice too high, reserve it for the next:
> My foes shall wish my Life a longer date,
> And ev'ry friend the less lament my fate.
> My head and heart thus flowing thro' my quill,
> Verse-man or Prose-man, term me which you will,
> Papist or Protestant, or both between,
> Like good Erasmus in an honest Mean,
> In moderation placing all my glory,
> While Tories call me Whig, and Whigs a Tory.
> POPE: *Imitations of Horace.*

Augustan Poetry

The first two chapters of this book have dealt mainly with
the prose of the Augustans, with the periodicals, pamphlets,
and prose satires from the Revolution of 1688 to the last
Jacobite rebellion and the death of Swift in 1745. A good
deal of our space was inevitably given up to political and
religio-political literature, though we stressed the purely
literary importance of the *Spectator* and *Gulliver's Travels.*
In this chapter and the next, we shall be leaving the politics
of the age almost completely, concentrating on poetry and
the growth of the novel. Defoe, it is true, was mixed up in
political affairs as much as Swift, but his main interest for us

is the part he played in the evolution of the novel from the newspaper and periodical; and, while Prior and Gay wrote some political verse, their importance for us is non-political and is, in any case, much subordinate to the importance of Pope, whose outstanding genius in satirical poetry was as much removed from politics as was possible in his time.

The chief poet of the Restoration period had died in 1700, and it is remarkable how the continuity of verse satire was preserved, with scarcely a break, after his death. If any poet can be said to have had a true successor, it was Dryden with Pope; not only in the improvement Pope made in the so-called "heroic couplet"—that is, the decasyllabic line used by Chaucer and modernised by Waller and Dryden—but in the greater range of Pope's satire compared with his acknowledged master's.*

Pope's Early Life

Alexander Pope (1688-1744) may be said to have had two setbacks from birth: he was weak physically, being partly crippled, and because of the Catholic religion of his parents he was debarred from the public schools and universities and from any employment by the State. What formal education he had was imparted by the family priest and by two private schools to which he went for short periods; but he was, in the main, self-educated, the wide reading in English poetry which he obtained at home being a better preparation for the business of his life than the exclusively classical education he would have received at a public school. His favourite poets were Spenser and Dryden, and when he was about ten or eleven he persuaded some friends to take him to Will's Coffee-house and was able to see the veteran poet in whose steps he was soon to tread.

* Writing to Thomas Warton in 1770, Gray outlined the plan of the History of English Poetry he had contemplated, observing that his scheme was partly taken from Pope's, who had also thought of writing such a history. Part V of this scheme is "School of France, introduced after the Restoration—Waller, Dryden, Addison, Prior, and Pope—which has continued to our own times".

He tells us in the *Epistle to Arbuthnot* that

> As yet a child, nor yet a fool to fame,
> I lisp'd in numbers, for the numbers came.*

The public part of his career began with the writing of his *Pastorals* at the age of sixteen. These were passed round in manuscript and admired by several influential people. William Walsh, whom Dryden had considered the best critic in England, wrote to the verteran dramatist Wycherley that "It is not flattery at all to say that Virgil had written nothing so good at his age". He advised Pope to aim at "correctness" above all things, saying that "The best of the modern poets in all languages are those that have nearest copied the ancients". Through the good offices of such men as Walsh and Congreve, it was not long before a publisher was found, Tonson requesting the honour to include the *Pastorals* in his *Miscellany* of 1709. The same year Pope began the *Essay on Criticism*, which is his first important poem; it was published in 1711 and praised by Addison in the *Spectator* as "a masterpiece in its kind".

Years of Experiment: 1704-13

Pope's poetry is commonly divided, for convenience of study, into three periods, which bear a more or less exact relation to the three principal divisions of his life. The first was a period of experiment, in which the young poet ventured into various fields, with varying success. This coincides with his life in Windsor Forest, in the village to which his father had retired; with his visits to London, where he met Steele, Addison, Swift, and other writers; and with his becoming

---

* "Numbers" was the contemporary word for verses or poetical measure. "It was Mr Waller," observed Dryden, "who first reformed our numbers"; meaning that Edmund Waller (1606-87) was the first to write, deliberately, rhymed couplets in which each line was marked by regular beats, so creating a greater "smoothness", as he called it, than in the verse of his predecessors Donne and Jonson. Pope is sometimes thought to have the same negative virtue, but this is true only of his early work; among the purposes of his later satires was to get the maximum flexibility out of the rhymed-couplet form, achieving a dramatic and conversational idiom which is more like the best of Donne than the best of Waller.

gradually recognised as Dryden's chief successor. The best-known works of this period are the *Essay on Criticism* and *The Rape of the Lock*. The second period is that of his great popularity with the Homer translation, during which time he was living with his parents at Chiswick, till the death of his father in 1717, after which he settled with his mother at Twickenham, his home for the rest of his life. The third period, the greatest, can be called the Twickenham or Horatian period, when he was writing his most masterly satires and carrying on a war of words with the hack-writers of Grub Street. The masterpieces of this period are the *Moral Essays*, the *Epistle to Arbuthnot*, and *The Dunciad*.

It is an extensive field altogether, Pope having the pro-lificity which often goes with supreme literary genius. Though he complains in the *Arbuthnot*,

> Why am I ask'd what next shall see the light?
> Heav'ns! was I born for nothing but to write?

there is no doubt that he enjoyed the satire in which he was so much a master and that, being deprived by health and religion of a more active part in the world, he found his genius for poetry a great compensation. As he wrote in the same autobiographical poem:

> I left no calling for this idle trade,
> No duty broke, no father disobey'd.
> The Muse but serv'd to ease some friend, not Wife,
> To help me thro' this long disease, my Life,
> To second, Arbuthnot! thy Art and Care,
> And teach the Being you preserv'd, to bear.

The first fruitful period—to take one meaning of that splendid pun in the last line—extended from the *Pastorals* of 1704 to the eve of the *Iliad* in 1713, and we must consider this period of mainly short pieces before we come to the Homer translation and the more extensive satires.

We can easily believe Pope when he tells us that his four *Pastorals*, celebrating the four seasons, were composed when he was only sixteen; for they are chiefly remarkable for the adolescent vigour with which he recreates the conventional imagery of nymphs and shepherds. The tradition of the

pastoral poem was becoming a little stale even in his day, and
Johnson was to pick holes in one of the greatest of English
pastorals, *Lycidas*, complaining of the convention that made
Milton see his friend and himself as shepherds,

> Battening our flocks with the fresh dews of night.

Pope, of course, at this time, had little of Milton's genius,
which could transform a conventional elegy into a most moving poem.   The best that can be said of this early work, and
of *Windsor Forest*, begun at the same time but not published till
1713, is that the poems still make pleasant reading and that
the invocations to the "gentle gales" and "ye sacred Nine!"
are not so frequent as to spoil the effect.   The high praise the
Pastorals originally received is chiefly important in that it
encouraged Pope to proceed to greater things.

Tonson's *Miscellany* also contained the *Pastorals* of Ambrose
Philips, besides contributions by Garth and Rowe.   Philips's
verses were greeted with acclamation by the *Guardian*, the
reviewer declaring that there had been only four masters of
the art of pastoral in two thousand years: "Theocritus, who
left his dominions to Virgil; Virgil, who left his to his son
Spenser; and Spenser, who was succeeded by his eldest born,
Philips".

In this eulogy Pope's *Pastorals* were not even mentioned,
and he went to the extraordinary device of sending an anonymous article to the *Guardian*, in which, while appearing to
praise Philips, he really lampooned him and exalted his own
verses.   Steele seems to have swallowed the bait, and actually
asked Pope for permission to publish an anonymous attack
upon him before inserting the article!   Perhaps this was a jest
in return, for Pope's satire here is obvious enough.   He
praises Philips, for instance, for having "by a poetical creation
. . . raised up finer beds of flowers than the most industrious
gardener; his roses, endives, lilies, kingcups, and daffodils
blow all in the same season".   And he quotes one of the
weakest couplets of his rival:

> O woeful day!   O day of woe! quoth he,
> And woeful I, who live the day to see!

and comments, with his tongue firmly in his cheek, on "the simplicity of the diction", "the melancholy flowing of the numbers", and "the solemnity of the sound".

The *Essay on Criticism* is Pope's first important work. Besides containing lines that have passed into the language—such as "A little learning is a dang'rous thing", "What oft was thought, but ne'er so well expressed", "To err is human, to forgive, divine", "For Fools rush in where Angels fear to tread "*—it is notable as the first poem in which we can see his genius for satire arising. The three-fold argument—the foundations of true criticism; the causes preventing its use; and true criticism exemplified in its most eminent practitioners —is not of great interest to-day, because few readers can share Pope's opinions on the subject. The interest for us is rather in the detail: in, for instance, this passage from the second part of the poem, where Pope seems to reply in advance to all those critics who have complained that his poetry is mere smoothness, that his "criticism of life was simply the heroic couplet":

> But most by Numbers judge a Poet's song;
> And smooth or rough, with them is right or wrong:
> In the bright Muse though thousand charms conspire,
> Her voice is all these tuneful fools admire;
> Who haunt Parnassus but to please their ear,
> Not mend their minds; as some to Church repair,
> Not for the doctrine, but the music there.
> These equal syllables alone require,
> Tho' oft the ear the open vowels tire;
> While expletives their feeble aid do join;
> And ten low words oft creep in one dull line:

---

* Pope's poetry, as the Dear Old Lady said of *Hamlet*, is "full of quotations": that is, of phrases that we commonly use without knowing their origin. He probably stands next to Shakespeare in this anonymous fame. Other common "quotations" in his poems include: "The proper study of Mankind is Man" and "An honest Man's the noblest work of God" from the *Essay on Man*; "Damn with faint praise" and "Who breaks a butterfly upon a wheel?" from the *Epistle to Arbuthnot*; "The Mob of Gentlemen who wrote with Ease" from the *Imitations of Horace*; "Do good by stealth, and blush to find it Fame" from *1738*; and "God said, Let Newton be! and all was Light" from the *Epitaph on Newton*.

> While they ring round the same unvary'd chimes,
> With sure returns of still expected rhymes;
> Where-e'er you find "the cooling western breeze",
> In the next line, it "whispers through the trees":
> If crystal streams "with pleasing murmurs creep",
> The reader's threaten'd (not in vain) with "sleep":
> Then, at the last and only couplet fraught
> With some unmeaning thing they call a thought,
> A needless Alexandrine ends the song
> That, like a wounded snake, drags its slow length along.

Though Pope praises Waller in the next few lines, it is clear that he was, even thus early, evolving from the merely "correct" use of the heroic couplet to a more dramatic and flexible use, in which he could "mend men's minds" not simply "please their ear". This early independence is as striking in its way as the precocity so often noticed of his tackling a subject already made famous by Horace and Boileau.*

The other principal work of this first period is the burlesque poem *The Rape of the Lock*, first printed anonymously in Lintot's *Miscellany* of 1712 and then published in an enlarged edition in 1714. Founded on an actual incident, when a nobleman had cut off a lock of a lady's hair, the subject is worked up by the poet to the heights of comic heroism, the prevailing attitude, of course, being the contrast between the sublimity of the style and what the eighteenth century called the "meanness" of the occasion. Pope was later to write with Arbuthnot a *Treatise on the Bathos*, and this poem is full of fine examples of this sometimes unconscious feat:

* In one of the satirical passages of this poem, Pope made a slighting reference to the dramatist and critic John Dennis, who attacked him in return in a coarse pamphlet entitled *Reflections upon a late Rhapsody*. The quarrel did not end there, for after Pope had written the Prologue to Addison's *Cato* and Dennis had criticised the play severely (and to some extent rightly), Pope took it upon himself to defend Addison in an equally coarse pamphlet called *The Narrative of Dr Robert Norris on the Frenzy of J.D.*—a pamphlet evidently imitated from the *Bickerstaff Papers* and possibly written with Swift's assistance. It was Addison's repudiation of this defence that caused a coolness to grow up between Pope and himself, leading in the end to the famous portrait of "Atticus" in the *Epistle to Arbuthnot*.

> Whether the nymph shall break Diana's law,
> Or some frail China jar receive a flaw;
> Or stain her honour or her new brocade;
> Forget her pray'rs, or miss a masquerade . . .
>
> Not louder shrieks to pitying heav'n are cast,
> When husbands, or when lapdogs breathe their last . . .

The poem has also a fine ease of manner, which Pope was afterwards to apply to more serious subjects.

Other poems of this early period include some "translations" of Chaucer, notably *The Temple of Fame* (1711); the Virgilian ecloque *The Messiah*, printed in the *Spectator* in 1712; and the *Ode on St Cecilia's Day*, written in 1708 at the request of Steele, set to music by Maurice Greene, and performed at Cambridge in 1730. This is a pleasant piece, but hardly bears comparison with Dryden's poem on the same subject.

Period of the Homer Translation: 1713-25

In later life Pope was sometimes to regret the years he spent translating the *Iliad* and the *Odyssey*, but there is no doubt that these laborious middle years of the poet's life were well worth while, for they gained him both an independence and a fame which must have made possible the last great period of the satires. When he was independent enough to write what he pleased, and famous enough to command the immediate attention of publishers and readers, his life must have been as happy as his various infirmities could permit, for now he was able both to pay off old scores in the *Dunciad* and "stoop to Truth and moralise his song".

He began the *Iliad* in 1713 and the first volume was published two years later, the remaining volumes coming out regularly till the last in 1720. Owing largely to Swift's advance publicity, in the brief years of his influence in London, the translation was an enormous financial as well as literary success, bringing in—the *Iliad* and the *Odyssey* together— close upon £10,000, which would be worth at least £100,000 in modern money. (The average stipend of a clergyman in the early eighteenth century was between £40 and £60 a year.)

Pope was no great scholar, and had to meet some criticism from those more versed in Greek.* For the *Odyssey* he had the assistance of two Cambridge scholars and minor poets, William Broome and Elijah Fenton.

Most of his early readers had read Homer in the original and required what he so admirably supplied: a version in English according to the spirit of the times. It had an extraordinary influence upon the standard of poetic style in the eighteenth century, so much so that Coleridge, seventy years later, claimed it as one of the main sources of that artificial poetic diction which he and Wordsworth rebelled against. The extent of Pope's audience is also remarkable here; for the Homer went into edition after edition, and was not only read by schoolboys but by those poorer-class readers who had not had the benefit of a classical education. To establish Homer—or an eighteenth-century Homer—for more than fifty years was no slight achievement for a poet whose own classical education had been so neglected.†

* Bentley remarked to him that it was a very pretty poem, but he must not call it Homer. Gibbon later referred to it as "a portrait endowed with every merit, excepting that of likeness to the original"; and Cowper, contemplating his own translation, wrote that "The literati are all agreed to a man, that, although Pope has given us two pretty poems under Homer's titles, there is not to be found in them the least portion of Homer's spirit, nor the least resemblance of his manner". On the other hand, Gray, one of the most learned men in England, thought that no other version would ever equal Pope's; and Boswell records Johnson's similar verdict: "I mentioned the vulgar saying, that Pope's Homer was not a good representation of the original. JOHNSON: 'Sir, it is the greatest work of the kind that has ever been produced'".

† During the same month that Pope published the first volume of the *Iliad* there came out a rival translation by Thomas Tickell, a friend of Addison's. Pope came to believe that Addison had written this translation himself, when (so far as is known) he had done no more than read it in manuscript and suggest corrections. Tickell himself comes out of the affair with credit, paying Pope the compliment of not finishing his own translation now that "an abler hand", as he said, had undertaken the work. In his *Life of Tickell* Johnson quotes from "Mr Spence's collection" (that is, the manuscript *Anecdotes* of Pope and other writers by Joseph Spence, not printed till 1820) the various reasons Pope had for thinking Tickell's translation mainly the work of Addison.

About this time, he and Arbuthnot assisted Gay in writing a farce entitled *Three Hours after Marriage*, and this was a decided failure when produced in 1717, owing mainly to a ridiculous scene which Colley Cibber later burlesqued in *The Rehearsal*—the then famous comedy by Buckingham to which (as to Sheridan's *Critic* in after years) topical allusions were often added. Cibber refused to withdraw the burlesque, and so began the quarrel which was to lead to his role of "hero" in the final version of the *Dunciad*. The first to occupy this unenviable position was Lewis Theobald, a scholar who had pointed out some mistakes in Pope's edition of Shakespeare. This was published in 1725, and was the second of the labours on which he afterwards lamented he had spent so much time.

But this middle period of Pope's life was not entirely void of original poetry. The first volume of his collected works, published in 1717, contained, besides the early poems mentioned, two of uncertain date, *Eloisa to Abelard* and the *Elegy to the Memory of an Unfortunate Lady*, which are his chief achievements in what we may call emotional rather than satirical poetry. (Warton singled them out, with *The Rape of the Lock*, as poems of imagination, not of wit.) The *Elegy* in particular is a very moving poem, as can be seen from this passage near the close:

> What tho' no friends in sable weeds appear,
> Grieve for an hour, perhaps, then mourn a year,
> And bear about the mockery of woe
> To midnight dances and the public show?
> What tho' no weeping Loves thy ashes grace,
> Nor polish'd marble emulate thy face?
> What tho' no sacred earth allow thee room,
> Nor hallow'd dirge be mutter'd o'er thy tomb?
> Yet shall thy grave with rising flow'rs be drest,
> And the green turf lie lightly on thy breast:
> There shall the morn her earliest tears bestow,
> There the first roses of the year shall blow;
> While Angels with their silver wings o'ershade
> The ground, now sacred by thy reliques made.

That the chief satirical poet of the early eighteenth century should have written those lines is an indication of how much

modification there must inevitably be when we talk, for
brevity, of "Pope's satirical manner" or "the satirical manner
of the Augustans".

The War with the Dunces

Pope's war with the "dunces", which is one main feature
of the last and greatest period of his poetry, can be said to
have started as early as 1714, when the Scriblerus Club was
founded, and extending to the time of his death was thus a
Thirty Years' War altogether. But the conflict did not
really get into its stride till the publication of the Scriblerus
Club's *Miscellanies* in 1727-8 and of the first three books of
the *Dunciad* in the same latter year. When Pope began the
Dunciad is not precisely known, but probably most of it was
written between 1725 and 1728, when both the Homer and
the Shakespeare had been completed.

The poem was dedicated to Swift, and Pope acknowledged
that he was, in a sense, its "author"—by which we can take
Pope as meaning that it was the Scriblerus Club, of which
Swift was the inspirer, which first mooted the idea of a general
satire upon the "dunces" of both Grub Street and the
Universities. The third volume of the Club's *Miscellanies*
included the *Treatise on the Bathos* by Pope and Arbuthnot,
in which the whole tribe of poetasters, from Philips down, were
effectively satirised by carefully-selected quotations from their
works (in the manner of Pope's anonymous letter to the
Guardian). The *Dunciad* itself took a wider sweep, lam-
pooning not only the minor poets of Grub Street, but Whig
journalists and historians like Welsted and Oldmixon, writers
of the official *Gazette* and Poets Laureate from Shadwell to
Cibber, scholars like Theobald, unscrupulous publishers like
Curll, and even the novelist Defoe and the Methodist preacher
Whitefield. In the fourth book, published in 1742, Pope
added to the list of his victims classical scholars like Bentley;
and the next year, the year before his death, he revised the
whole satire, putting the current Poet Laureate, Cibber, into
Theobald's place as "hero" of the mock-epic. This was an
unfortunate revision, for few people could have been less

suitable as a hero of Dullness than the lively actor-dramatist who had the dubious honour—in those days—of writing official odes on the king's birthday.* Theobald took his own "bad eminence" good-humouredly, and Cibber was too old a hand to care; it was the lesser victims, by their furious counter-attacks, who made the *Dunciad* such a huge success. The war continued at its height some years, and a weekly paper, the *Grub-Street Journal*, written by Pope and his allies, came out in 1730 and continued till 1737.

Pope's model in the *Dunciad* was Dryden's *MacFlecknoe* (1682), in which the minor poet and dramatist Shadwell had been held up to ridicule. But Pope was more serious than his master here, the *Dunciad*, in spite of the many private scores paid off incidentally, being conceived as a public defence of Wit against Dullness. The privacies bulk too large, admittedly; only in the *Moral Essays* was Pope able to give us genuine types instead of persons. But if we become rather irritated at the ceaseless flow of invective—especially in Book I—we should remember that Pope had had to suffer a good deal of personal abuse himself, abuse that was not above dwelling on his crippled state and on the fact that he was a Catholic who refused to abjure his parents' faith. Reading some of the remarks of Dennis, for instance, we are surprised

* The Laureateship in the eighteenth century was often granted for political rather than literary services. Thus it came to be regarded as a questionable distinction. Not one of the century's Laureates— Nahum Tate, Nicholas Rowe, Laurence Eusden, Colley Cibber, William Whitehead, Thomas Warton, Henry Pye—is judged now to be more than a very minor poet, though several of them were distinguished in other ways, as Cibber in the theatre and Warton in criticism. Jonson and Dryden had lent real honour to the Laureateship in the seventeenth century, as Wordsworth and Tennyson were to do in the Victorian Age; but the attitude of the eighteenth century is seen in Gray's amusing letter to Mason, after he had refused the laurel wreath: "Though I very well know the bland emollient saponaceous qualities both of sack and silver, yet if any great man would say to me, 'I make you rat-catcher to his Majesty, with a salary of £300 a year and two butts of the best Malaga; and though it has been usual to catch a mouse or two, for form's sake, in public once a year, yet to you, sir, we shall not stand upon these things', I cannot say I should jump at it; nay, if they would drop the very name of the office, and call me Sinecure to the King's Majesty, I should still feel a little awkward, and think everybody I saw smelt a rat about me".

rather that Pope was able to keep his more general purpose in view at all, with the temptation he must have had to hit back at his abusers in their own coin.

There are many passages worth quoting in this mock-epic masterpiece, whose title, of course, glances at the real epics of the *Iliad* and the *Aeneid*. (Among the counter-attacks was the *Popiad*, compiled by Curll from various satires against the poet.)   In Book I, there is the invocation to Swift:

> O Thou! whatever title please thine ear,
> Dean, Drapier, Bickerstaff, or Gulliver . . .

and the character of Cibber, ending with the dramatist's apostrophe to his own works:

> "O born in sin, and forth in folly brought!
> Works damn'd, or to be damn'd! (your father's fault)
> Go, purify'd by flames ascend the sky,
> My better and more Christian progeny!
> Unstain'd, untouch'd, and yet in maiden sheets;
> While all your smutty sisters walk the streets . . ."

In Book II, there is the Miltonic opening ("High on a gorgeous seat . . .") and the superb passage where the tribe of poetasters and Gazetteers troop down Fleet Street

> To where Fleet-ditch with disemboguing streams
> Rolls the large tribute of dead dogs to Thames . . .

and are encouraged by the Goddess of Dullness to leap into the dirty water and see who can swim the best.   Book III traces the historical background of Dullness, ending with a contrast between the rewards of the Dunces and those of the Wits:

> Hibernian Politics, O Swift! thy fate;
> And Pope's, ten years to comment and translate . . .

But the best book is probably the fourth, with its impressive opening and even more impressive close.   Written much later than its predecessors, it has the quality rather of the *Moral Essays* than the earlier *Dunciad*, its characters being more types than personalities.   It celebrates the Dullness lying in "Wisdom's grave disguise", among the objects of satire being "a hundred head of Aristotle's friends" at the universities:

> As many quit the streams that murm'ring fall
> To lull the sons of Marg'ret and Clare-hall,
> Where Bentley late tempestuous wont to sport
> In troubled waters, but now sleeps in Port.

It may seem easy to write such satire, whether of individuals or of types. "It is easy to shoot," said Thackeray; "but not as Pope did; the shafts of his satire rise sublimely: no poet's verse ever mounted higher than that wonderful flight with which *The Dunciad* concludes . . . It is a wonderful and victorious single combat, in that great battle which has always been waging since society began":

> She comes! she comes! the sable Throne behold
> Of Night primaeval and of Chaos old!
> Before her Fancy's gilded clouds decay,
> And all its varying Rain-bows die away.
> Wit shoots in vain its momentary fires,
> The meteor drops, and in a flash expires.
> As one by one, at dread Medea's strain,
> The sick'ning stars fade off th'ethereal plain;
> As Argus' eyes by Hermes' wand opprest,
> Clos'd one by one to everlasting rest;
> Thus at her felt approach, and secret might,
> Art after Art goes out, and all is Night.
> See skulking Truth to her old cavern fled,
> Mountains of Casuistry heap'd o'er her head!
> Philosophy, that lean'd on Heav'n before,
> Shrinks to her second cause, and is no more.
> Physic of Metaphysic begs defence,
> And Metaphysic calls for aid on Sense!
> See Mystery to Mathematics fly!
> In vain! they gaze, turn giddy, rave, and die.
> Religion blushing veils her sacred fires,
> And unawares Morality expires.
> Nor public flame, nor private, dares to shine;
> Nor human Spark is left, nor Glimpse divine!
> Lo! thy dread Empire, Chaos! is restor'd;
> Light dies before thy uncreating word;
> Thy hand, great Anarch! lets the curtain fall,
> And universal Darkness buries All.

Essays and Epistles

Between the original three books of the *Dunciad* and the *New Dunciad*, with the fourth book added, Pope had been writing some of his most masterly work, in the Essay or Epistle form. To this period belong the *Moral Essays* (1731-5), the *Essay on Man* (1732-4), the *Imitations of Horace* (1733-7), the *Epistle to Dr Arbuthnot* (1735) and the two dialogues entitled *1738*. Pope's first editor, Bishop Warburton, renamed the *Arbuthnot* as the *Prologue to the Satires* and the *1738* dialogues as the *Epilogue*; it is a pity that many later editors have followed this lead, for nothing is gained by the substitution.

The *Essay on Man* stands somewhat apart from the other work of the 'thirties, though the original idea of Pope's was for this poem to form part of a much wider scheme, in which the last book was to be divided into several epistles on the cardinal virtues. This ambitious undertaking was never completely realised, but out of the conception grew what are usually called the *Moral Essays* (or *Ethic Epistles*). The *Essay on Man* itself—dedicated to, as it was inspired by, Bolingbroke—is not one of Pope's most successful works. Philosophical poetry has always had more casualties than victors, and Pope had not the enthusiasm or the faith of a Dante or a Milton. His genius was for character rather than exposition, and it is the characters of the *Moral Essays* whom we remember, not the philosophical scheme for which they and the *Essay* were originally devised.

The chief link between the two poems is the doctrine of the Ruling Passion:

> Search then the Ruling Passion: there, alone,
> The Wild are constant, and the Cunning known . . .

Whatever the philosophical limitations of this doctrine, Pope certainly makes magnificent use of it. The close of the First Epistle of the *Moral Essays* is surely one of the supreme heights of satirical poetry:

> Time, that on all things lays his lenient hand,
> Yet tames not this; it sticks to our last sand.

> Consistent in our follies and our sins,
> Here honest Nature ends as she begins . . .
> The frugal Crone, whom praying priests attend,
> Still tries to save the hallow'd taper's end,
> Collects her breath, as ebbing life retires,
> For one puff more, and in that puff expires.
> "Odious! in woollen! 'twould a saint provoke,"
> (Were the last words that poor Narcissa spoke)
> "No, let a charming Chintz, and Brussels lace,
> Wrap my cold limbs and shade my lifeless face:
> One would not, sure, be frightful when one's dead—
> And—Betty—give this Cheek a little Red . . ."

The universal application of the *Moral Essays* is particularly evident in the Third and Fourth Epistles, dealing with the use of riches. Though there is certainly some topical application in Pope's social criticism in the opening dialogue of Epistle III:

> B.   What nature wants, commodious Gold bestows,
> 'Tis thus we eat the bread another sows.
> P.   But how unequal it bestows, observe,
> 'Tis thus we riot, while, who sow it, starve . . .

the remedy of wealth being more evenly distributed is not one the Augustan Age only had need to be reminded of:

> Wealth in the gross is death, but life diffus'd;
> As Poison heals, in just proportion us'd:
> In heaps, like Ambergrise, a stink it lies,
> But well-dispers'd is Incense to the Skies.

And when Pope joins Swift in his contemptuous treatment of "men of pelf"—we remember the Houyhnhnm informing Gulliver of the "unnatural appetite" of the Yahoos, who are "violently fond" of "certain shining stones of several colours" which they carry away and "hide them by heaps in their kennels"—the particular personalities concerned seem unimportant beside the universal application of the satire:

> Perhaps you think the Poor might have their part?
> Bond damns the Poor, and hates them from his heart:
> The grave Sir Gilbert holds it for a rule,
> That "ev'ry man in want is knave or fool":

> " God cannot love (says Blunt, with tearless eyes)
> The wretch he starves "—and piously denies:
> But the good Bishop, with a meeker air,
> Admits, and leaves them, Providence's care.
> Yet, to be just to these poor men of pelf,
> Each does but hate his neighbour as himself:
> Damn'd to the mines, an equal fate betides
> The Slave that digs it, and the Slave that hides.

The superb story of Sir Balaam which closes this Epistle is another fine instance of Pope's universal satire in these *Moral Essays*, as is the character of Timon in Epistle IV.

The *Imitations of Horace*, the *Epistle to Dr Arbuthnot*, and the dialogues called *1738* are the most autobiographical of Pope's writings, so can be suitably considered last, together with our brief reflections on his character and genius. The so-called "Imitations" are really as original as Fielding's *Joseph Andrews*, modestly described on its title-page as "Written in Imitation of the Manner of Cervantes". Perhaps the best is the ironical *Epistle to Augustus*, in which Pope, appearing to praise the patronage of the arts by George II, makes it plain that since the reign of Anne the arts had been almost entirely neglected. The most amusing passage in *1738* is in the second dialogue, where a friend (F) asks Pope (P) to leave personalities alone and concentrate on exposing the vice. This is what Pope had succeeded in doing in the *Moral Essays*, but in this dialogue the poet takes, for argument, the other side:

> Spare then the Person, and expose the Vice.
> P.   How, Sir? not damn the Sharper, but the Dice?
> Come on, then, Satire! gen'ral, unconfin'd,
> Spread thy broad wing, and souse on all the kind.
> Ye Statesmen, Priests, of one Religion all!
> Ye Tradesmen vile, in Army, Court, or Hall,
> Ye Rev'rend Atheists—F. Scandal! name them!   Who?
> P.   Why that's the thing you bid me not to do.
> Who starv'd a Sister, who forswore a Debt,
> I never nam'd; the Town's enquiring yet.
> The pois'ning Dame—F.   You mean—P. I don't—F. You do!
> P.   See, now I keep the Secret, and not you!

The *Imitations of Horace* had led to two counter-attacks by persons satirised therein, both of whom were formerly friends of the poet. Lady Mary Wortley Montagu—best known to-day for her *Letters*—wrote *Verses to the Imitator of Horace*, in collaboration with Lord Hervey—remembered for his shrewd *Memoirs of the Reign of George II*—who also wrote a prose attack on Pope. It was partly to answer these attacks, and partly to sum up his career, that Pope wrote the famous *Epistle to Dr Arbuthnot*, one of his most pleasant poems and one of his most important. Some of the lines in which he praises himself will not be accepted by most readers, but in general he gives us a self-portrait which contemporary opinion bears out. His lines on his parents, for instance, are not affected; for all witnesses testify to his great respect for his father and the tender care he had for his widowed mother. That he was a good friend to many of the best men of the time is also unquestioned,* as is the ultra-sensitivity that made him rush into quarrels and linger over injuries. But, considering the physical handicaps which he suffered throughout his life, it is his courage which is the most remarkable thing about him. His personal bravery is testified by observers of his coolness during the *Dunciad* storm; and it was a bravery no less remarkable that allowed him to poke fun at his own infirmities in that wonderful passage in the *Arbuthnot* where he complains ironically that some of his flatterers even pay compliments to his face and figure. It must have needed a great effort of detachment, as well as a great comic genius, to see himself in perspective like this:

---

* Hazlitt's essay *Of Persons one would wish to have seen* gives us the opinion of Lamb upon Pope's friendships: "'I thought,' said A——, turning short round upon B—— [Lamb], 'that you of the Lake School did not like Pope?'—'Not like Pope! My dear sir, you must be under a mistake—I can read him over and over for ever!'—'Why certainly, the *Essay on Man* must be allowed to be a masterpiece.'—'It may be so, but I seldom look into it.'—'Oh! then it's his Satires you admire?'—'No, not his Satires, but his friendly Epistles and his compliments.'—'Compliments! I did not know he ever made any.' 'The finest,' said B——, 'that were ever paid by the wit of man ...'"— and Lamb goes on to quote, among other examples, Pope's lines on his early friends in the *Epistle to Arbuthnot*.

> There are, who to my person pay their court:
> I cough like Horace, and, tho' lean, am short;
> Ammon's great son one shoulder had too high,
> Such Ovid's nose, and "Sir! you have an Eye"—
> Go on, obliging creatures, make me see
> All that disgrac'd my Betters, met in me.
> Say for my comfort, languishing in bed,
> "Just so immortal Maro held his head":
> And when I die, be sure you let me know
> Great Homer died three thousand years ago.

Gay and the Street-Ballad

The genius of Pope so much overshadows the poetry of his
contemporaries and immediate successors that it is tempting
to dismiss them all as his followers or weak imitators.   But we
shall be false to the facts of Augustan poetry if we do not
recognise that there were other sorts of verse practised at the
time besides the rhymed-couplet satires and epistles in which
Pope had no real rival.   He himself wrote a few ballads, for
instance, and his friend John Gay was one of the masters in
that street-balladry, the tradition of which had been kept up in
London and the market-towns since the Middle Ages.   It had
suffered under the Commonwealth, but had sprung to life again
with the Restoration; and it is pleasing to note that all the
Wits of the Augustan Age—Swift and Gay in particular—wrote
ballads of various kinds.*   Lord Wharton boasted that by
his famous ballad *Lilibullero* (a favourite song of Sterne's Uncle
Toby) he had rhymed King James out of the country in 1688.

* Cowper observed in a letter, in 1783, that "The ballad is a species
of poetry . . . equally adapted to the drollest and the most tragical
subjects.   Simplicity and ease are its proper characteristics.   Our
forefathers excelled in it; but we moderns have lost the art . . . I
inherit a taste for it from my father, who succeeded well in it himself,
and who lived at a time when the best pieces in that way were produced.
What can be prettier than Gay's ballad, or rather Swift's, Arbuthnot's,
Pope's, and Gay's, in [the farce] *The What d'ye Call It*—'*Twas when
the seas were roaring*?   I have been well informed that they all contributed, and that the most celebrated association of clever fellows
this country ever saw did not think it beneath them to unite their
strength and abilities in the composition of a song.   The success,
however, answered to their wishes, and our puny days will never
produce such another".   Unknown to Cowper, Burns was then
writing his songs in Scotland.

Gay, like Pope, was born in that reign of revolution, and died in 1723, twelve years before his friend. His first notable work was *The Shepherd's Week* (1714), in which he burlesqued the pastoral manner of Philips and incidentally gave some glimpses of rustic life nearer the reality than the conventional picture of either Philips or Pope. *Trivia, or The Art of Walking the Streets of London* followed in 1715; and in 1720 he celebrated the completion of the *Iliad* by a graceful tribute entitled *Mr Pope's Welcome from Greece*. The same year he published his collected poems by subscription, which brought him in a thousand pounds—most of which he lost in the fiasco known as the South Sea Bubble. In 1727 he won a great reputation by his *Fables*, which, though not to be compared in point of subtlety with those of La Fontaine, are probably the best in English. The even greater success of *The Beggar's Opera* followed the year after.

The Beggar's Opera is often thought to have been intended as a parody on the Italian operas then in vogue in London; it is truer to say that it had the more serious intention of being a rival to them. As Arbuthnot put it, writing in the *Daily Journal*: "I take *The Beggar's Opera* to be the touchstone to try the British taste on, and it has accordingly proved effectual in discovering our true inclinations, which, how artfully soever they may be disguised by a childish fondness for Italian poetry and music in preference to our own, will in one way or another start up and disclose themselves".

Gay had not Arbuthnot's knowledge of music, but (like Goldsmith) he played the flute and was as much a lover of the traditional English airs as Goldsmith was to be of the Irish. He probably chose himself the majority of the tunes to which he had written such admirable words (some of them came from D'Urfey's collection *Wit and Mirth*); and it is the songs of the *Opera*—combining traditional airs with Gay's own mastery of the street-ballad—that have lasted longest, though part of the popularity of the piece at the time was due to the realistic treatment of the Newgate scenes and to the political implications of the character Macheath, who was thought to be a portrait of Walpole. The suspicion was sufficient for the

Government to ban from the stage Gay's much inferior sequel, *Polly*, which, however, sold even better than the original play in book form.

The success of *The Beggar's Opera* was extraordinary. Hogarth painted a scene from it, and also a portrait of the actress who created the part of Polly (who, incidentally, by becoming the Duchess of Bolton, initiated the long line of matrimony between the peerage and the stage); and the greatest ballad-writer of the age, Henry Carey, wrote a song *Polly Peachum* to the tune of his *Sally in our Alley*. The usual imitations followed the success, and Gay was even so fortunate as to have influential Dissenting ministers preaching against the *Opera*, on the ground that it showed vice in too pleasant a light—reminiscent of Elizabethan times, when dramatists and actors were pleased at the publicity inadvertently given them from Puritan pulpits. The *Opera*, of course, is hardly to be compared, as a play, with even minor Elizabethan comedies; but it admirably fulfilled its purpose, and the sixty songs in it—among the best being *Can Love be controlled by advice, Were I laid on Greenland's coast, Youth's the season made for joys, How happy could I be with either*—are among the pleasantest literature of the Augustan Age.

Gay's other ballads include *Black-ey'd Susan, The Lady's Lamentation, Molly Mog, Sleep, O Sleep* (from *Polly*), and, most famous of all, the song *O ruddier than the Cherry*, from the opera *Acis and Galatea* (1732) which had the distinction of being set to music by Handel.*

* Gay's immediate followers in the ballad-opera included Cibber and Carey, but the best, from the literary point of view, was undoubtedly Fielding, who in his early years wrote several comedies interspersed with original ballads to traditional tunes: for instance, *The Intriguing Chambermaid* (1733), *Don Quixote in England* (1733), and *An Old Man Taught Wisdom* (1734). The *Quixote* includes the famous ballads *The Roast Beef of Old England* and (to the tune of *There was a jovial beggar*)

> The dusky night rides down the sky,
>   And ushers in the morn:
> The hounds all join in glorious cry,
>   The huntsman winds his horn:
>   And a hunting we will go, will go, will go,
>   And a hunting we will go.

The Hymn-Writers

To pass from ballads to hymns is not so great a step as it might seem at first glance. Handel set both; both are among the most popular forms of literature; and both probably nourished the genius of one of the greatest of English poets, William Blake. The fact that the century of Erastianism, when the Church of England became almost a branch of the civil service, should also have been the century when our greatest hymns were written, is certainly surprising; but we have noted the genuine, if perhaps somewhat shallow, Christianity of such men as Steele and Addison, and the Augustan Age can claim to have begun the century of hymnsinging, even if its greatest hosanna was to come immediately afterwards, with the Methodist revival.

Addison himself, we observed, wrote two hymns which have retained their popularity. More astonishing is the fact that Nahum Tate, who wrote that melodramatic "improvement" of *Lear* and who was one of the victims of the *Dunciad,* wrote a hymn which is known to millions who have only heard dimly of Shakespeare and have never heard of Pope. This is the famous *While shepherds watched their flocks by night,* undoubtedly one of the best of our Christmas carols and, furthermore, one of the few eighteenth-century hymns which have not been altered in later years. The carol which will be piped by thousands of children next Christmas is exactly the same as that published by Tate in 1702.

But the greatest figure is Isaac Watts (1674-1748), a Nonconformist minister who is only excelled in English hymnwriting by Charles Wesley. He wrote some ambitious poems, as well as moral verses for children which retained their popularity for more than a hundred years (to be eventually burlesqued in *Alice in Wonderland*); but his *Hymns and Spiritual Songs* (1716) and *Psalms of David* (1719) have outlasted his other works. If occasionally they fall into bathos:

> Sing to the Lord with joyful voice;
> Let every land his Name adore;
> The British Isles shall send the noise
> Across the ocean to the shore . . .

more frequently they rise to the sublimest heights in this field of Ken, Wesley, Cowper, and Newman; as in *Our God, our help in ages past*, *Jesus shall reign where'er the sun*, and *When I survey the wondrous Cross*. Watts is a much lesser figure in literature than Milton or Bunyan, but his influence on popular religion and culture in the eighteenth century must have been nearly as great.*

Prior and Minor Augustans

Matthew Prior (1664-1721) was one of the intimate circle of Swift and Bolingbroke, Pope and Gay. The son of an artisan, he had an astonishing career, rising to be Ambassador to France and being mainly responsible for the Treaty of Utrecht, popularly known at the time as "Matt's Peace". His early appointment to the Embassy at the Hague produced his amusing poem *The Secretary* (1696), and other light pieces were written regularly in the intervals of public business and collected in *Poems on Several Occasions* (1709) and in a larger publication of the same name, issued by subscription in 1718. This latter volume brought him in over £4,000, and the money was needed, for by this time Prior had fallen with the rest of the Tory ministry and had, in fact, only just been released from prison.

He is mainly remembered to-day by these light pieces, in which he seems almost to anticipate Byron in the deliberate coolness and impudent wit of his verse; among the best known are the ode *The merchant, to secure his treasure* and *A Better Answer*. He also wrote two lengthier serious poems, *Alma, or The Progress of the Mind* (written in prison) and *Solomon on the Vanity of the World*, a work which Johnson found tedious but Cowper and Scott admired. His epigrams are among the best of their kind; they were mostly printed posthumously, together with the poems *To a Child of Quality*

---

* He was one of several minor poets added to the famous collection for which Johnson wrote his prefaces, at Johnson's recommendation. Cowper records that Pope "had placed him once in the *Dunciad*; but on being advised to read before he judged him, was convinced that he deserved other treatment, and thrust somebody's blockhead into the gap, whose name, consisting of a monosyllable, happened to fit it".

and *For my Own Monument* and the song *Accept, my love, as true a heart*. His tales in verse, popular at the time, were later censured by Lord Hales as "impure"; but John Wesley admired them, and Johnson declared that "there is nothing in Prior that will excite to lewdness. If Lord Hales thinks there is, he must be more combustible than other people".

Prior's two collections, and the poems by Gay mentioned, were the principal minor verse produced between 1700 and 1720; parts of William Diaper's *Sea-Eclogues* (1712) and Lady Winchilsea's *Miscellaneous Poems* (1713) are also well worth reading. The 'twenties produced some interesting minor poems, at a time when Pope was mainly engaged on the *Odyssey* and the edition of Shakespeare. Before the *Dunciad* and the *Beggar's Opera* took the town by storm in the late 'twenties, there appeared *Poems on Several Occasions* (1722) by Thomas Parnell, friend of Pope and Swift and member of the Scriblerus Club; John Dyer's *Grongar Hill* (1726), a pleasant poem much admired by Wordsworth and reminiscent in manner of Milton's *L'Allegro* and *Il Penseroso*; and *Poems on Several Occasions* (1727) by Pope's assistant in the *Odyssey* translation, William Broome. This collection contains the poem *The Rosebud: To a Young Lady*, in which this memorable passage reminds us of the impressive lyrics of the seventeenth century:

> Tho' Sickness yet a while forbears,
> Yet Time destroys what Sickness spares;
> Now Helen lives alone in Fame,
> And Cleopatra's but a Name;
> Time must indent that heav'nly Brow,
> And thou must be what Helen's now.

One of the most interesting minor poems of the following decade was *The Spleen* (1737), written "by the late Mr Matthew Green, of the Custom-House, London". Green was a Quaker of independent mind, and his poem, in octosyllabic couplets, is similar to Swift's verse in ease and manner. Its philosophy is one that takes the Augustan dread of enthusiasm to its furthest, if logical, extreme:

> I rail not with mock-patriot grace
> At folks, because they are in place,
> Nor, hir'd to praise with stallion pen,
> Serve the ear-lechery of men;
> But to avoid religious jars
> The laws are my expositors,
> Which in my doubting mind create
> Conformity to church and state.
> I go, pursuant to my plan,
> To Mecca with the caravan,
> And think it right in common sense
> But for diversion and defence.

An age that could produce both that passage and the hymns of Isaac Watts is evidently not a simple age to understand, either in literature or philosophy.

James Thomson

The most original of Pope's younger contemporaries was his friend Thomson, whose life covers exactly the period taken by this chapter and who, in the age of the heroic couplet, wrote mainly in blank verse and in the age of the town wrote of the country. He was by no means a "rival" to Pope, for not only did the two men admire each other's poetry but the younger owed a good deal to the elder poet, accepting some corrections from him when his chief poem *The Seasons* was in manuscript. What makes him original is that he succeeded to a large extent in making his country themes live, even though hampered—to a modern eye brought up on Wordsworth and Keats—by eighteenth-century diction. If we compare his four *Seasons* with Pope's in the *Pastorals*, we see what a gain he made in realistic description of the countryside; how many useless conventions, furthermore, he discarded. He is not, of course, quite at his ease; he feels it necessary, in the opening lines of *Spring*, to mention classical precedents:

> Such themes as these the rural Maro sung
> To wide-imperial Rome, in the full height
> Of elegance and taste, by Greece refined.

But before long we come to such passages as this, which were more original in the Augustan Age than they seem to-day:

> The Black-bird whistles from the thorny brake;
> The mellow Bullfinch answers from the grove:
> Nor are the Linnets, o'er the flowering furze
> Pour'd out profusely, silent.   Join'd to these
> Innumerous songsters, in the freshening shade
> Of new-sprung leaves, their modulations mix
> Mellifluous.   The Jay, the Rook, the Daw,
> And each harsh pipe, discordant heard alone,
> Aid the full concert: while the Stock-dove breathes
> A melancholy murmur through the whole.

The poet who could write such passages evidently ranks with Gray and Collins and Akenside in the transition from the conventional pastoral of Pope and Philips to the true natural feeling of Wordsworth's *Tintern Abbey* and Keats's *Autumn*.

To a modern eye, of course, such passages are rather spoilt by the "poetic diction" which Wordsworth was to criticise. To us Thomson is bound to appear curiously mixed: at one moment, writing naturally of what he had observed, at others resorting to "the Finny-race" and "the vocal woods" and "the hoary Fen", conventional pairings that the dullest of poetasters could achieve.   When he writes of the rainbow:

> Here, awful Newton, the dissolving Clouds
> Form, fronting on the Sun, thy showery Prism;
> And to the sage-instructed Eye unfold
> The various Twine of Light, by thee disclosed . . .

he is in the most unhappy region of eighteenth-century verse, that could lead to such monstrous diction as Gilbert White's

> Push'd by the weightier atmosphere, up springs
> The ponderous Mercury, from scale to scale
> Mounting, amidst the Torricellian tube . . .

and Erasmus Darwin's

> So where the Hummingbird in Chile's bowers
> On murmuring pinions robs the pendent flowers;
> Seeks where fine pods their dulcet balm distil,
> And sucks the treasure with proboscis bill.

The fact that distinguished naturalists like White and Darwin could write such unnatural verse is a justification in itself for the revolution that Wordsworth was eventually to make.

Thomson was born in Scotland, son of a Presbyterian
minister, and was sent to Edinburgh University with the
object of following the same vocation.   While there, in 1720,
he wrote an essay on "A Country Life" for the *Edinburgh
Miscellany*; and five years later he abandoned his clerical
studies and followed his friend David Mallet to London, hoping
to find a patron and make a living by literature.   The scheme
was not so venturesome in those days, of course, as it would
be to-day; it was the last great age of patronage, before the
publishers assumed the role almost entirely.   Thomson found
first some employment as tutor with a noble family, and then,
after the success of his *Winter* (1726), dedicated to Sir Spencer
Compton, found his path clear to advancement by the usual
means.   *Winter* was followed by *Summer* (1727), dedicated to
Bubb Dodington, the future Lord Melcombe; *Spring* (1728)
was dedicated to the Countess of Hartford; and *Autumn*,
dedicated to the Speaker of the House of Commons, completed
the collected volume published as *The Seasons* in 1730.   His
Poem sacred to the Memory of Sir Isaac Newton (1727) was
dedicated to Walpole, and—with a fine disregard of contemporary political manoeuvres—his *Britannia* (1729) flattered
the Prince of Wales.*

The Seasons was for many years the most popular volume
of poetry in the country, found like the *Pilgrim's Progress* in
nearly every cottage and rivalling Pope's Homer in the wide
extent of its influence.   It was undoubtedly the originality we
have noticed that caused this popular success; and Johnson
made that the burden of his discriminating praise in his *Life
of Thomson*:

> As a writer, he is entitled to one praise of the highest
> kind: his mode of thinking, and of expressing his
> thoughts, is original. His blank verse is no more the blank
> verse of Milton, or of any other poet, than the rhymes of
> Prior are the rhymes of Cowley . . . He thinks in a peculiar
> train, and he thinks always as a man of genius; he looks
> round on Nature and on Life with the eye which Nature
> bestows only on a poet . . . The reader of the *Seasons*

* Son of George II, father of George III, at that time the supposed
centre of the anti-Walpole faction.

wonders that he never saw before what Thomson shows
him, and that he never yet has felt what Thomson
impresses . . . His diction is in the highest degree florid
and luxuriant . . . It is too exuberant, and sometimes
may be charged with filling the ear more than the mind.*

Thomson's later work includes the ambitious poem
Liberty (1734-6); five tragedies, of which *Tancred and
Sigismunda* (1745) was the most successful on the stage; and
the *Masque of Alfred* (1740), written with Mallet, with music
by Thomas Arne, a piece which contains the famous patriotic
song *Rule, Britannia*. Less well known, and perhaps more
deserving to be known, is this passage from the unfinished
Elegy upon James Therburn, which is so striking an anticipation of Burns that one wonders why it is not commonly
included in the Scottish background of that great poet:

> Having his paternoster said,
> He took a dram and went to bed;
> He fell asleep, and death was glad
> > That he had catch'd him;
> For Therburn was e'en ill bested,
> > That none did watch him.
>
> For had the carl but been aware,
> That meagre death, who none does spare,
> T'attempt sic things should ever dare,
> > As stop his pipe;
> He might have come to flee or skare:
> > The greedy gipe . . .
>
> Therefore they say he got some help
> In getting of the little whelp;
> But passing that, it makes me yelp,
> > But what remead?
> Death lent him sic a cursed skelp,
> > That now he's dead.

---

* Compare Johnson's opinion in conversation, as recorded by
Boswell: "Thomson had a true poetical genius, the power of viewing
every thing in a poetical light. His fault is such a cloud of words
sometimes, that the sense can hardly peep through. Shiels . . . was
one day sitting with me. I took down Thomson, and read aloud a
large portion of him, and then asked,—Is not this fine? Shiels having
expressed the highest admiration, 'Well, Sir, (said I,) I have omitted
every other line'".

Coffee-House to Country-Churchyard

Thomson's last work was a romantic poem called *The Castle of Indolence* (1748), a poem written in the Spenserian stanza and in conscious imitation of the Elizabethan poet. This has its place in the line of Spenserian imitations of the 'forties and onward which is discussed in our seventh chapter (see below, pp. 196-7). For now we are moving out of the Augustan Age into an age of very different preoccupations in poetry. With Collins's *Ode on the Death of Thomson* (1749) we seem to be right in the heart of eighteenth-century romance; and this poem expresses, far better than any commentary can do, how far we are now from Addison and Pope, and how Thomson, more than his contemporaries Young and Blair, is the true link between the Coffee-House and the Country-Churchyard:

> In yonder grave a Druid lies,
>   Where slowly winds the stealing wave!
> The year's best sweets shall duteous rise
>   To deck its Poet's sylvan grave!
>
> In yon deep bed of whisp'ring reeds
>   His airy harp shall now be laid,
> That he, whose heart in sorrow bleeds,
>   May love thro' life the soothing shade.
>
> Then maids and youths shall linger here,
>   And while its sounds at distance swell,
> Shall sadly seem in Pity's ear
>   To hear the Woodland Pilgrim's knell . . .
>
> The genial meads assign'd to bless
>   Thy life, shall mourn thy early doom;
> Their hinds and shepherd-girls shall dress
>   With simple hands thy rural tomb.
>
> Long, long, thy stone and pointed clay
>   Shall melt the musing Briton's eyes;
> O! vales, and wild woods, shall he say,
>   In yonder grave your Druid lies!

CHAPTER IV

DEFOE: FROM THE NEWSPAPER TO THE NOVEL
1704-1754

> "The world is so taken up of late with novels and romances that it will be hard for a private history to be taken for genuine, where the names and other circumstances of the person are concealed; and on this account we must be content to leave the reader to pass his own opinion upon the ensuing sheets, and to take it just as he pleases."
>
> DEFOE: Preface to *Moll Flanders*.

> "The Editor has been much pressed with importunities and conjectures in relation to the person and family of the gentleman, who are the principal persons in the work; all he thinks himself at liberty to say, or is necessary to be said, is only to repeat what has already been hinted, that the story has its foundation in truth: and that there was a necessity, for obvious reasons, to vary and disguise some facts and circumstances, as also the names of persons, places, etc."
>
> RICHARDSON: Preface to *Pamela*, Volume II.

The Newspaper before Defoe

We have seen something of the periodical literature of the Augustan Age and have observed that some of the essays in the *Spectator* were among the ancestors of the Georgian novel. But Steele and Addison were primarily critics and essay-writers and never attempted full-length fiction; it is to their more versatile contemporary Daniel Defoe that we must look for the real evolution of the novel from periodical journalism.

Though Defoe had some influence, we noted, on the character of Steele's *Tatler*, his journalism was very different from that of his coffee-house rivals. We read the *Tatler* and the *Spectator* to-day, partly it is true for their picture of contemporary society, but also as literature in their own right.

Defoe's journalism is not often literature in this sense,* but it was his flair for news—more developed even than Steele's—that eventually led him to the writing of *Robinson Crusoe* and *Moll Flanders*.

When he founded his *Review* in 1704, the newspaper in England was less than a hundred years old, and its history had been one of constant struggle against the government. Under the Commonwealth, Cromwell—like more recent dictators—had banned all the newspapers except a few that were sympathetic to the new regime; and this ban continued at the Restoration, the only journal of any significance permitted to appear being the *London Gazette*—a Court paper which still prints official news—and Roger L'Estrange being appointed Surveyor of the Press. It was not till 1695 that Parliament repealed the Licensing Act, which had allowed only twenty printing presses for the whole of England; and several new journals at once appeared, among them the Whig *Flying Post* and the Tory *Post Bag*. These papers approximated more than their predecessors to the modern pattern: they contained ordinary news as well as party propaganda, together with such lighter fare as the racing results and the betting odds.

The first daily newspaper came out in 1702. It was called the *Daily Courant*, was produced "next door to the King's Arms Tavern at Fleet-Bridge", and managed to live for over thirty years. Meanwhile other journals had begun to spring up outside London, among them two which still exist: the *Worcester Postman* (1690), now called *Berrow's Worcester Journal*, and the *Lincoln, Rutland, and Stamford Mercury* (1695). The first real newspaper in Scotland was the *Edinburgh Gazette* (1699), and Scotland produced the first evening newspaper in the *Edinburgh Evening Courant* (1705), the *Evening Post* (mentioned in *Tom Jones*) following in London a year later.

---

* The contrary opinion of Coleridge should, however, be noted: he claimed that he could select from Defoe's periodical writings "a volume equal in size to Addison's collected papers, little inferior in wit and humour, and greatly superior in vigour of style and thought".

Among the less celebrated literary achievements of the Augustan Age, therefore, was the production of newspapers all over the country.* Some towns produced more than one: there were three papers, for instance, in Exeter. It is injudicious to compare modern newspapers with the periodicals of Steele and Addison; the proper comparison is with the *Flying Post* or the *Daily Courant*.

Defoe and the " Review "

Daniel Defoe (*c.* 1660-1731) was the son of a London butcher and was educated for the Nonconformist ministry. Like Thomson forty years later, he preferred a less exacting if more precarious livelihood; and, after taking part in the unsuccessful rebellion of the Duke of Monmouth against James II, he was in turn a dealer in hosiery, a minor civil servant, the manager of a brick factory, a secret agent, and— through almost the whole of his life—a prolific journalist in prose and verse.

We are interested here in the work of his middle and later years, from 1704 onwards. But two of his earlier productions can be mentioned in passing. The first is that amusing defence of the King entitled *The True-Born Englishman* (1701). This is easily the best of his journalistic efforts in verse, and it has a universal touch in its common-sense irony that makes it less merely topical than the journalism of such contemporary verse-writers as Ned Ward. William III had had to put up with much criticism for establishing some of his Dutch followers in high positions at Court; Defoe's defence, masterly

* Among the survivals are: the *Nottingham Journal* (1710); the *Newcastle Journal* (1711); the *Bristol Times* (1713), now incorporated in the *Western Daily Press*; the *Norwich Mercury* (1714); the *Kentish Gazette* (1717); the *Leeds Mercury* (1718), now part of the *Yorkshire Post*; the *Gloucester Journal* (1722); the *Reading Mercury* (1723); and the *Salisbury and Winchester Journal* (1729). *Lloyd's List and Shipping Gazette* started from Edward Lloyd's Coffee-house in 1734. It was not till 1772 that the famous *Morning Post*, for which Coleridge later wrote, came into existence, followed in 1785 by the still more famous *Times*, originally called the *Daily Universal Register*. The first Sunday newspaper, founded by a woman, was E. Johnson's *British Gazette and Sunday Monitor* (1783), the still flourishing *Observer* following nine years later.

in its simplicity and immediately popular, was a reminder of the Englishman's own extremely varied pedigree:

> Fate jumbled them together, God knows how;
> Whate'er they were, they're true-born English now.

Whether Defoe's personal background suggested this defence is not clear: his father was named plain "Foe", but there may have been some Huguenot ancestry in the family which led the writer to adopt, about this time, the prefix by which he is always known.

His next attempt at irony was not so fortunate. With the succession of Anne, the Dissenters felt themselves in immediate danger of repressive measures; Dr Sacheverell preached his famous sermon against them, and Bills were being discussed among Tory statesmen that were to suppress their chapels and schools. Defoe had earlier annoyed his fellow-Dissenters by writing pamphlets against the practice of "occasional conformity", which he likened, in a phrase that would have pleased Bunyan, to "playing bo-peep with God Almighty". But now that the times had changed, "the Author of the True-Born Englishman" published an ironical pamphlet called *The Shortest Way with the Dissenters* (1702). He assumed for himself the character of an extreme High Church-man, one who had no doubt whatever that there should be only one form of religion allowed in England (and that, by a fortunate coincidence, his own). Under this disguise, Defoe pursued an apparently logical argument: the Puritans had used persecution to make England entirely Calvinist; now the time had come to make England entirely Episcopalian. To fine a man a shilling for not going to church was a paltry measure; the one way to secure the unity of the Church of England was to get rid of the Dissenters altogether, by sending them out of the country and hanging their ministers. If this should appear to some an unmerciful act, "is it unmerciful", asked the disguised Defoe, "to kill a serpent, a toad, a viper? It is an act of mercy to our neighbours; much more to get rid of those who poison the soul, corrupt our life, and destroy our peace".

Defoe's intention here was to show what the spirit of intolerance would lead to if it were fully unleashed. But the irony missed fire, in one sense; though the outcome was to reveal how serious were the dangers to which the courageous author had drawn attention. For the pamphlet, at first, was taken by both sides at its face value: the Dissenters were alarmed at what they took to be the serious proposal of one of their enemies, while some High Churchmen publicly expressed their approval of the measures apparently advocated. "I join with that author in all he says," wrote a Fellow of a Cambridge college; "I pray God put into Her Majesty's heart to put what is there proposed in execution."

When the real intention of the pamphlet was perceived, the printer was arrested; and Defoe was sentenced, for "seditious libel", to stand three times in the pillory, to pay a considerable fine, and to be imprisoned in Newgate during the Queen's pleasure.

"Earless on high stood unabash'd Defoe," wrote Pope in the *Dunciad*; and though "earless" is an error, "unabashed" certainly described his attitude. For the government had overreached itself, and Defoe's intended humiliation was turned into a triumph. He pilloried his persecutors in his *Hymn to the Pillory*, written from Newgate and hawked as a ballad among the crowd that came to watch his exposure—and instead of pelting him with rotten eggs, as was hoped, covered him with flowers. And while still in prison, he began his newspaper, the *Review*, which lasted for nearly ten years.

Ironically enough, by the editor's secret negotiation with the more moderate Tories, who promised him his release, the paper became for some years an unofficial organ of the Coalition Government, and later of the Tory Government. But Defoe was given a free hand, being able to criticise the government on many matters—such as the terms of the Treaty of Utrecht and the measures against Dissent—even while drawing its pay. He pursued, in fact, with remarkable success, the ideal of moderation set forth both in the title and the manifesto of the *Review*. It was to be, Defoe claimed, "A Weekly Review of the Affairs of France, purged from the errors and partialities of news-writers and petty-statesmen of all sides". Some of its objects were to set the affairs of France and Europe in a clearer light, with no bias towards any side: "Nor shall we embroil ourselves with parties, but pursue the truth, find her out, when a crowd of lies and nonsense has almost smothered her, and set her up so as she may be both seen and heard".

The extent to which Defoe was successful in pursuing this ideal made the *Review* very different from most of the other papers of the time. There were probably occasions, of course, when he differed so deeply from the government that he did not dare to express his full mind; but, on the other hand, he never expressed opinions that were not his own, he counselled moderation in all things, and he wrote in favour of every scheme of social improvement that was mooted in his time. The compliment that is often paid him, of dating the history of English journalism from the foundation of the *Review*, has much justification behind it.

His literary activity during these middle years of his life was astonishing. Besides his ordinary journalism, he found time to produce several pamphlets every year; to write *The Consolidator* (1704), a satirical account of a journey to the moon; *The Apparition of Mrs Veal* (1706); a *History of the Union of Great Britain* (1709); a *General History of Trade* (1713); and several pieces of journalism in verse. He contributed to the *Mercator* after the *Review* had been killed by the newspaper tax, and for a time edited the *Flying Post*. He wrote a manual of conduct, *The Family Instructor*, which for more than a century after its publication in 1715 had a place in the devout Dissenting home alongside the Bible and the *Pilgrim's Progress*.

About this time he appears to have become involved in another prosecution and to have escaped a further term of imprisonment by a similar negotiation with the triumphant Whig party to that he had earlier made with the moderate Tories and the war Coalition. He entered again into government service, and from 1718 was employed to contribute to Jacobite papers with the secret intention of modifying their opinions and steering them round towards some reconciliation with the Hanoverian dynasty and the Whig Government. He appears to have ceased to be a secret agent and journalist about 1725-6 and to have written little for the periodical press during the last few years of his life.

Towards the Novel

Defoe is often called the Father of the English Novel as well as the Father of the English Newspaper. Both titles are to some extent inaccurate, for there were newspapers before the *Review* and novels before *Crusoe*. A combination of the honours is more relevant to the facts, for Defoe was certainly the first novelist of any importance to base his stories on the same methods he had found so useful in journalism.

One of the features of the *Review*, we noted, had been the supplement at the end which had an influence on the *Tatler* and *Spectator*. Though it was his rivals who improved on his design in the periodical press, it was Defoe himself who came to evolve from imaginary clubs and letters and types a form of fiction in which one character tells a story which is made as circumstantial as possible. To enter into the life of an imaginary character, to relate a story from his or her point of view, the author remaining apparently in the background: this suited Defoe's peculiar genius and must have been encouraged by the unintended success of his High-Church impersonation in *The Shortest Way with the Dissenters* as much as by the intended camouflage of his later Jacobite writings. His talent as a novelist and as a secret agent and journalist were evidently part of the same power of impersonation.

The first sign of the journalist turning into the novelist is as early as 1706, when Defoe wrote *A True Relation of the Apparition of one Mrs Veal, the Next Day after her Death, to one Mrs Bargrave at Canterbury, the 18th of September, 1705*. This Canterbury tale was based on a ghost story current at the time, but Defoe, in the manner of his later fictions, assures us in the Preface that every word of it is true:

> This relation is matter of fact, and attended with such circumstances as may induce any reasonable man to believe it. It was sent by a gentleman, a Justice of Peace at Maidstone, in Kent, and a very intelligent person, to his friend in London, as it is here worded; which discourse is here attested by a very sober and understanding gentleman, who had it from his kinswoman who lives in Canterbury, within a few doors of the house in which the within-named Mrs Bargrave lives . . . and who positively assured him that the whole matter as it is related and laid down is really true and what she herself had in the same words, as near as may be, from Mrs Bargrave's own mouth.

Assurances like this are in the tradition of the popular ballad and novelette of the early seventeenth century, as we see from the scene in *The Winter's Tale* where Autolycus is selling his wares to the shepherd-girls:

> AUTOLYCUS: Here's one to a very doleful tune: how a usurer's wife was brought to bed of twenty money-bags at a burden, and how she longed to eat adders' heads and toads carbonadoed.
> MOPSA: Is it true, think you?
> AUTOLYCUS: Very true, and but a month old.
> DORCAS: Bless me from marrying a usurer!
> AUTOLYCUS: Here's the midwife's name to it, one Mistress Taleporter, and five or six honest wives that were present. Why should I carry lies abroad?

Defoe liked to get all the circumstantial evidence available, the appearance of Mrs Veal after her death being confirmed by the fact that she wore a scoured silk gown, newly made up, which, as Mrs Bargrave told a friend, she felt and admired. "Then Mrs Watson cried out, 'You have seen her indeed, for none knew but Mrs Veal and myself that the gown was scoured.'" The ghost came chiefly for the purpose of commending a popular work of piety called *A Christian's Defence against the Fear of Death*; and later editions of this work contained Defoe's story as an appendix. To the appeal of the marvellous for the ordinary sinful reader he thus added, for the more devout, a religious appeal; and this combination of the sensational and the pious was to have a great deal to do with the popularity of his later novels.

Defoe's celebrated "realism" is, then, partly a trick, a trick that reaches back to the traditional ballads and forward to the detective story. Why we should demand apparent realism in a tale meant wholly or primarily for our entertainment is a curious problem in psychology; but that the fact is so will not be disputed. Defoe, however, was also genuinely interested in the behaviour of ordinary people in extraordinary circumstances, and he wanted to replace the old romances by stories more in keeping with his readers' experience. He came himself—like his successors Richardson and Dickens and George Eliot—from the lower-middle-class, the class of small tradesmen, small masters, and minor officials; and he had had experience in Newgate of what was later to be known as "the submerged tenth". At the time he was writing *Moll Flanders*, there was an extensive underworld in London, a region of vice and misery vividly portrayed in some of Hogarth's prints and that only began to be reformed after Defoe's death by the efforts of magistrates like the Fieldings and practical saints like Howard. A good deal of the true realism of the later English novel can be traced back to Defoe, as surely as the sensational fiction of modern times that is disguised as fact.

"*Robinson Crusoe*"

Although Defoe was moving towards the novel as early as 1706, it was not till 1719, when he was nearly sixty, that he opened the line of his true novels with the world-famous *Robinson Crusoe*. After the deserved success of this first venture, novels competed with histories and pamphlets and works of instruction in the astonishingly prolific period of the 'twenties. He published in this single decade about thirty books, besides lesser pamphlets and articles: among the best known are *Memoirs of a Cavalier* (1720), *Life of Captain Singleton* (1720), *Moll Flanders* (1722), *Journal of the Plague Year* (1722), *History of Colonel Jacque* (1722), *History of Peter the Great* (1723), *Roxana; or the Fortunate Mistress* (1724),

Life of John Sheppard (1724), *A Tour through Great Britain* (1724-6), *An Account of Jonathan Wild* (1725), *The Complete English Tradesman* (1725-7), and *A Plan of English Commerce* (1728). From a mere glance through this list, we can see how histories of actual persons, like Peter the Great and Jonathan Wild the Great, were written side by side with "histories" of fictitious characters like Moll Flanders and Colonel Jacque. It is almost impossible, with Defoe, to know where fact ends and fiction begins; and there is no doubt that this confusion was deliberate.

Crusoe itself was founded on fact, on some account Defoe had read of the adventures of Alexander Selkirk, a sailor who served in 1704 as a privateer under Dampier and was marooned on Juan Fernandez island, where he remained till rescued in 1709. (Cowper later wrote a poem on the same subject.) But Defoe's *Crusoe* was also intended as a moral fable; and the moral purpose, together with all the circumstantial details, came out of the novelist's own mind. It is intriguing to speculate what Selkirk thought of these embellishments if he happened to read *Crusoe* before he died in 1721.

What everyone remembers about the novel is the desert island, Crusoe's efforts to make himself a home, and the sudden appearance of Friday. But the adventures of Crusoe before he reaches the island are meant to be more important than those of Gulliver before he reaches Lilliput or Brobdingnag. Swift's story really starts only when Gulliver is shipwrecked, whereas it was Defoe's intention that the central story of self-help should follow as retribution for Crusoe's earlier life.

His early idleness is stressed by the novelist to form a contrast with his later activity. He starts out in life with the sole purpose of gratifying his own inclinations. Bent on a life of adventure, he wants it on the easiest terms. He runs away to sea, but with no intention of learning seamanship: "Having money in my pocket, and good clothes on my back, I would always go on board in the habit of a gentleman; and so I neither had any business in the ship nor learnt to do any". He begins to trade on the Guinea coast, is taken prisoner by a Turkish pirate, and is made a slave. With the boy Xury, he escapes in a small boat, and suffers great hardships; but is rescued by a ship going to Brazil. He sells Xury to the captain as a slave, and determines to become a planter. It is while he is sailing back to Guinea to capture some negro slaves for the plantations that he meets the storm in which he is shipwrecked and is cast, the only survivor, on a desert island. This is the first part of the story—largely forgotten in our memory—to which the life on the island bears a strict relation.

He first sees nothing but death before him, and in his misery calls upon God with the first prayer he has uttered since his youth. Later, when a Bible is among the things he has salvaged from the wreck, he turns to the passage "Call upon me in the day of trouble, and I will deliver thee . . .". He first takes the words to mean only deliverance from the island:

> But soon I learnt to take it in another sense; now I looked back on my past life with such horror, and my sins appeared so dreadful, that my soul sought nothing of God but deliverance from the sin that bore down all my comfort. As for my solitary life, it was nothing; I did not so much as pray to be delivered from it, or think of it; it was all of no consideration in comparison with this.

He then resolves to make the best of his life on the island, to "fight the good fight" even under the most distressing circumstances. Defoe's faith was the practical sort, and his hero is rescued from his early life of vice and idleness by leading a life of duty and labour.

Crusoe's humane treatment of Friday is similarly contrasted with his treatment of Xury and his employment of slaves for the American plantations. Defoe's concern for the victims of the slave-trade—expressed earlier in the *Review*—was not a common one at that time; it was not till much later on in the eighteenth century that the outcry against slavery reached such proportions as to have, eventually, an effect upon governments. It is pleasing to reflect that the tremendous popularity of *Crusoe*—easily the most widely-read work of the century—had as one of its incidental virtues an influence upon the greatest moral revolution of modern times.

"*Moll Flanders*"

The novels which followed *Crusoe* have never been so popular, partly because they were not considered, either in the eighteenth century or in Victorian times, entirely suitable for family reading. They certainly deal with the side of life furthest removed from that of the classics on the juvenile shelf; yet between these later novels and *Crusoe* there are distinct points of resemblance. To begin with, they are all, like *Crusoe*, stories of self-help. Crusoe is cast upon a desert island, and comes near to death; the later protagonists start off even earlier in similar, though varied, predicaments. Captain Singleton was stolen as a child and sold to the gipsies; Moll Flanders was born in Newgate of a mother who was shortly afterwards transported to the American plantations for petty theft; Colonel Jacque, born a gentleman, was through early misfortune apprenticed to a pickpocket; while Roxana, married at fifteen, sees her husband ruined and is left "in a condition the most deplorable that words can express". The basis of each novel is clearly the same; and the narrative, in the hero's or heroine's own words, tells of their efforts to rise out of their material or spiritual misery.

Moll Flanders, supposed to be "written in the year 1683", is the best of these successors to *Crusoe* and can be discussed here as typical of them all. We should note, first, the full title of this novel: "The Fortunes and Misfortunes of the famous Moll Flanders, etc., who was born in Newgate, and during a life of continued variety, for three-score years, besides her childhood, was twelve years a Whore, five times a Wife (whereof once to her own brother), twelve years a thief, eight years a transported Felon in Virginia, at last grew rich, lived honest, and died a Penitent. Written from her own Memorandums". This lengthy title, with its summary of sensations within, reminds us of the preliminary "Roll up!" to a travelling variety-show. It was Defoe's evident intention, as it was that of the Elizabethan ballad-monger and the modern barker, to attract his audience by dwelling on the sensational characters and incidents that were for sale. To attract the ordinary sinner, there was the promise of a woman married five times, once to her own brother (thus outdoing the Wife of Bath); to attract the more pious, there was the promise of a final repentance. And, as a last inducement to buy, the whole story was "written from her own memorandums", was indeed based upon fact! "Why should I carry lies abroad?"

Whether there was a real Moll Flanders has intrigued Defoe's biographers as much as the genuineness of his *Memoirs of a Cavalier* or the authenticity of his *Journal of the Plague Year*. From what we know of Defoe's methods, it seems wasted labour to try to pin down a real Moll who might have suggested to him—while he was in Newgate—some features of the story. "The Life and Strange Surprising Adventures of Robinson Crusoe, of York, Mariner" bears, after all, only a superficial resemblance to the life and adventures of Alexander Selkirk; so we may be permitted to doubt whether there was a real Moll Flanders in any other sense.

What makes the novel "realistic" is rather Defoe's interest in the everyday affairs of common humanity. Moll has truly adventures more than life-size—there is no deception; there is nothing up Defoe's sleeve save the whole bag of tricks —but her character seems, like Crusoe's, so much like our own that we can sympathise with her emotions even in the most extraordinary circumstances. To get this prevailing sympathy for his characters was Defoe's real achievement. He is not among the greatest novelists, but his genius is more than just a flare for the sensational and the topical. His importance in literary history is his leading role in the evolution of the novel from periodical journalism; but he is also a novelist who is still widely read. (Whereas the plays of Kyd, to take an example of a pioneer in the drama, are as seldom read as performed.) By comparison with such masters as Dickens and George Eliot, he sometimes seems crude enough; and where he has in each novel only one real character, the narrator, it is the achievement of masterpieces like *Little Dorrit* or *Middlemarch* that a single episode can be seen through the eyes of several contrasted characters.   There is no harm in suggesting his comparative crudity, providing we remember that his work came first and that more subtle fictions were raised to some extent on his foundations.

The moral purpose of *Moll Flanders* is not so clear as that of *Crusoe*.   It is difficult not to see some disingenuousness in the Author's Preface:

> The pen employed in finishing her story, and making it what you now see it to be, has had no little difficulty to put it into a dress fit to be seen, and to make it speak language fit to be read.   When a woman debauched from her youth . . . comes to give an account of all her vicious practices . . . an author must be hard put to it to wrap it up so clean as not to give room, especially for vicious readers, to turn it to his disadvantage.
>
> All possible care, however, has been taken to give no lewd ideas, no immodest turns, in the new dressing up this story . . .

The last sentence is clearly a lie; for on scores of occasions in the actual narrative "all possible care has been taken" to give as many salacious details as possible for the amusement of the reader.   To defend either Defoe or Richardson from the charge of deliberate pornography is a waste of time. "Other times, other manners", certainly; but as certainly could the pious reader, to whom the stage was a sink of vice, get the near-equivalent of Restoration Comedy from the bedroom scenes of *Moll Flanders* or *Roxana* or *Pamela*, with the simple alteration of a moral instead of an immoral argument attached.   But the attitude of the Restoration play-goer had been one of studied cynicism; the attitude of the contemporary readers of *Moll Flanders* must have one of half regretful fascination.   When the stage was truly popular, audiences could delight in the low comedy of Falstaff without being anxious to imitate it; only in the Restoration theatre did the vice depicted on the boards bear any strict relation to the actual practice of a certain section of the upper classes. Defoe's readers must have been more like Shakespeare's audience than Wycherley's; they could appreciate the humanity and the vigour of a Moll Flanders, and were so far "fallen" themselves as to approve of the author's kindness in giving as many details of her doings as possible; but they had no real wish to emulate her adventures and their sympathy lay with her misfortunes rather than with her debaucheries.

Defoe, furthermore, had been cast into Newgate for advocating toleration, and he must have reflected that many of the thieves and prostitutes who were his fellow-prisoners had been the victims of heredity and environment rather than of vicious disposition. His tenderness towards the underworld has to be contrasted with the terrible penal code of the time, to be fully appreciated; as his courageous stand for religious freedom and political moderation has to be seen against the prejudices left over from the seventeenth century for his contribution to Augustan toleration to be realised. The limitations of his novels, and the pornography of parts of them, seem small criticisms to make of a writer who anticipated Fielding and Dickens on so many points in literature and life.

Moll Flanders is commonly considered his best novel after *Crusoe*; and the *Journal of the Plague Year* is probably the best example of his power of relating past events as if he himself had witnessed them. Historians no longer take the *Journal* as an authority, but for ordinary readers the narrative remains the best introduction to its subject. Among the other productions of Defoe's prolific old age can be singled out, in conclusion, the *Tour through Great Britain*, which is one of his most careful works and gives the only full picture of the commerce of this country in the Augustan Age.

Defoe and Richardson

Samuel Richardson (1689-1761) was almost the exact contemporary of Pope, but, like Defoe, he wrote the novels by which he is remembered late in life. He is connected with Defoe not by the accident of his having published an edition of the *Tour through Great Britain* in 1742, but by the fact that they were both of lower-middle-class stock, both became tradesmen, and turned to the novel in middle-age, both managed to combine piety with pornography, and both won immediate and enormous popularity. Richardson, furthermore, wrote his novels in the form of letters, an interesting throw-back to the original method of Defoe in the *Review* supplement and of Addison and Steele in the *Spectator*.

Son of a Derbyshire carpenter, Richardson was apprenticed to a London printer and spent most of his life in the neighbourhood of Fleet Street, where he set up his own business in 1719. According to his own account, he was "not more than thirteen" when he was employed by three young women "unknown to each other" to write answers to their lovers' letters. This early anticipation of *Pamela* and *Clarissa* is certainly remarkable, but it was not till he was fifty that the incident occurred which led to his writing fiction in letter-form. The *Spectator* had set the fashion for letter-writing, and naturally enough it took some forty years for the fashion to spread from the leisured classes to the common people in London and the provinces. Richardson was asked by two printer-friends to prepare for them "a little volume of letters, in a common style, on such subjects as might be of use to those country readers who were unable to indite for themselves". This book bore the lengthy, Defoe-like title: "Letters written to and for particular friends, on the most important occasions. Directing not only the requisite Style and Forms to be observed in writing Familiar Letters; but how to think and act justly and prudently in the common Concerns of Human Life". One of the subjects treated was the danger attending an attractive and pious girl employed as a domestic servant; and out of this subject grew the novel of *Pamela; or Virtue Rewarded,* which in its initial conception was simply a series of letters professing to be written by a servant-girl to her father and mother in the country. From a somewhat clumsy combination of instruction and entertainment Richardson evolved a form of fiction which, owing something to Defoe, was nevertheless an original creation, destined to have a tremendous influence on not only English but European literature.

His flair for capturing the reader's attention exceeded even his predecessor's. Defoe had certainly known how to construct his story so that the reader would constantly be in the position of wanting to learn what would happen next. It was left to Richardson to exploit anew the dodge known to every popular entertainer: that of keeping the audience in a fever of suspense. Anyone anxious to learn the fate of Moll Flanders in her successive predicaments can cheat the author by turning to the end of the episode; we can cheat in the same way now with Richardson—but his original readers could not. For he published *Pamela* in four separate volumes, during 1741-2, and its even more popular successor, *Clarissa Harlowe*, in no less than seven volumes, from November 1747 to December 1748. Dickens was later to create the same suspense with the monthly numbers in which nearly all of his novels originally appeared.

The success of *Pamela* was as immense as that of *Crusoe*, if more temporary. Richardson had a similar moral purpose, and he created in his extremely prudent maidservant a character more akin to his readers' personal experience than Moll Flanders (who had, in her turn, been more credible than the heroines of the old romances). Ladies of easy virtue were no doubt attractive to meet in print, but a maid as pretty as pious who manages to marry her employer and would-be seducer was a figure more easily to be identified with. It is one of the themes of popular literature that every man is plotting seduction, and every woman marriage; and when the issue of class is added, so that the woman can gain a material as well as a moral victory, the theme becomes irresistible. There is a touch of this combination in the way Moll Flanders becomes penitent only after she has grown rich; but in Richardson the material and the moral are so interwoven that it is difficult to decide whether Pamela is what her creator meant her to be or just a young calculator who intends to sell her virtue at the highest price. Moll Flanders in much the same situation loses hers to her employer's son, but marries his brother; she confesses she fell from grace through vanity and greed. Pamela is supposed to be without vanity or greed, but she never seems to question whether it might be undesirable to marry a man who has sought her "person" by the same means as Moll Flanders's seducer. There is no doubt that Richardson was clumsier here than Defoe, though he was equally proficient at "taking all possible care" to paint the details of the attempted seduction in the liveliest colours. The heroine is not a very life-like figure, compared with the creations of later novelists; and the ultimately-repentant Mr B. is a mere sketch. The central character is not really Pamela herself, but her Virtue: this Virtue is exposed to the most terrible dangers that the mind of Richardson can imagine; storms blow upon this Virtue, high seas almost wreck it. It is only at the close of the second volume that Virtue is Rewarded, two more volumes being devoted to Pamela's trials as wife and mother.

"Clarissa"

So far Richardson had not improved much on the novel as left by Defoe. His invention was poorer, and his characters no more subtle; the only foreshadowing of the comparative masterpiece of *Clarissa*—and subsequently of Fanny Burney's and Jane Austen's novels—was in the recorded conversation, as natural as Defoe's and much more highly developed. It was the combination of this genius for conversation with the creation of more life-like characters and greater subtlety of analysis that led to the success of *Clarissa* and its even more widely-spread popularity.

The motive of Richardson here was the same as in *Pamela*, but his moral purpose was now the master of a much greater range of feeling. It is not simply that Clarissa is a more appealing character than Pamela, or that the graceful but perfidious Lovelace has taken the place of the hero-villain Mr B. The earlier novel had been, after all, a storm in a teacup: the villain had repented and become a hero, and Pamela had sacrificed her much-troubled Virtue on the altar of Hymen. It was all very satisfactory, and according to the rules of popular romance. But something more like the dilemma of Clarissa is truer to the facts of ordinary existence than the situations from which Pamela and Moll Flanders emerge in their different ways.

Clarissa's early letter to her friend Anna Howe, giving her reasons for preferring Lovelace to Solmes, and yet repudiating any suggestion that she is in love with the one preferred, is a good illustration both of the comparative complexity of this novel and of Richardson's mature style:

> But, pray now, is it saying so much, when one who has no very particular regard to *any* man, says there are *some* who are preferable to *others*? And is it blameable to say *they* are the preferable, who are not well used by one's relations, yet dispense with that usage out of regard to one's self which they would otherwise resent? Mr Lovelace, for instance, I may be allowed to say, is a man to be preferred to Mr Solmes, and that I *do* prefer him to that man; but surely, this may be said without its being a necessary consequence that I must be in love with him.
>
> Indeed, I would not be *in love* with him, as it is called, for the world: first, because I have no opinion of his morals, and think it a fault in which our whole family (my brother excepted) has had a share, that he was permitted to visit us with a hope, which, however, being distant, did not, as I have observed heretofore, entitle any of us to call him to account for such of his immoralities as came to our ears. Next, because I think him to be a vain man, capable of triumphing (secretly at least) over a person whose heart he thinks he has engaged. And thirdly, because the assiduities and veneration which you impute to him seem to carry a haughtiness in them, as if he thought his address had a merit in it that would be more than an equivalent to a woman's love. In short, his very politeness, notwithstanding the advantages he must have had from his birth and education, appears to me to be constrained, and with the most remarkably easy and genteel person, something, at times, seems to be behind in his *manner* that is too studiously kept in.

In such passages, which are common in *Clarissa*, we are a long way from Defoe, almost in the carefully cultivated territory of a Meredith or a Henry James (or in the love-letter style of the Brownings). There are at least two sentences in the above which could be mistaken for James—who can be described perhaps as the modern or the American Richardson —and that beginning with the Micawber-like "in short" approaches the superfluous caution of his later style.

The events in *Pamela* are seen almost entirely from Pamela's own point of view. Where Richardson pointed the way forward for some of his successors was in treating the events in *Clarissa* from the angle of several characters with different motives. This may seem an obvious development, but all literary developments seem obvious when once they have been followed up; no further developments in the nineteenth century should allow us to minimise Richardson's achievement here, for he was the pioneer in this evolution as truly as Defoe in the prior evolution of the novel from the newspaper.

The overwhelming success of *Clarissa* was partly due to the genuine artistry of the book, partly to the artful way the author kept his readers fluctuating between hope and despair of the heroine's fate. Letters were written to Richardson imploring him to spare Clarissa—as later they were to be written to Dickens beseeching him to save poor Smike—but "the author of *Pamela*" kept his more serious purpose in view, and Clarissa was duly sacrificed after more than a year's anxiety in the hearts of her admirers.*

The tears from *Clarissa* spread across the Channel and the North Sea to inundate the Continent. The popularity of Richardson in Europe was greater than that of any English writer before Byron. He was among the chief pioneers of the cult of sensibility in France, of romance in Germany. *Clarissa* was imitated by Rousseau in *La Nouvelle Héloise*; and the critic Diderot in his *Éloge de Richardson* presented the English novelist as one of the great creative spirits of the age. In Italy, two plays adapted from *Pamela* by Goldoni had a great success.

---

* Among the mourners were not only society ladies and kitchen-maids but men of the world like the veteran actor-manager Colley Cibber. When a friend told him of the end of the story, Cibber flung down the book and vowed he would not read another line: "What!" he exclaimed, "shall I, who had loved and revered the virtuous, the beautiful Clarissa, from the same motives I loved Mr Richardson, bear to stand a patient spectator of her ruin, her final destruction? No! My heart suffers as strongly for her as if word was brought me that his house was on fire, and himself, and his wife and little ones, likely to perish in the flame!"

This universal fame appears not to have shaken Richardson from the modest path he was treading. He wrote only one more novel, *The History of Sir Charles Grandison: in a Series of Letters published from the Originals by the Editor of Pamela and Clarissa*. This appeared in the customary several volumes between November 1753 and March 1754. To the last, we see, he kept up his Defoe-like pretence of merely being the "editor" of letters copied from the "originals". But he had done much to shake off the trammels of journalism, to create the novel more as we know it, to evolve a form of fiction of a complexity comparable to that of life from a simple narrative disguised as fact. His popularity has not been maintained, for the rather ironical reason of that long-windedness which was among the causes of his original fame. Johnson, his friend and great admirer, said that if you read him for the story you would hang yourself before the end; and it has been not unfairly added that if you read Defoe for anything but the story you would be in the same mortal state of irritation. But the problem does not arise in the great novelists of the nineteenth century; and there is no doubt that the waning of Richardson's popularity is mainly due to our being able to read later novels which combine his subtlety of analysis with Defoe's power of narration.

Richardson and Fielding

There is, however, another tradition in the English novel, which, while owing something to Defoe, owes nothing at all to Richardson. We cannot treat adequately of the English novel without giving a good deal of attention to the genius of Dickens; and behind Dickens stands, not Richardson, Fanny Burney and Jane Austen, but Fielding, Smollett, Sterne, Goldsmith and Scott. The comic, as we know from Shakespeare and Jonson, can be as essentially serious a form of literature as the tragic or epic. The tradition of comedy in English literature changed its main expression in the eighteenth century from the drama to the novel; and the point of separation came with Fielding. It is this tradition which will be our main interest in the following chapter.

There was some incidental relation between Richardson and Fielding, but it was entirely antipathetic. From the first there were some dissenting voices amid the clamour of applause that greeted *Pamela*; and among the burlesques was one entitled *An Apology for the Life of Mrs Shamela Andrews, etc., by Conny Keyber*. The title of this skit glances at Cibber's autobiography as well as *Pamela*; and the probability of Fielding having written it—or had a hand in it—is confirmed by the first chapter of *Joseph Andrews*, which came out the next year. In this chapter Fielding refers to "two books lately published, which represent an admirable pattern of the amiable in either sex"; and continues ironically:

> The former of these, which deals in male-virtue, was written by the great person himself, who lived the life he has recorded, and is by many thought to have lived such a life only in order to write it. The other is communicated to us by an historian who borrows his lights, as the common method is, from authentic papers and records. The reader, I believe, already conjectures I mean the lives of Mr Colley Cibber and of Mrs Pamela Andrews . . .
>
> What the female readers are taught by the memoirs of Mrs Andrews is so well set forth in the excellent essays or letters prefixed to the second and subsequent editions of that work, that it would be here a needless repetition. The authentic history with which I now present the public is an instance of the great good that book is likely to do . . . since it will appear that it was by keeping the excellent pattern of his sister's virtues before his eyes that Mr Joseph Andrews was chiefly enabled to preserve his purity in the midst of such great temptations . . .

It was a good joke, to satirise Richardson's obsession with female virtue by setting beside Pamela's rejection of Mr B.'s immoral proposals, her brother's no less indignant rejection of Lady Booby's advances. But if *Joseph Andrews* had not speedily developed from this topical jest into the first of Fielding's immortal comedies, it would be as unimportant in literature as the skit of *Shamela*. Richardson is said to have been hurt by what he called the "lewd and ungenerous engraftment" of *Joseph Andrews*, for the two men had been friendly and among Richardson's wide circle of female admirers were Fielding's sisters. But at this distance of time we can see it as an addition to our gratitude to the author of *Clarissa* that he should, by the faults of his earlier work, have provoked the first achievement of another great novelist in a very different field.

CHAPTER V

FIELDING: TO THE NOVEL FROM THE DRAMA
1728-1771

> "The Epic, as well as the Drama, is divided into
> tragedy and comedy . . . it may be likewise either in
> verse or prose . . . it is much fairer and more reasonable
> to give it a name common with that species from which
> it differs only in a single instance, than to confound
> it with those which it resembles in no other; such as
> those voluminous works, commonly called Romances,
> namely *Clelia, Cleopatra, Astraea, Cassandra,* the *Grand
> Cyrus,* and innumerable others, which contain, as I
> apprehend, very little instruction or entertainment."
>
> FIELDING: Preface to *Joseph Andrews.*

The Drama before Fielding

The dramatic literature of the early eighteenth century is
more important for its connection with the novel than for any
intrinsic merits of its own. It is not an accident that the two
most distinguished dramatists at the turn of the century—
William Congreve and George Farquhar—are regarded to-day
as the last of the "Restoration dramatists" rather than as
contributors to any distinctive drama of the Augustan Age.
If, indeed, we take Augustan literature as dating from 1688,
it is remarkable how many plays commonly regarded as
"typically Restoration" fall within the period: not only
Congreve's *Love for Love* (1695) and *The Way of the World*
(1700) and Farquhar's *The Beaux Stratagem* (1706) but Sir
John Vanbrugh's *The Relapse* and *The Provoked Wife,* both
produced in 1697. Such plays are usually co-opted into
"Restoration Comedy", along with their predecessors, the
plays of Dryden, Etherege, and Wycherley.

There is much to be said for this co-optation. For the
stage at the end of the seventeenth century was getting more
and more out of touch with the tastes of the general public.
The comedies of Congreve and Vanbrugh were among the main

targets of Jeremy Collier's pamphlet *A Short View of the Immorality and Profaneness of the English Stage*, which came out in 1698. Although this pamphlet is in many ways "a short-sighted view"—and is hardly read nowadays, while *Love for Love* and *The Way of the World* are still performed —it created at the time an immense sensation, the majority of the public being on the side of the author in the ensuing controversy.

The veteran dramatist Dryden, who was one of the writers attacked, surrendered to the onslaught in the Preface to his *Fables*, dated 1699. While he complained of the harshness with which he had been treated, he frankly acknowledged that, on the whole, his plays had been justly reproved. "If Mr Collier be my enemy," he concluded, "let him triumph. If he be my friend, as I have given him no personal occasion to be otherwise, he will be glad of my repentance."

Congreve and Vanbrugh answered Collier in a different manner, but it was acknowledged even in the coffee-houses that in wit, as well as in argument, "the clergyman", as Dryden called him, came off best. One of Congreve's counter-arguments was that, though he and his fellow-dramatists were guilty of a little levity, they were always careful to put a moral at the end of every play. Yes, indeed, replied Collier, and the moral of *The Old Bachelor* can be found in Heartwell's triplet at the close of the fifth act:

> What rugged ways attend the noon of life!
> Our sun declines, and with what anxious strife,
> What pain we tug that galling load, a wife!

Love for Love, continued Collier, "may have a somewhat better farewell, but it would do a man little service should he remember it to his dying day:

> The miracle to-day is that we find
> A lover true, not that a woman's kind".

For the time being, the clergyman's triumph was complete.* But when William Law followed him by writing *The Absolute*

* Congreve wrote nothing for the stage after 1700; Farquhar ended his brief life in 1707; while Vanbrugh spent his later years chiefly as an architect. Fielding was the only later dramatist to

Unlawfulness of the Stage-Entertainment fully demonstrated (1726), he was effectively answered by John Dennis in a pamphlet entitled *The Stage defended from Scripture, Reason, Experience, and the Common Sense of Mankind for Two Thousand Years*. Law had written that "Plays are contrary to Scripture as the devil is to God, as the worship of images is to the second commandment" and that "The actors and spectators must all be damned: the playhouse is the porch of hell, the place of the devil's abode, where he holds his filthy court of evil spirits . . .". Meeting this High-Church puritan on his own ground, Dennis pointed out that

> when St Paul was at Athens, the very source of dramatic poetry, he said a great deal publicly against the idolatry of the Athenians, but not one word against their stage. At Corinth he said as little against theirs. He quoted on one occasion an Athenian dramatic poet, and on others Aratus and Epimenides. He was educated in all the learning of the Grecians, and could not but have read their dramatic poems; and yet, so far from speaking a word against them, he makes use of them for the instruction and conversion of mankind.

All these skirmishes, however, are really beside the point. Granted that the typical "Restoration" play was based upon the rather loose and empty moral character of certain elements in high society, and that it was therefore inferior to the best comedy of Shakespeare and Jonson, even of Middleton and Massinger, we should ask ourselves the question whether the "reformed" drama, which succeeded Collier's original attack, was better or worse. The argument from survival is conclusive here. *Love for Love* and *The Way of the World* have

---

attempt the "Restoration" manner: witness Mondish's curtain speech at the end of Act I of *The Universal Gallant* (1734): "Damn her! I was weary of the affair, and she has found out the only way to renew my eagerness—the whole pleasure of life is pursuit,

> Our game though we are eager to embrace,
> The pleasure's always over with the chase".

Sir Simon Raffler's outburst against marriage in Act II has a similar connection with scores of passages in the comedies of Wycherley and Vanbrugh, Dryden and Congreve. A later play by Fielding, *Miss Lucy in Town*, the scene of which is set in a high-class brothel, is a curious cross-breed of Restoration Comedy with *The Beggar's Opera*.

been successfully performed in recent years, as have *The Beaux Stratagem* and Wycherley's *Country Wife*, but neither the comedies of Steele nor the tragedies of Rowe have held the stage in modern times. Steele is known for his *Tatler* rather than for his *Conscious Lovers*, and Rowe for his pioneer editing of Shakespeare rather than for his own *Fair Penitent* (1703) or *Tragedy of Lady Jane Grey* (1715). Similarly, Addison lives for his *Spectator* essays, not for *Cato*; and Colley Cibber because of his *Apology*, still full of interest for its picture of the Augustan theatre, not for his comedies *Love's Last Shift* (1696) or *The Careless Husband* (1704). While the plays of Susannah Centlivre, long successful on the eighteenth-century boards, are not likely ever again to be revived.

So there must have been something in Congreve and Farquhar, in Wycherley and Vanbrugh, that was lacking in their younger contemporaries and successors. However immoral or absurd the argument of their plays might be—especially when set out in plain prose by Collier (we should remember that Tolstoy found no difficulty in proving the absurdity and immorality of *King Lear*)—it is not, after all, the argument of a play, particularly of a comedy, that matters most, it is its treatment by the dramatist. From any strictly moral point of view, *The Conscious Lovers* is superior to *Love for Love*; but Steele's wit and dialogue are much inferior to Congreve's. Plays which could be mistaken for sermons were no doubt as pleasing to Collier as to Parson Adams, but we are entitled to wonder whether the most serious, the most moral comedies—such as *Measure for Measure*, *Volpone*, or *Le Misanthrope*—would have been much more to their taste than the plays they condemned. By comparison with the master comedies of Shakespeare, Jonson, and Molière, *Love for Love* and *The Beaux Stratagem* seem, it is true, pretty small beer; but there are not more than a dozen of such master comedies in English, and to condemn Congreve or Farquhar for ranking high among the comparatively second-rate is to be in the position of the duke's butler, who looked down his nose at anyone less than a duke.

The changes in the language that we observed in the first chapter of this book had a great deal to do with the decline in comedy from Jonson to Congreve. It was not nearly so steep a decline, however, as in tragedy. Congreve and Farquhar have still something in common with Jonson, but the tragedies of Rowe have little in common with *Macbeth.** Congreve's one tragedy, *The Mourning Bride* (1697), had as great a contemporary success as *Cato*; but, apart from the opening line—"Music has charms to soothe a savage breast"— and the other famous quotation about hell having no fury like a woman scorned, it is equally forgotten. As comedy turned into sentimentality on the stage, while retaining some of its old life in the new medium of the novel, so tragedy turned into melodrama, from Rowe's so-called "imitations of Shakespeare" to the brave attempt by Fielding's friend George Lillo in *The London Merchant; or The History of George Barnwell* (1731) to give a domestic tragedy, with an apprentice for the hero, in what was intended to be, but hardly was, ordinary contemporary speech.

The situation in the drama when Fielding came to it in the late 'twenties was not, therefore, a very encouraging one. Comedy had listened to Collier, but in banishing Restoration immorality had also taken leave of Restoration wit. Tragedy had listened to those, like Rowe, who wanted to return to the Elizabethans from the classical rules of the French, but the actual "imitations of Shakespeare"—ridiculed in *Tom Jones*— were almost as devoid of life as *Cato*. The one really new and interesting thing on the stage at about the time Fielding approached it was, significantly, not a play at all, but Gay's ballad-opera. The theatre was steadily losing its power as a serious—if often outwardly "comic"—criticism of life; and

* "Shakespeare's language is one of his principal beauties", Gray wrote to Richard West in 1742; "and he has no less advantage over your Addisons and Rowes in this, than in those other great excellencies you mention. Every word in him is a picture . . ." Gray proceeds to quote the famous speech in *Richard III*—"But I, that am not shaped for sportive tricks . . ."—and asks whether those lines can be put "into the tongue of our modern Dramatics". He concludes: "To me they appear untranslatable; and if this be the case, our language is greatly degenerated".

Fielding's somewhat haphazard attempts to revive some of the old tradition were to be frustrated both by government pressure and by the discrepancy between his natural genius for comedy and the meagre opportunities presented to him on the boards.

Fielding and the Censorship

Henry Fielding (1707-54) was born in Squire Allworthy's county of Somerset and was educated at Eton, afterwards studying law at Leyden University in Holland. On coming to London about 1726, he seems to have led the life of a fashionable man about town, to have run into debt like his character Captain Booth, and to have turned to the writing of stage pieces purely at first as a means of maintaining his position. If one comes to his plays after reading his novels, they are bound to seem very disappointing, and there is no doubt that most of them were written hastily. We have noticed that he attempted to revive the Restoration manner in comedy, also that some of his plays were attempts to repeat the success of the *Beggar's Opera*. *Love in Several Masques* (1728), *The Universal Gallant* (1735), and *The Wedding Day* (1743) are examples in the Congreve tradition; *The Intriguing Chambermaid* (1733), *Don Quixote in England* (1733), *An Old Man Taught Wisdom* (1734), and *Tumble-down Dick* (1737) are examples of comedies or farces interspersed with original ballads to traditional tunes. He also adapted some plays by Molière, notably *The Miser* (1733); and wrote several burlesques, one of which, *Tom Thumb the Great* (1731), has sufficient real humour in it to be still well worth performing.

There is not very much of literary interest in his "Restoration" comedies. Some of them were successful at the time, partly owing, one presumes, to the excellent acting of, for instance, Kitty Clive as the intriguing chambermaid and Garrick and Peg Woffington in *The Wedding Day*. The ballad-comedies are more interesting, particularly *Don Quixote in England*. Squire Badger in this play seems to be a first rough version of Squire Western in *Tom Jones*. Though leaning heavily, of course, on Cervantes, the play has some of the comic eloquence of the English comedy of Shakespeare and Jonson. Sancho has a little of the true Falstaff spirit, while the Don's madness has something reminiscent of Epicure Mammon's and even a touch of Lear's. The scene where Don Quixote meets the supposed Princess Dulcinea, really the maid Jezebel, at a country inn which he believes to be a castle, is a good example of Fielding's not entirely unsuccessful attempts to recapture the spirit of Elizabethan comedy:

> QUIX.   O most illustrious and most mighty princess, with what looks shall I behold you? with what words shall I thank you for this infinite goodness to your unworthy knight?
>
> JEZ.   Rise, Sir.
>
> QUIX.   Do not overwhelm me with too much goodness; though to see you be inexpressible happiness, yet to see you here gives me some uneasiness; for, O most adorable princess, this castle is enchanted, giants and captive ladies inhabit only here.
>
> JEZ.   Could I but be assured of your constancy, I should have no fear; but, alas! there are so many instances of perjured men.
> (*sings*) A virgin once was walking along,
>   In the sweet month of July,
>   Blooming, beautiful and young,
>   She met with a swain unruly;
>   Within his arms the nymph he caught,
>   And swore he'd love her truly;
>   The maid remembered, the man forgot,
>   What passed in the month of July.
>
> QUIX.   Eternal curses light on all such perjured wretches!

Early in 1736 Fielding took over the Little Theatre in the Haymarket, forming, like Molière, his own company of players. The two plays he produced with this company during 1736-7— *Pasquin: A Dramatic Satire on the Times* and *The Historical Register for the Year 1736*—were his first attempts at political burlesque and were destined also to be his last.   Read to-day, when most of the topical allusions have lost their point, these burlesques are difficult to get through; and there is no doubt that here and elsewhere Fielding much overdoes the device of "the play within the play". There is a limit to the number of times an audience can be surprised at finding a rehearsal in progress upon the stage, with the author and actors getting into difficulties with the candid criticisms of their friends. *Pasquin*, in fact, presents us with two rehearsals, one of a comedy called *The Election*, the other of a tragedy called *The Life and Death of Common Sense*. The two authors naturally pick holes in each other's efforts:

> FUSTIAN. Is there nothing but bribery in this play of yours, Mr Trapwit?
>
> TRAPWIT. Sir, this play is an exact representation of nature; I hope the audience will date the time of action before the bill of bribery and corruption took place.

The *Historical Register* is the better of these political burlesques. In the Dedication to the Public, Fielding pretends that so far from the play being aimed at overthrowing the Government, it is

> a ministerial pamphlet, calculated to infuse into the minds of the people a great opinion of their ministry, and thereby procure an employment for the author, who has been often promised one, whenever he would write on that side . . . But I am aware I shall be asked, who is this Quidam, that turns the patriots into ridicule, and bribes them out of their honesty? Who but the devil could act such a part? . . . Indeed, it is so plain who is meant by this Quidam, that he who maketh any wrong application thereof might as well mistake the name of Thomas for John, or old Nick for old Bob.

The best scene is that of the mock auction, where Hen the auctioneer tries to dispose of some very peculiar property:

> Lot 1. A most curious remnant of Political Honesty . . . It will make you a very good cloak, you see it's both sides alike, so you may turn it as often as

you will . . . Lot 7. A very clear Conscience, which
has been worn by a judge and a bishop . . . Pray
observe how capacious it is . . . put as much as you
will into it, it is never full . . . Come, lot 8, a very
considerable quantity of Interest at Court . . . two hundred pound . . . five hundred . . . a thousand . . . All
the Cardinal Virtues, lot 9 . . . Eighteenpence is bid for
these Cardinal Virtues . . . all going for eighteenpence . . .

We have seen that *Polly*, Gay's sequel to the *Beggar's
Opera*, was refused permission to be acted because of its
incidental satire of Walpole and the government. In
Pasquin and the *Historical Register* Fielding made a more
frontal attack on government corruption, and the reaction
of "old Bob" was swift. In 1737 was introduced a Licensing
Act, which brought all plays, prologues, and epilogues under
the censorship of the Lord Chamberlain—an Act which still
exists in the guise of a moral censor—and furthermore reduced
the London theatres to the original two, Drury Lane and Covent
Garden, allowed at the Restoration. So Fielding lost at one
stroke all further opportunities for political burlesque and all
chance of writing further plays for his own company.
Although his dramatic career was not over—his last play was
produced, at Drury Lane, in 1743—it was no longer his chief
occupation. He turned to the law and to journalism, being
called to the bar in 1740 and editing, with his American
friend James Ralph, a paper called the *Champion* (1739-41) in
which he attacked the social abuses of the age.

It has often been said that it was only the censorship
which turned Fielding's attention from the drama to the
novel. But there is some evidence, as we shall see, that he
was dissatisfied not only with the contemporary stage but
with his own contributions to it and that the censorship
merely acted as the last straw.

Towards the Novel

In the Preface to *Joseph Andrews*, Fielding spoke of the
difference between his novel and "the productions of romance

writers on the one hand and burlesque writers on the other".
The characters, he wrote, are drawn from life, but "in the
diction" burlesque is admitted. He might have made the
same statement of *Tom Jones*: Squire Western is as much
drawn from life as Parson Adams, and for the burlesque
diction of "some very fine writing", as Fielding calls it, in
Joseph Andrews—"Now the rake Hesperus has called for his
breeches . . .", etc.—we have in *Tom Jones* not only the
celebrated parody of heroic writing in the account of the
village fight ("He thumps the verdant floor with his carcase
. . .") but several pieces of burlesque diction such as this:

> Hushed be every ruder breath. May the heathen
> ruler of the winds confine in iron chains the boisterous
> limbs of noisy Boreas, and the sharp-pointing nose of
> bitter-biting Eurus. Do thou, sweet Zephyrus, rising
> from thy fragrant bed, mount the western sky, and lead
> on those delicious gales, the charm of which call forth
> the lovely Flora from her chamber, perfumed with
> pearly dews, when on the 1st of June, her birthday, the
> blooming maid, in loose attire, gently trips it over the
> verdant mead . . .

This kind of thing could easily become irksome, but
nobody would claim that his enjoyment of *Joseph Andrews* or
Tom Jones is seriously disturbed by such passages, any more
than our enjoyment of *Chuzzlewit* is marred by Dickens's
similar burlesque diction at the opening of Chapter VI:
"It was morning; and the beautiful Aurora, of whom so
much hath been written, said and sung, did, with her rosy
fingers, nip and tweak Miss Pecksniff's nose". Our enjoyment of *Chuzzlewit* is based upon the character and dialogue
of Mr Pecksniff, Mrs Gamp, etc., as our enjoyment of Fielding
is based upon the character and dialogue of Parson Adams
and Mrs Slipslop, of Squire Western and Partridge. Such
persons and conversation are certainly larger than life, being
heightened by literature and having something of the comic
dramatist's touch upon them still; but they cannot be called
"burlesque" in the same way as the diction quoted. Even
as early as *Joseph Andrews*, Fielding seems to have made good

his intention of leaving behind the stage conventions of such a piece as the *Historical Register*.

But was *Joseph Andrews* his first attempt at novel-writing? It was the first to be published, in 1742, but the three volumes of *Miscellanies* that came out a year later probably contained pieces written a good deal earlier.   There is so strong a relation between *Joseph Andrews* and *Tom Jones* that *The Life of Mr Jonathan Wild the Great* and *A Journey from this World to the Next*—the two principal items in the *Miscellanies*—seem rather strange productions to come in between.   They are so strongly related, in their turn, to the burlesque tradition of the theatre that we may be permitted to regard them as Fielding's "Mrs Veal"—that is, as bearing the same link between Fielding's stage burlesques and *Joseph Andrews* as Defoe's *Mrs Veal* between his journalism and *Robinson Crusoe*.

Jonathan Wild is the more famous of these *nouvelles*, possibly being written or started at the time when Fielding first became professionally interested in criminals.   The burlesque nature of the characters suggests that Fielding had not yet advanced from the conventions of *Tom Thumb* and the *Historical Register* to give us more life-like figures such as Parson Adams.   The ironic argument is rightly admired, as are such touches as "the ruling passion" of Wild even at the last—he picks the chaplain's pocket of his corkscrew "which he carried out of the world in his hand"—but the story is too dependent on the author's running commentary to be entirely successful as a novel.   Though there are many phrases of a Swiftian point—for instance, "It is a pity that those for whose pleasure and profit mankind are to labour and sweat, to be hacked and hewed, to be pillaged, plundered, and every way destroyed, should reap so little advantage from all the miseries they occasion to others"—on the whole the work suffers from prolixity, the very nature of the contrast between the good and the great preventing Fielding from developing his interest in character beyond the point of simple personification.

The introduction to the unfinished *Journey from This World to the Next* refers to "my friend, Parson Adams", which seems to indicate that the story was written after *Joseph Andrews*. But the discrepancy between the Introduction and the *Journey* itself suggests that Fielding grew tired of the work and afterwards produced an ingenious explanation of its remaining incomplete:

> Whether the ensuing pages [runs the Introduction] were really the dream or vision of some very pious and holy person, or whether they were really written in the other world, and sent back to this . . . or lastly, whether . . they were really the production of some choice inhabitant of New Bethlehem, it is not necessary nor easy to determine. It will be abundantly sufficient if I give the reader an account by what means they came into my possession . . .

Fielding proceeds to do so, presenting the reader with the ingenious hoax that he had procured the manuscript from "Mr Robert Powney, stationer, who dwells opposite to Catherine Street in the Strand". It was the bad debt of an impecunious author who had "since gone to the West Indies", and the stationer had used the sheets for wrapping up pens, by which means one or two had got into Fielding's possession:

> He said I was welcome to what remained, and he was heartily sorry for what was missing, as I seemed to set some value on it. I desired him to name a price: but he would receive no consideration farther than the payment of a small bill I owed him, which at that time he said he looked on as so much money given him.

This is the amusing theory advanced in the Introduction, and the story itself bears it out save in one particular, which is important for dating the work. In Chapter IX Fielding is talking about the spirits of "the heroes who here frequently pay their respects to the several bards, the recorders of their actions". Achilles and Ulysses go up to Homer, Aeneas and Caesar to Virgil, Adam (but not Satan, Fielding observes) to Milton, Henry V and others to Shakespeare. And here

Fielding "forgets" the theory he has advanced in the Introduction: "a very small spirit came up to me, shook me heartily by the hand, and told me his name was Thomas Thumb. I expressed great satisfaction in seeing him . . .". Evidently there was no reason why Tom Thumb should present himself to the supposed writer of the manuscript found in Powney's shop, whether he was "a choice inhabitant of New Bethlehem" or any other. The reference is clearly to Fielding himself and his burlesque tragedy *Tom Thumb the Great*. So not only must the Introduction have been written after the book, which is common, the story must originally have been meant as the adventures in the other world of Fielding himself and the date given for the writer's death— the book begins "On the first day of December 1741 I departed this life at my lodgings in Cheapside"—must have been originally a date later (perhaps much later) than the date of composition. Fielding forgot to omit the reference to Tom Thumb when publishing the work with the ingenious introduction, but put a footnote to "1741" to the effect that this may be really a hundred years earlier.

The evidence seems to suggest a book begun early (any time between 1731 and 1741) and left unfinished, then published in the *Miscellanies* of 1743 with an introduction meant to explain its incomplete state. The following generalisation can now perhaps be risked: that Fielding came to regard the stage seriously, became genuinely anxious to hold the mirror up to nature, and his dissatisfaction, aggravated by the Censorship, both with the stage conditions of the time and his own achievements (there is a painful sense of strain in *Pasquin* and the *Historical Register*) led him to the law and the novel for treatment of the vices of the age. In this view, *Jonathan Wild* and the *Journey* were his first attempts to move from the atmosphere of the stage to that of the novel; and their composition may have coincided, more or less, with his being called to the bar in 1740, as the publication of *Tom Jones* in 1749 coincided with his becoming a magistrate for the City of Westminster.

"Joseph Andrews"

Fielding's first real novel is in some ways his most attractive. Though begun as a skit upon *Pamela*, he cast that shackle aside almost as completely as Dickens was to do with the original conception of *Pickwick*. Joseph's letters to his sister are an obvious thrust against Richardson, as is this early dialogue between Joseph and Lady Booby:

> "Your virtue!" said the lady, recovering after a silence of two minutes, "I shall never survive it . . . Did ever mortal hear of a man's virtue! Did ever the greatest or the gravest men pretend to anything of this kind! . . . And can a boy, a stripling, have the confidence to talk of his virtue?"
>
> "Madam," says Joseph, "that boy is the brother of Pamela, and would be ashamed that the chastity of his family, which is preserved in her, should be stained in him . . ."

And when Fielding, in this early chapter, speaks of Lady Booby as "the heroine of our tale", he evidently still thought the novel was to revolve round Joseph's relations with his mistress, as *Pamela* had with his sister's relations with Lady Booby's nephew. In the event, this is no more than an episode in the novel, the point of departure from the original plan being when Joseph is turned out of Lady Booby's service. From this time forward, the original motive is almost forgotten, and Fielding is able to deal with a whole series of events and persons quite outside the narrow range of *Pamela*.

Parson Adams has been introduced in the third chapter, but it is not until he and Joseph unexpectedly meet at the Dragon that he begins to dominate the novel. He is one of the first examples—owing much to *Don Quixote*—of that long line of innocents in English fiction which includes the Vicar of Wakefield, My Uncle Toby, Dominie Sampson, Mr Pickwick, and Captain Cuttle:

> Mr Abraham Adams was an excellent scholar. He was a perfect master of the Greek and Latin languages; to which he added a great share of knowledge in the Oriental tongues; and could read and translate French, Italian, and Spanish. He had applied many years to the

> most severe study, and had treasured up a fund of learn-
> ing rarely to be met with in a university. He was,
> besides, a man of good sense, good parts, and good-
> nature; but was at the same time as entirely ignorant of
> the ways of this world as an infant just entered into it
> could possibly be. As he never had any intention to
> deceive, so he never suspected such a design in
> others . . .

The adventures of Adams and Joseph take their chief source
from the honesty and innocence of the two friends, as they
are thrust into the company of those not conspicuous for
either quality. Though the characters and incidents are
drawn from observation, there is little pretence that they are
factual; Fielding's remark on the dinner of the convalescent
Joseph—"he ate either a rabbit or a fowl, I never could with
any tolerable certainty discover which"—is one of the few
instances of the method of Defoe and Richardson and may have
been written with a satirical eye on *Pamela*. (Fielding, of
course, calls himself an "historian" in *Tom Jones* and *Amelia*,
but the persons and events are not usually pretended to be
based on fact.)

"The only source of the true Ridiculous", Fielding observes
in the Preface, "is affectation". Joseph and Adams are
straightforward persons, but almost all the minor characters
afford opportunities, by their various affectations, for Fielding's
genius for ridicule. Mrs Slipslop, for instance, "was a mighty
affector of hard words":

> "Sure nothing can be a more simple contract in a
> woman than to place her affections on a boy . . . If we
> like a man, the lightest hint sophisticates. Whereas a
> boy proposes upon us to break through all the regula-
> tions of modesty, before we can make any oppression
> upon him." Joseph, who did not understand a word she
> said, answered, "Yes, madam."—"Yes, madam!"
> replied Mrs Slipslop with some warmth, "Do you intend
> to result my passion? Is it not enough, ungrateful as
> you are, to make no return to all the favours I have done
> you; but you must treat me with ironing?"

This is where Fielding's comedy in *Joseph Andrews* is most
connected with the stage. It is not a weakness here, for the

stage dialogue has been successfully adapted to the novel.*
The speech of Mrs Slipslop looks back to Shakespeare's Mrs
Quickly, but forward, not only to Sheridan's Mrs Malaprop,
but to Dickens's Mrs Gamp. In such passages, Fielding is
the link between the comedy of the Elizabethan stage and that
of Smollett, Sterne, Scott, and Dickens. The jargon of the
doctor who attends Joseph (compare the surgeon's jargon in
Book VIII, Chap. iii, of *Tom Jones*) is another typical instance:

> "Sir," says the doctor, "his case is that of a dead
> man. The contusion on his head has perforated the
> internal membrane of the occiput and divellicated that
> radical small minute invisible nerve which coheres to the
> pericranium; and this was attended with a fever at first
> symptomatic, then pneumatic; and he is at length grown
> deliriuus, or delirious as the vulgar express it."

The fascination with jargon is one of the universal traits of
comic genius; and, in general, where the serious novelist,
like Richardson, is more concerned with the argument and
motive of his dialogue, the comic novelist, like the writer of
stage comedies, is more concerned with the actual wording.
The professional jargon that so delighted Fielding, Smollett,
Sterne, and Dickens has many parallels in the Elizabethan
theatre, particularly, of course, in Jonson's *Alchemist*.

Fielding was as well fitted for "the comic epic in prose",
to use his own long-winded expression, as Richardson for the
detailed scrutiny of motive and character. In some moods,
Richardson (or Henry James) will seem unbearably tedious
to us; in others, Fielding (or Dickens) will appear too frivolous.
Richardson's experience of the world was narrower than
Fielding's, but at certain points much more intense; Fielding's
range was wide, but frequently superficial. The conventional
statement of the distinction between the men and their

---

* Though not so successfully as in *Tom Jones*: for instance, in
the dialogue between Squire Western and his sister in Book VI, Chap.
ii, and that between Sophia and Mrs Honour in Book VII, Chap.
vii ("Dear ma'am, consider, that to be denied Christian burial, and
to have your corpse buried in the highway, and a stake drove through
you, as farmer Halfpenny was served at Ox Cross . . ."), besides the
examples given below.

novels* is not perhaps very well expressed, but it does point to what is surely the main difference: that Fielding excels in *public* scenes, Richardson in *private*. Even when Fielding is telling us about Joseph's early education, he has to put in the reason for his father's not being able to get him into a charity school: "because a cousin of his father's landlord did not vote on the right side for a churchwarden in a borough town"! Such matters did not concern Richardson; nor was he greatly interested in the public life of inns and prisons, in the jargon of doctors and hunting men, in the social abuses of the time, in the idiosyncrasies of the law. Some of Fielding's treatment of such things is, admittedly, superficial; and some was, of course, mainly of interest to the contemporary reader. But a fine example of universal irony, unequalled in its field before Dickens, is the passage where Joseph, beaten up and left naked by the robbers, refuses to get into the coach (which has a lady inside) unless he is provided with some covering. Nobody, on account of his bloody condition, is willing to lend him a coat,

> and it is more than probable that Joseph, who obstin-
> ately adhered to his modest resolution, must have
> perished, unless the postilion (a lad who hath been since
> transported for robbing a hen roost) had voluntarily
> stripped off a great-coat, his only garment, at the same
> time swearing a great oath (for which he was rebuked by
> the passengers) that he would rather ride in his shirt all
> his life than suffer a fellow-creature to lie in so miserable
> a condition.

Though lads are no longer transported for robbing hen-roosts —thanks partly to the influence of Fielding himself and later enlightened magistrates—this passage loses nothing in its criticism of some universal traits in human nature.

* For example, by Coleridge in his *Literary Remains*: "I do loathe the cant which can recommend *Pamela* and *Clarissa Harlowe* as strictly moral, although they poison the imagination of the young with continued doses of *tinct. lyttae*, while *Tom Jones* is prohibited as loose. I do not speak of young women; but a young man whose heart or feelings can be injured, or even his passions excited by this novel, is already thoroughly corrupt. There is a cheerful, sunshiny, breezy spirit, that prevails everywhere, strongly contrasted with the close, hot, day-dreamy continuity of Richardson".

"Tom Jones"

"Human nature" is what we are explicitly offered in the first chapter of *Joseph Andrews*'s lengthier successor.* There is a strong likeness between the two novels, but nevertheless some significant points of difference. *Joseph Andrews* is still rather weakened by its initial parody of *Pamela*; we feel that Fielding "made the story up" as he went along. *Tom Jones* was evidently conceived as a whole from the beginning, only certain details being altered in the process of composition. The *Pamela* parody had much limited the interest of Joseph himself. A young man spurning the advances of his mistress, and talking of his virtue, was an excellent joke and an even more excellent skit; but "human nature" could have been probed to its lowest depths without such an extraordinary figure being found. There is no doubt that Fielding felt the burden he had laid upon his hero and that he determined to make Tom Jones—and Captain Booth in *Amelia*—a young man as generous and brave as Joseph but without his prudery. Jones, in fact, is as fond of the women as any hero of Restoration comedy, but differs greatly from such heroes in being entirely free from cynicism. He is no man of fashion, but a country-bred youth whose virtues and failings are as near to the reality as we can expect from "a comic epic in prose". That is, both are a little heightened by the comic pencil, but not sufficiently to make them unrecognisable.

Though Jones is the principal character of his "history", and though Fielding declared himself "greatly in love" with Sophia (an interesting example of that sentimental touch which is often thought to be the prerogative of Victorian

* That Fielding succeeded in his aim can be judged from the celebrated opinion of the historian Gibbon, a man of European education and interests who is not likely to have been biased in favour of the novel's very English atmosphere. Referring to Fielding's supposed connection with Austrian royalty, Gibbon made the following prophecy, which came true in 1918: "Our immortal Fielding was of the younger branch of the Earls of Denbigh, who drew their origin from the Counts of Hapsburgh. The successors of Charles V may disdain their brethren of England: but the romance of *Tom Jones*, that exquisite picture of human manners, will outlive the palace of the Escurial and the Imperial Eagle of Austria".

novelists), they do not monopolise the novel. There is no comic character, it is true, of quite the stature of Parson Adams; but there are Squire Western, who loves his daughter almost as much as his horses and dogs; his political sister, who so scorns the Squire's Jacobite notions; the barber-surgeon Partridge, who begins the accompaniment in English fiction— borrowed from Cervantes—of a faithful but eccentric servant to the hero on the road (compare Mark Tapley and Martin Chuzzlewit among later examples); the two maids, Sophia's and Mrs Western's; the two landladies, who, though criticised by some as indistinguishable, are, protests Fielding, "most carefully differentiated from each other"; and the two learned men of Mr Allworthy's household, Mr Thwackum and Mr Square:

> Square held human nature to be the perfection of all virtue, and that vice was a deviation from our nature, in the same manner as deformity of body is. Thwackum, on the contrary, maintained that the human mind, since the fall, was nothing but a sink of iniquity, till purified and redeemed by grace. In one point only they agreed, which was, in all their discourses on morality, never to mention the word goodness. The favourite phrase of the former was the natural beauty of virtue; that of the latter was the divine power of grace. The former measured all actions by the unalterable rule of right, and the eternal fitness of things; the latter decided all matters by authority; but in doing this, he always used the scriptures and their commentators as the lawyer does his Coke upon Lyttleton, where the comment is of equal authority with the text.

Thwackum makes a distinction which would save trouble were it made by other clerical propagandists: "When I mention religion, I mean the Christian religion; and not only the Christian religion, but the Protestant religion; and not only the Protestant religion, but the Church of England". He is even more of a rascal than Square, who is at any rate human enough to become one of Jones's rivals in the affections of Molly Seagrim and who—caught in the act—reasons that "to murder one's own reputation is a kind of suicide, a detestable and odious vice".

Squire Western is the most memorable of these humorous characters. His curses, his anxiety to lend an opponent a "flick" or a "douse", his oscillation from storming rage to high gaiety: all have the mark of truth upon them. Fielding knew his Somerset squires, and also the side of life that was as much closed to Dickens as to Richardson—the sporting and gaming side, so popular with the painters and caricaturists of the century. The Squire's dialogues with his Hanoverian sister are among the best things in the book:

> "To be sure," said the squire, "I am always in the wrong." "Brother," answered the lady, "you are not in the wrong unless when you meddle with matters beyond your knowledge. You must agree that I have seen most of the world; and happy had it been for my niece if she had not been taken from under my care. It is by living at home with you that she has learnt romantic notions of love and nonsense." "You don't imagine, I hope," cries the squire, "that I have taught her any such things." "Your ignorance, brother," returned she, "as the great Milton says, almost subdues my patience." "Damn Milton!" answered the squire: "if he had the impudence to say so to my face, I'd lend him a douse, though he was never so great a man . . . The world is come to a fine pass indeed, if we are all fools, except a parcel of roundheds and Hanover rats. Pox! I hope the times are a coming when we shall make fools of them, and every man shall enjoy his own . . . I hope to zee it, sister, before the Hanover rats have eat up all our corn, and left us nothing but turneps to feed upon."—"I protest, brother," cries she, "you are now got beyond my understanding. Your jargon of turneps and Hanover rats is to me perfectly unintelligible."—"I believe," cries he, "you don't care to hear o'em; but the country interest may succeed one day or other for all that."

The dramatic bent of Fielding's mind is seen in some of these conversations, as in the kind of "chorus" he has before each section of the book. The famous exchange between Partridge and the sergeant—so admired by Keats—is evidently, too, of a dramatic character:

> "Excuse me there, Mr Sergeant," quoth Partridge,
> "that's a *non sequitur*."—"None of your outlandish
> lingo," answered the sergeant, leaping from his seat; "I
> will not sit still and hear the cloth abused."—"You
> mistake me, friend," cries Partridge. "I did not mean
> to abuse the cloth; I only said your conclusion was a
> *non sequitur*."—"You are another," cries the sergeant,
> "an you come to that . . ."

In general, though, *Tom Jones* is a great advance upon *Joseph Andrews* in what we have come to think of as the natural method of the novel. And it contains certain reflections on public life that were soon to engage Fielding's interests further, both in his capacity as magistrate and in his third and last novel, *Amelia*.

"Amelia" and Bow Street

The dedication of *Amelia* is dated from "Bow Street, Dec. 12, 1751"; and there is more than this incidental relationship between Fielding's last novel and his remarkable career as magistrate at Westminster. Jonathan Wild had combined the office of a magistrate with the reception of stolen goods on a large scale; and though later magistrates did not reach this height of "greatness", the fact that the office was paid by fees encouraged corruption. As Fielding himself said, in the Introduction to his *Journal of a Voyage to Lisbon* (posthumously published in 1755):

> I will confess that my private affairs . . . had but a
> gloomy aspect; for I had not plundered the public or
> the poor of those sums, which men who are always ready
> to plunder both as much as they can, have been pleased
> to suspect me of taking; on the contrary, by composing,
> instead of inflaming, the quarrels of porters and
> beggars . . . and by refusing to take a shilling from a
> man who most undoubtedly would not have had another
> left, I had reduced an income of about £500 a year of
> the dirtiest money upon earth, to little more than £300, a
> considerable portion of which remained with my clerk.

The extent to which money could relieve the rigours of the law can be seen in that passage in *Amelia* where Miss Matthews asks the governor of the prison by what means she might procure Captain Booth his liberty:

> The governor answered, "As he cannot get bail, it will be a difficult matter; and money, to be sure, there must be; for people, no doubt, expect to touch on these occasions. When prisoners have not wherewithal as the law requires to entitle themselves to justice, why, they must be beholden to other people to give them their liberty; and people will not, to be sure, suffer others to be beholden to them for nothing, whereof there is good reason; for how should we all live if it was not for these things?"—"Well, well," said she, "and how much will it cost?"—"How much?" answered he; "how much? why, let me see . . . I will be content with five guineas; and I am sure that's little enough. What other people will expect, I cannot exactly say. To be sure, his worship's clerk will expect to touch pretty handsomely: as for his worship himself, he never touches anything, that is, not to speak of; but then the constable will expect something, and the watchman must have something, and the lawyers on both sides, they must have their fees for finishing."

Defoe had seen something of this while in Newgate; but Fielding knew it from the other side and had the grace to be thoroughly ashamed of a profession which could interpret justice in terms of cash. By his personal example as magistrate—together with that of his blind half-brother, the remarkable Sir John Fielding—he was able to begin the movement for reform; and in several pamphlets of his last years, notably *Proposals for making an Effectual Provision for the Poor* (1753), he began an agitation that was to occupy the attention of reformers for more than a hundred years. The brothers Fielding also had their eye on the criminal, and on the protection of the ordinary citizen, their "Bow-Street runners" being the first effective attempt at a police force in England. Some of the papers in *The Covent Garden Journal*, which Fielding edited throughout its brief career in 1752, touch on this topic.

Tom Jones had contained certain reflections on morality which were to engage Fielding's attention more and more during this last period of his life.   The following, for instance, was a disturbing thought to come from a lawyer who was soon to be made a magistrate:

> There are a set of religious or rather moral writers, who teach that virtue is the certain road to happiness, and vice to misery, in this world.   A very wholesome and comfortable doctrine, and to which we have but one objection, namely, that it is not true . . .
>
> If by virtue is meant (as I almost think it ought) a certain relative quality, which is always busying itself without-doors, and seems as much interested in pursuing the good of others as its own; I cannot so easily agree that this is the surest way to human happiness; because I am afraid we must then include poverty and contempt, with all the mischiefs which backbiting, envy, and ingratitude can bring on mankind, in our idea of happiness; nay, sometimes perhaps we shall be obliged to wait upon the said happiness to a jail; since many by the above virtue have brought themselves thither.

Part of the conception of *Amelia* is seen in that passage. "The following book," said Fielding in the dedication, "is sincerely designed to promote the cause of virtue, and to expose some of the most glaring evils, as well public as private, which at present infest the country."   Much of the action of the novel takes place in prison;* and there are few forms of contemporary injustice that Fielding does not manage to include in his indictment.   The very first person to be introduced is a justice of the peace named Jonathan Thrasher, who "had too great an honour for Truth, to suspect that she ever appeared in sordid apparel; nor did he ever sully his sublime notions of that virtue, by uniting them with the mean ideas of poverty and distress".

It is remarkable that Fielding, of upper-class birth, had so little of the snobbery of his age that he could go out of his way to counteract the idea that the nobility were usually

---

* Prison-scenes in English fiction are remarkably common: they occur, for instance, in *Moll Flanders*, *The Vicar of Wakefield*, *Caleb Williams*, *Pickwick*, and *Little Dorrit*; and the very title of one of Scott's best novels, *The Heart of Mid-Lothian*, refers to a prison.

noble and the common people mean in their behaviour. Not only does he put a footnote to his use of the word "mob" in *Tom Jones*—"Whenever this word occurs in our writings, it intends persons without virtue or sense, in all stations; and many of the highest rank are often meant by it"—he makes Captain Booth reflect in *Amelia* "why we should be more surprised to see greatness of mind discover itself in one degree or rank of life than in another . . .". He had seen poverty at close quarters during his early years in London, and when he became professionally interested in the law he discovered—what Defoe had discovered before him—how many "criminals" were either altogether innocent or else the victims of misfortune.* There must have been few Englishmen of his aristocratic connections whose interests were less bounded by class. The character of Amelia was founded on his first wife—even to the accident which left a scar on her nose—and after she died he married her maid, who became an excellent mother to his children. Both in private life and public, he seems to have judged people entirely on their merits—a point of view, to put it mildly, that was not very common among the eighteenth-century aristocracy.

Regarded as a comic novel, *Amelia* is not so successful as its predecessors. That passionate concern for injustice can co-exist with achievement in comedy we know from Dickens—and indeed partly from *Tom Jones* and *Joseph Andrews*. But there is too much statement in *Amelia*, and not enough creation; the novel, furthermore, is rather clumsily put together, with (for instance) Booth's long narrative following hard upon Miss Matthews's long narrative. There is no humorous character of the quality of Adams or Western; and there is not the variety of *Tom Jones*. Its purpose of exposing

---

* In *Tom Jones* he refers to "the house of correction" as "that house where the inferior sort of people may learn one good lesson, viz., respect and deference to their superiors; since it must show them the wide distinction Fortune intends between those persons who are to be corrected for their faults, and those who are not". Compare the remark of the mayor's wife to her daughter in *Pasquin*: "People are punished for doing naughty things; but people of quality are never punished; therefore they never do any naughty things".

public and private evils is, however, successfully carried through; and Amelia and Booth are, at least, brave attempts to create characters more "in the round" than Fanny and Joseph or Sophia and Tom. The novel is, in some ways, so different from its predecessors that it is intriguing to speculate what the fourth novel would have been like. But Fielding, worn out with his professional duties, fell seriously ill in 1754, was ordered south by his doctors, and died at Lisbon only three months later at the age of forty-seven.

His novels were generally admired by his contemporaries, but there were a few dissenting voices, among them Richardson, Johnson, and Horace Walpole. Richardson said that "the virtues of Fielding's heroes were the vices of a truly good man"; Johnson called him "a blockhead" and "a barren rascal" and said that "there is more knowledge of the human heart in one letter of Richardson's than in all *Tom Jones*"; while Walpole (the son of Fielding's enemy, "old Bob") spoke of the novels as vulgar and stupid. Fielding's cousin, Lady Mary Wortley Montagu—who had been rather scandalised at his second marriage—allowed he had "a fund of true humour" but lamented that he was "forced by his necessities to publish without correction" and rated him below Congreve and Smollett. It is hardly necessary to answer these charges in detail, particularly as we have given the contrary estimate of Gibbon and Coleridge. The first observation quoted is simply untrue (unless we take courage and generosity and good-humour to be "the vices of a truly good man") and the grain of truth behind Johnson's comparison has been admitted in our judging Richardson to have succeeded pre-eminently in treating of private life and Fielding in treating of public. Taking him altogether, in conclusion, considering his achievement in evolving a form of comedy in fiction from the degenerate comedy of the stage, his creation of such comic characters as Parson Adams and Squire Western, his concern for justice shown in novels and pamphlets and in his admirable career as magistrate and reformer, we shall not be far wrong if we conclude that Fielding, though inferior in certain respects to some other writers of his time, was one of the greatest men—

in a sense different from that used in *Jonathan Wild*—in the
life and literature of the eighteenth century.

The Novels of Smollett

Fielding's principal successor in the comic novel was his
younger contemporary Tobias Smollett (1721-71), whose work
bears an interesting relationship to both Fielding's own and
to Defoe's. He was the grandson of Sir James Smollett of
Bonhill, one of the commissioners appointed by the Scots for
framing the Union with England. Educated at Dumbarton
Grammar School and afterwards apprenticed to a surgeon in
Glasgow, he came to London at the age of eighteen, hoping to
find a manager who would produce a tragedy he had written
called *The Regicide*. Finding no manager at all interested,
he obtained an appointment as surgeon in the Navy, sailing
in 1740 to the West Indies. After taking part in the Car-
thagena expedition, he left the service, lived for some time in
Jamaica, then returned to England in 1746 to set up as a
surgeon in London. He was at first as unsuccessful in his
profession as in the reception accorded some verse satires he
had written; but when he turned to prose fiction and published
in 1748 his first novel, *The Adventures of Roderick Random*,
he at once made a hit.

He was as well qualified to write this kind of story—the
so-called "picaresque novel", dealing with the adventures of
rogues and vagabonds—as Richardson was to treat of domestic
problems and Fielding of the public life of England. He
probably owed something to *Joseph Andrews* and *Jonathan
Wild*, but where Fielding had acknowledged his debt to *Don
Quixote*, Smollett acknowledged *Gil Blas* as the literary parent
of *Roderick Random*. He must have been influenced, too, by
the example of Defoe; but his personal experience and his
eye for comic detail enabled him to add something fresh to
the novel of adventure. If we describe his work briefly as
being a combination of Defoe and Fielding—of the story of
low life with the tradition of English comedy—his individual
contribution must not be forgotten. He was, for instance,
the first novelist of the Navy, the literary father of the

"British tar" (Dickens's Captain Cuttle owes a great deal to him); and by casting overboard Defoe's concern with morality and "original documents", he managed to create that kind of frankly fictional story, based on personal experience but not pretending to be either factual or to point a moral, which had so great an influence on the lesser literature of the early nineteenth century.   Scott and Dickens also acknowledged a debt to him, but in their case the debtors were greater than the creditor.

They both read him first in boyhood, and though there are certain things in *Roderick Random* and *Peregrine Pickle* not very suitable for boys, Smollett clearly shares with Defoe the parentage of much of the juvenile fiction that was produced in so great a flood during the Victorian Age.   Neither *Random* nor *Pickle* has any great subtlety in it, both are full of violence and horseplay, yet there was a good deal in actual eighteenth-century life of which these novels are the record.   If Defoe and Fielding are the Hogarths of English literature, Smollett can perhaps be called the Rowlandson.

The Adventures of Peregrine Pickle (1751) is his best comedy, and the novel most clearly related to Fielding (who, ironically enough, was one of the authors attacked in the Preface to the first edition).   It contains his most memorable comic characters, Commodore Trunnion, Lieutenant Hatchway, and Tom Pipes; and the account of the Commodore's wedding is not only a good example of his humour at its best but perhaps the finest comic episode in the whole of eighteenth-century fiction:

> The commodore, to give a specimen of his gallantry, by the advice of his friend Hatchway, resolved to appear on horseback, on the grand occasion, at the head of all his male attendants, whom he had rigged with the white shirts and black caps formerly belonging to his barge's crew; and he bought a couple of hunters for the accommodation of himself and his lieutenant.   With this equipage, then, he set out from the garrison for the church, after having dispatched a messenger to apprise the bride that he and his company were mounted.   She got immediately into the coach . . . and drove directly to the place of assignation . . . Thus arrived at the altar,

and the priest in attendance, they waited a whole half-hour for the commodore, at whose slowness they began to be under some apprehension, and accordingly dismissed a servant to quicken his pace. The valet having rode somewhat more than a mile, espied the whole troop disposed in a long field, crossing the road obliquely, and headed by the bridegroom and his friend Hatchway, who, finding himself hindered by a hedge from proceeding further in the same direction, fired a pistol and stood over to the other side, making an obtuse angle with the line of his former course; and the rest of the squadron followed his example, keeping always in the rear of each other, like a flight of wild geese.

Surprised at this strange method of journeying, the messenger came up and told the commodore that his lady and her company expected him at church . . . and were beginning to be very uneasy at his delay; and therefore desired he would proceed with more expedition. To this messenger Mr Trunnion replied, "Hark ye, brother, don't you see we make all possible speed? Go back and tell those who sent you that the wind has shifted since we weighed anchor, and that we are obliged to make very short trips in tacking, by reason of the narrowness of the channel; and that as we lie within six points of the wind, they must make allowance for variation and lee-way."—"Lord, sir!" said the valet, "what occasion have you to go zigzag in that manner? Do but clap spurs to your horses and ride straight forward, and I'll engage you shall be at the church porch in less than a quarter of an hour."—"What! right in the wind's eye?" answered the commander; "ahey! brother, where did you learn your navigation? Hawser Trunnion is not to be taught at his time of day how to lie his course, or keep his own reckoning. And as for you, brother, you best know the trim of your own frigate." The courier, finding he had to do with people who would not be easily persuaded out of their own opinions, returned to the temple, and made a report of what he had seen and heard, to the no small consolation of the bride . . .

It was evidently such passages as this which made Dickens so great an admirer of Smollett. In many of Dickens's novels we find scenes of a similar absurdity that have, nevertheless, a certain truth in them. Fielding has no purely comic incident superior to this; and even in this short extract we can see something of Smollett's easy flow of narrative, which is one of his principal qualities.

His middle years were filled with comparative hack-work. He established a kind of literary factory at Chelsea, which turned out, among other things, translations of *Don Quixote* and Voltaire and a *Complete History of England*. In 1756 he began the *Critical Review*, in which he expressed himself freely about public affairs. His criticism of Admiral Knowles —"an admiral without conduct, an engineer without knowledge, an officer without resolution, and a man without veracity"—led to his spending three months without liberty. His two minor novels of this period—*The Adventures of Ferdinand Count Fathom* and *The Adventures of Sir Lancelot Greaves*—are still quite amusing to read, but hardly in the class of *Peregrine Pickle*.

Ordered south for his health, like Fielding, he spent the years 1763-6 travelling in France and Italy, afterwards publishing a volume of *Travels* in letter-form. In 1769 appeared his *Adventures of an Atom*, a satire on public affairs. The next year he set out again for Italy, wrote there his last novel, *The Expedition of Humphry Clinker* (1771), and died soon after at Leghorn at the age of fifty.

He thus, like Richardson and Fielding, wrote only three major novels; and *Humphry Clinker*, in some ways his most agreeable work, is interesting because it was written, in the Richardson manner, in letter-form. One would not have supposed this method to have suited Smollett, and we cannot imagine *Random* or *Pickle* written in this way; but *Humphry Clinker* is a decided success in a much quieter vein, the two principal humorous characters—the old bachelor Bramble and the Scotch soldier Lismahago—being among his best creations. His Morgan in *Roderick Random* had been drawn from stage comedy, the traditional "Taffy" of Fluellen's inferior descendants; Lismahago is more of an individual Scotsman, less of a national type. Though the novel contains no comic scenes quite equal to the best in *Peregrine Pickle*, it is Smollett's most mature work, where he shows most observation of human nature.

Scott preferred Smollett to Fielding; and his narrative power was certainly superior to both Fielding's and Richardson's. But he did not have the deep interest of Richardson in ordinary family life, nor Fielding's wide interests in public morality. If we place him next to Fielding in comic achievement, and add that there were certain sides of eighteenth-century life of which he was the chief portrayer in fiction, we shall not be doing his memory any great injustice.

CHAPTER VI

THE AGE OF JOHNSON

1738-1784

> "Mr Sober's chief pleasure is conversation; there is
> no end of his talk or his attention; to speak or to hear is
> equally pleasing; for he still fancies that he is teaching
> or learning something, and is free for the time from his
> own reproaches."
>
> JOHNSON: in the *Idler*.

After the Augustans

There is a wide difference of opinion among literary
historians as to the limit of the Augustan Age. Some take
the term as covering almost the whole of the eighteenth
century, others restrict it to the reign of Queen Anne. The
former seems too vague to be of much significance, while if
we take the latter in its strict sense we shall be excluding from
Augustan literature such works as the *Dunciad* and *Gulliver's
Travels*. In this book we have taken the Augustan Age as
extending roughly from the birth of Pope to the death of
Swift, or in political terms from the Revolution of 1688 to
the last Jacobite rebellion in 1745. This includes all the
writers commonly thought of as "Augustan", and the succeeding age, which overlaps it by a few years, can best be
named after its greatest and most representative writer,
Samuel Johnson.

The mid-eighteenth century is, after all, very different in
its customary outlook from both the preceding Augustan Age
and the succeeding age of social and political revolution; so
if we are to divide "the eighteenth century"—itself, of course,
merely a term used for convenience—into three more manage-
able parts, then those named appear the most suitable. We
shall only be in error if we forget that such periods are merely
useful abstractions and that they run into one another, as

ages and centuries naturally do. The changes that occur from one age to the next are like the "dial hand", which "steals from his figure, and no pace perceived". If we were ideal historians we should be in the position of the Lilliputians, who could plainly perceive the movement of the hands of Gulliver's watch. Our eyesight not being so sharp, we have to tell the time of literary history by such clumsier methods as those mentioned.

Perhaps the most distinctive feature of the Age of Johnson, compared both with its predecessor and its successor, was the gap between literature and politics. We have seen how important was political literature during the Augustan Age, and it was to become important again in the closing years of the century; the middle period was a breathing space between the last age of religious politics and the first age of democratic. If we wish to put our finger on the change, we can do no better than consider Boswell's urbane statement of Johnson's position: "He had a tenderness for the unfortunate House of Stuart"! Such a remark could not have been made of Atterbury or Bolingbroke thirty years before; for in their day to be a supporter of the Stuarts was an act of treason, not simply an opportunity to differ from Jack Wilkes. The fact that Johnson could accept a pension from the fortunate House of Hanover indicates in itself the change that had come over English life. Not till the "Jacobin menace" had succeeded the "Jacobite" were writers to line up once more in opposing camps.

The position in regard to religion will concern us more directly later on. The Methodist agitation began in the late 'thirties, but was not to reach its full proportions till the 'fifties and 'sixties. Johnson himself was an orthodox Anglican, but—like Fielding's Parson Adams—could speak with respect of some of the ideas of Wesley and Whitefield. He had been much influenced in his early life by reading William Law's *Serious Call to a Devout and Holy Life*; and Law, though a High Churchman, was one of the fathers of Methodism. The Augustan compromise had given place to a body of pious Anglicanism on the one hand—a body which could approve of some of the un-Augustan "enthusiasm" of the Methodists—and on the other to a species of rationalism more developed than the vague "religion of nature" of such philosophers as Shaftesbury. The central figure of an Addison, with his gentlemanly contempt for vice, had branched out into the piety of a Johnson and the scepticism of a Hume. If politics had for the moment left the literary field, the deeper questions of religion had become divorced from politics and were beginning to affect literature more directly. Mysticism had had little place in the religious philosophy of the Augustans; with Law and Johnson and the Methodists it began to challenge the easy-going ways of the Church of England no less than the avowed unorthodoxy of the English disciples of Voltaire. To speak of the mid-eighteenth century, the Age of Johnson, as a period tranquil both in politics and religion is, then, only partly true; for beneath the placid religious exterior there was a "reformation" proceeding which was to have almost as great an influence on English life and character as the Puritan revolution of the seventeenth century.

To turn to more strictly literary matters: there was no poet of the mid-eighteenth century in the dominant position of Pope among the Augustans. The fact that Johnson is commonly accepted as the chief literary figure of the age is significant, for he was the first great professional writer, a writer who turned his hand to almost every branch of literature—poetry, drama, criticism, biography, journalism, lexicography, translation, even philosophical fiction. When we think of Augustan poetry, we think of Pope; when of Augustan satire, of Swift. But neither the Age of Johnson nor Johnson himself is so readily summed up. He failed, it is true, in drama; and there is little of interest in the dramatic literature of the age between Fielding's *Historical Register* (1737) and Goldsmith's *She Stoops to Conquer* (1773). But Johnson himself is remembered for his *Vanity of Human Wishes*, for his *Rambler*, for his *Dictionary*, for his *Rasselas*, for his *Lives of the Poets*; and his age is remembered for its poetry and its novels, its criticism and its biography and its history. There were historians before Gibbon, and biographers before Boswell, and certainly there were novelists before Richardson and Fielding; but these men gave to their different forms of literature a power and a grace not previously given in England, as Johnson brought to his *Lives of the Poets* a critical equipment not brought by his predecessors and thus deserves the title, Father of English Criticism, more than his namesake or Dryden. There is one dominant figure in the age, then, but he dominates it because of his wide range of literary achievement; and the age itself is remarkable for a similar range, in which no one form of literature predominates and in which such different writers as Fielding, Gray, Gibbon, Sterne, Goldsmith, are held in equal literary esteem. We have considered the achievements in the novel of Richardson, Fielding, and Smollett; this chapter will be concerned mostly with Johnson himself, and the background of his age; and the three succeeding chapters with his younger contemporaries.

Johnson: Early Life and Literature

Samuel Johnson (1709-84) was born at Lichfield, the son of a bookseller, and was educated at local grammar schools. His family were too poor themselves to be able to give him a university education, and it was only by the assistance of his godfather, Dr Swinfen, who was lodging in his parents' house, that he was enabled to spend two years at Pembroke College, Oxford, which, however, he had to leave without taking his degree. He later told Boswell that he had idled his time away at Oxford, and while this may have been a somewhat exaggerated statement—throughout his life he was subject to self-reproaches—there is no doubt that he received the real foundations of his learning in his wide reading in his father's shop.*

* In this respect, he rather resembled Pope, who was also a splendid example of the benefit of self-education for a literary career. He resembled Pope, too, in his bodily afflictions and in the brave way he overcame them; though tall and massively built, Johnson suffered all his life from a nervous disease, which disfigured his face, impaired his eyesight, and caused him involuntary twitchings in his limbs. The comparative poverty of his family makes his victory over distressing circumstances even more impressive than Pope's.

In 1731 his father died, leaving him £20, and the next year he obtained a post as assistant teacher in a school at Market Bosworth. He left this to live at Birmingham with a friend, and there translated Lobo's *Voyage to Abyssinia*, with a Preface (1735), which was his first published work. The same year he married a widow almost twice his age, with a grown-up family. The marriage proved a very happy one, and with the £800 his wife had brought him he set up a school at Lichfield, which, however, only three pupils—one of whom was David Garrick—appear to have attended. In the intervals of this not very laborious teaching duty, he wrote the greater part of his tragedy of *Irene*, and in 1737 gave up his school altogether and accompanied Garrick to London.

It was not till 1749 that *Irene* was acted, when Garrick had become manager of Drury Lane and the most celebrated actor in England. It had then but a moderate success, for among Johnson's many literary gifts was never to be found any gift for the drama, and *Irene* is even more classically dead than *Cato*. Johnson's real career in literature began with his contributions to the *Gentleman's Magazine* and with the publication in 1738 of his poem *London*.

The *Gentleman's Magazine* had been founded in 1731 by a printer named Edward Cave, son of a Warwickshire shoemaker. Johnson began to contribute regularly in 1738, and in the early 'forties was the "sole composer" of the Parliamentary debates. There was then no Press Gallery in the House of Commons, and it was forbidden even to take notes. So Cave and his assistants had to attend the public gallery, listen attentively, and then write up the debates at the nearest coffee-house. Cave had got into trouble with Parliament for reporting Members' speeches too faithfully, and by the time Johnson came to work for him the proceedings were disguised as "Debates in the Senate of Great Lilliput", with the speakers given fancy names. Johnson gave them so much of his own learned eloquence that Voltaire exclaimed that the glories of ancient Greece had been revived at Westminster.

Johnson continued very poor during these early years of journalism. One of his letters to Cave is signed "Yours,

impransus . . ."—that is, "dinnerless". His contributions
to the *Magazine* were many and various; he wrote biographies,
essays, prefaces, poems, translations, editorials—in fact, anything that Cave required or that they agreed the public might
be glad to read. This labour must have been often irksome,
but much of his later readiness to write or speak on any
subject at short notice was no doubt due to this painful
training.

His first work of importance was his *London, a Poem, in
Imitation of the Third Satire of Juvenal*—"written in 1738",
according to his own account, and published the same year.
He was in great distress at this time, and that he was bitterly
conscious of it can be seen from a couplet in this poem, the
second line of which he marked by capitals:

> This mournful truth is everywhere confess'd,
> SLOW RISES WORTH, BY POVERTY DEPRESS'D!

The poem came out the same morning as Pope's *1738,* so that
England, as Boswell remarks, "had at once its Juvenal and
Horace as poetical monitors". It was published anonymously, made a great sensation, and the public, who bought
two editions in one week, were anxious to know the name of
this "unknown poet, greater even than Pope". Pope himself
admired the poem, and tried to do Johnson some service.
Hearing that the author of *London* wished to apply for the
headmastership of a school and that he must have the degree
of Master of Arts to be eligible, Pope endeavoured through
Earl Gower and Swift to obtain for him the necessary degree
from Dublin. This petition failed, as did that of Johnson
himself to his own university; so he was forced to continue
in the path of journalism and authorship upon which he had
started.*

London is one of the few political pieces that Johnson ever
wrote. The Whigs were in power, so the Tories naturally
thought (as the Whigs would have done in their place) that

---

* It was not till 1755 that Oxford made him Master of Arts, and
ten years later he received the degree of LL.D. from Dublin. As often
happens in human life, when he had got the qualifications necessary
for a certain position, he no longer needed it.

the government were ruining the country; and the poem is full of spirited invective against Walpole and his fellow-ministers—who fell from office four years later after more than twenty years of power—and of appeals to patriotism and liberty. The political theme seems more than a little rusty now—many other governments have ruined the country since —and the poem lives rather by Johnson's record in it of his own personal struggles in the city of the title. The liberty and independence he really was qualified to write about were not political but literary; for one thing in particular marks off his early career in literature from that of his predecessors like Thomson—that he was resolved to go his own way, to produce his work through magazines and publishers, without the name of some patron to recommend it. The one exception he made to this rule was in addressing the plan of his dictionary to the Earl of Chesterfield, and that ended in the famous letter which is said—with pardonable exaggeration—to have given the death-blow to literary patronage altogether.

The Dictionary and Chesterfield

The idea of compiling a dictionary of the English language was first suggested to Johnson by the publisher Dodsley. For a long time literary men in England had been concerned by the absence here of a book comparable to the French dictionary of 1694. It says a good deal for Johnson's reputation with the publishers that he should have been considered capable of compiling single-handed a work that in France had been effected by the combined labours of forty scholars. He had not, after all, written very much: a poem, *London*; the life of his friend Savage (1744); contributions to the *Gentleman's Magazine*; the still unacted tragedy of *Irene*; and a few minor pieces. He had no degree, had failed as a school-master, and had spent almost all his early life as a journalist, writing whatever was required of him. It must have been partly that capability to write on any subject, partly the learning he revealed in private conversation, that convinced Dodsley and his associates—among whom was the firm of Longmans, still flourishing to-day—that he was the man for the job.   The group of publishers offered him 1,500 guineas, and at Dodsley's request his *Plan of a Dictionary of the English Language* (1747) was addressed to the Earl of Chesterfield.

The aims set out in the plan were for the compiling a dictionary "by which the pronunciation of our language may be fixed, and its attainment facilitated; by which its purity may be preserved, its use ascertained, and its duration lengthened".   Johnson's most original idea was to include quotations, to show the actual literary use of the language. He had a mastery of definition, and also a mastery of the difficulties of definition.   As he wrote in the Preface:

> To explain requires the use of terms less abstruse than that which is to be explained, and such terms cannot always be found.   For as nothing can be proved but by supposing something intuitively known, and evident without proof, so nothing can be defined but by the use of words too plain to admit of definition. Sometimes easier words are changed into harder . . . for the *easiest* word, whatever it be, can never be translated into one more easy.

Sometimes he was to indulge himself by defining political words in a prejudiced or humorous manner; but his humour could also be turned against himself, as when he defined "Grub Street" as "the name of a street in London much inhabited by writers of small histories, dictionaries, and temporary poems; whence any mean production is called Grub-street"; or when he defined "lexicographer" as "a writer of dictionaries, a harmless drudge".

He employed six assistants in the more mechanical part of the drudgery, but his estimate of three years' work was quickly seen to be over optimistic, and it was not until 1755 that the Dictionary was published.   It had a deserved success, and Johnson's pension from the Crown seven years later was meant to be taken as the country's acknowledgment of his labours.

Chesterfield had meanwhile rather neglected his duties as patron.   Possibly with the intention to make amends, possibly with the desire to be connected at little cost with so reputable a work, he now wrote two essays in Dodsley's paper, the *World*, highly recommending the Dictionary to the notice of the public. The first essay opened:

> I heard the other day with great pleasure from my worthy friend Mr Dodsley that Mr Johnson's English dictionary, with a grammar and history of our language prefixed, will be published this winter, in two large volumes in folio . . .
>
> Many people have imagined that so extensive a work would have been performed by a number of persons . . . incorporating their respective funds into one joint stock. But whether this opinion be true or false, I think the public in general, and the republic of letters in particular, greatly obliged to Mr Johnson for having undertaken and executed so great and desirable a work. Perfection is not to be expected from man; but if we are to judge by the various works of Mr Johnson already published, we have good reason to believe that he will bring this as near to perfection as any one man could do . . .

There was a postscript to this essay:

> P.S. I hope that none of my courteous readers will upon this occasion be so uncourteous as to suspect me of being a hired and interested puff of this work; for I most solemnly protest that neither Mr Johnson nor . . . any bookseller or booksellers concerned . . . have ever offered me the usual compliment of a pair of gloves or a bottle of wine; nor has even Mr Dodsley . . . so much as invited me to take a bit of mutton with him.

These two essays were written anonymously—under the fictitious name of "Adam Fitz-Adam" who was supposed to write every number of the *World*—but Johnson soon discovered, through Dodsley, who the author was. Coming after Chesterfield's long indifference to the project, the essays seemed to Johnson not so much a flattering amends as a kind of insult. He said to Garrick: "I have sailed a long and painful voyage round the world of English language; and does he now send out two cock-boats to tow me into harbour?" And to Boswell: "Sir, after making great professions, he had, for many years, taken no notice of me; but when my

Dictionary was coming out, he fell a scribbling in the *World* about it. Upon which I wrote him a letter expressed in civil terms, but such as might show him that I did not mind what he said or wrote, and that I had done with him".

The famous letter was certainly "expressed in civil terms", but few more deadly civilities have ever been written. It concludes:

> Is not a patron, my Lord, one who looks with uncon-
> cern on a man struggling for life in the water, and,
> when he has reached ground, encumbers him with help?
> The notice which you have been pleased to take of my
> labours, had it been early, had been kind; but it has
> been delayed till I am indifferent, and cannot enjoy it;
> till I am solitary,* and cannot impart it; till I am
> known, and do not want it. I hope it is no very cynical
> asperity, not to confess obligations where no benefit has
> been received, or to be unwilling that the public should
> consider me as owing that to a patron which providence
> has enabled me to do for myself.
>
> Having carried on my work thus far with so little
> obligation to any favourer of learning, I shall not be
> disappointed though I should conclude it, if less be
> possible, with less; for I have been long wakened from
> that dream of hope, in which I once boasted myself with
> so much exaltation,
>
> My Lord,
> Your Lordship's most humble,
> Most obedient servant,
> SAM. JOHNSON.

Changes in Literature and Society

Whether Chesterfield was quite so guilty in this respect as Johnson supposed is of no great importance to-day. The interest of the quarrel lies rather in its contribution to the decline of patronage and its relation to the increasing independence of even the poorest author.† Johnson was not the

* His wife had died three years before.

† Goldsmith observed in his *Citizen of the World* that the poets of England "no longer depend on the great for subsistence; they have now no other patrons but the public, and the public, collectively considered, is a good and a generous master". And Gibbon was later

man to deride the nobility: an ultra Tory, he believed firmly in the spirit of the Catechism, but he also evidently held the doctrine of *noblesse oblige* and thought it proper for a nobleman who had accepted the address of a work to take some interest in its progress and assist the author to the best of his ability. If we say with truth that no poor author in the Augustan Age could have written such a letter, we must add that no nobleman of the age of Halifax and Somers would have so neglected the first duty of a patron. Such men as Chesterfield seem to have wanted the honours of patronage without the responsibilities.

The quarrel was also part of the increasing "democracy" of the age. Though Johnson was no democrat in the political sense—in his later years he wrote a pamphlet against the American Congress entitled *Taxation no Tyranny*—he was one of the hard-working individualists of comparatively humble birth who make the literature (and also the art and science) of the mid-eighteenth century so different in its social aspects from that of the Augustan Age. Pope, it is true, valued his independence as much as Johnson; and in general Augustan literature was far less aristocratic than its predecessor; but there was, nevertheless, a decided gap between such men as Pope and Addison and Swift and the "hacks" of Grub Street, and the *Dunciad* is not entirely free from some ordinary, if natural, social snobbery. Johnson's humorous reference to Grub Street in his Dictionary, and the fact that a hard-working journalist could become the chief literary figure of the age, were indications of a changed state of affairs. "Grub Street" was next door to the *Gentleman's Magazine*, which had been founded by a shoemaker's son who was to defy the power of Parliament itself. The greatest publisher of the age, the "worthy friend" of earls and "hacks" alike, was a former footman; and the author with the widest reputation in Europe was a carpenter's son who had become a

to write in his *Autobiography*: "I cannot boast of the friendship or favour of princes; the patronage of English literature has long since devolved on our booksellers, and the measure of their liberality is the least ambiguous test of our common success".

printer in that very street down which Pope's Dunces had
hurried to their muddy doom.   Johnson's position has thus
to be seen in its contemporary setting for its representative
nature to be realised; his Age was also the Age of Hogarth,
the painter whose genius was beyond the grasp of the average
nobleman, whose tastes had been formed—or whose prejudices
had been fixed—by the Grand Tour.

Besides this decline of patronage, and increasing independence of authors, there was a change in public opinion.   No
longer were the gentlemen-critics in the coffee-houses the
arbiters of taste.   Johnson could write to a friend in the
country, soon after the Dictionary had come out:

> I have, indeed, published my book, of which I beg
> to know your father's judgment, and yours; and I have
> now stayed long enough to watch its progress in the
> world.   It has, you see, no patrons, and, I think, has
> yet had no opponents, except the critics of the coffee-
> house, whose outcries are soon dispersed into the air,
> and are thought on no more . . .

In place of the coffee-house, and its Spectators and Guardians,
there was growing up a more independent public opinion, still
led by London but by the authors and publishers and professional reviewers rather than by any social or political
aristocracy.   Such a change was the inevitable result of a
wider reading public and the growth of printing all over the
country.   London, steadily increasing in population, was still
first in the publishing and newspaper trade; but between
1726 and 1775 there had been established about 150 publishing
firms in the provinces, which was about the same number as
in the capital.

Circulating libraries and book clubs were beginning in the
chief provincial cities, supplying mainly, it is presumed, the more
leisured members of the middle class.   Whitefield, the great
Methodist preacher, found the proportion of illiterates in the
slum areas of London and Bristol alarmingly high; but there
is no doubt that many of the lower classes were readers,
particularly of the Bible, of course, and also of the English
classics, of which edition after edition was produced in these

years. At the end of our period, in 1782, a German visitor compared the English knowledge of our classics with the German knowledge of theirs:

> Certain it is that English classical authors are read more generally, beyond all comparison, than the German; which in general are read only by the learned; or at most by the middle class of people. The English national authors are in all hands, and read by all people, of which the innumerable editions they have gone through are a sufficient proof. My landlady, who is only a tailor's widow, reads her Milton; and tells me that her late husband first fell in love with her on this very account; because she read Milton with such proper emphasis. This single instance would prove but little; but I have conversed with several people of the lower class, who all knew their national authors, and who all have read many, if not all of them.

"The Vanity of Human Wishes"

Between the Plan of the Dictionary and its publication, Johnson had been engaged on two other works which brought him even more applause. When he remarked in the letter to Chesterfield that his patron's help had been delayed "till I am known, and do not want it", he must have been thinking mainly of his poem *The Vanity of Human Wishes* (1749) and of his periodical *The Rambler* (1750-2). These two works have lasted longer than the Dictionary. Johnson's humorous comparison of dictionary-making with "temporary poems" had some truth in it; of its very nature, a dictionary is bound to be superseded, and the most a lexicographer can hope for is that his work will sometimes be consulted by future lexicographers. Johnson's modest hopes in this respect have been fulfilled, and no later publication can rob him of the initial honours.

The Vanity of Human Wishes, being the Tenth Satire of Juvenal imitated is not a "temporary poem" but Johnson's chief achievement in verse and one of the most readable long poems of the century. Between the *Epistle to Arbuthnot* and Goldsmith's *Deserted Village* there were not a great many poems written of any length which can still be read with pleasure without needing to be skipped. Young's *Night Thoughts* and Blair's *Grave* are examples of lengthy poems written in the 'forties which the utmost respect is hardly sufficient to read through to-day in full. Johnson's poem, in length, is somewhere between these poems and Gray's *Elegy*; and though hardly to be compared with the latter masterpiece in genius, shares with it a noble simplicity and a constant readability not given to the former. How far it and *London* are "imitations" can only be decided by classical scholars, but the presumption is that they are as much original literature as Pope's imitations of Horace or Fielding's imitations of Cervantes.*

The theme is one that came to interest Johnson more and more during these middle years of his life; we meet with it again in *Rasselas* and in some of the papers in the *Rambler* and the *Idler*. It was a theme, too, popular with other poets of the time, particularly with Young and Gray. The optimism of the Augustans is often exaggerated, but there were certainly experiences in human life not easily to be fitted into the more shallow of the philosophies of that age. Johnson had had some bitter disappointments himself, and had come to see that the desires of men do not often reach fruition or create the happiness anticipated. Even the most fortunate of students, for instance, must not expect to have a life free from care:

> Should tempting Novelty thy cell refrain,
> And Sloth effuse her opiate fumes in vain;
> Should Beauty blunt on fops her fatal dart,
> Nor claim the triumph of a letter'd heart;
> Should no Disease thy torpid veins invade,

---

* The opinion of Gray, one of the greatest scholars of the century as well as one of the greatest poets, is probably conclusive: dissenting from the opinion of his friend Horace Walpole, he wrote that "*London* is to me one of those few imitations that have all the ease and all the spirit of an original". Technically, of course, both poems owe a good deal to Pope, particularly to the *Moral Essays*; but probably Johnson owes no more to Pope than Pope to Dryden. In each case, the creditor has a large independent account of his own, and no one could mistake a typical piece of Johnson for Pope or a typical piece of Pope for Dryden. In the same tradition, they nevertheless speak with different accents.

> Nor Melancholy's phantoms haunt thy shade;
> Yet hope not life from grief or danger free,
> Nor think the doom of man revers'd for thee.

But Johnson was a convinced Christian, and to despair was to him, as to Christian theology, one of the gravest of sins. He had to reconcile his pessimistic (or realistic) view of life with the need to fight against despair, to take comfort in the inscrutable workings of providence. (Compare Cowper's hymn *God moves in a mysterious way*, especially the last two verses.) The conclusion of the poem, which has given examples of the title's theme from the lives of statesmen and scholars and soldiers, is a fine antithesis, a supreme instance of the power that comes to a writer who can, without paradox and with perfect sincerity, destroy—as he feels he has to—the whole of his previous argument:

> Where then shall Hope and Fear their objects find?
> Shall dull Suspense corrupt the stagnant mind?
> Must helpless man, in ignorance sedate,
> Roll darkling down the torrent of his fate?
> Shall no dislike alarm, no wishes rise,
> No cries attempt the mercy of the skies?
> Inquirer, cease; petitions yet remain,
> Which Heav'n may hear, nor deem Religion vain.
> Still raise for good the supplicating voice,
> But leave to Heaven the measure and the choice.
> Safe in His hand, whose eye discerns afar
> The secret ambush of a specious pray'r;
> Implore His aid, in His decisions rest,
> Secure, whate'er He gives, He gives the best:
> Yet when the sense of sacred presence fires,
> And strong devotion to the skies aspires,
> Pour forth thy fervours for a healthful mind,
> Obedient passions, and a will resign'd;
> For love, which scarce collective man can fill;
> For patience, sovereign o'er transmuted ill;
> For faith, which panting for a happier seat,
> Counts death kind Nature's signal for retreat.
> These goods for man the laws of Heaven ordain,
> These goods He grants, who grants the power to gain;
> With these celestial wisdom calms the mind,
> And makes the happiness she does not find.

The " Rambler "

The year after this poem was published, Johnson turned from Pope to Pope's contemporaries Steele and Addison, starting a bi-weekly journal called the *Rambler*, with the intention of doing for his age what the *Tatler* and the *Spectator* had done for theirs. His contributions to the *Gentleman's Magazine* had been numerous and varied, but he often had to write what was required of him rather than what he personally wished to say. He was as eminently qualified as Addison to be a moral teacher, and though he refused in 1756 a living offered to him in Lincolnshire he was as fitted to preach the kind of lay-sermon which up till now had been Addison's speciality. The title he chose was not a very happy one, and was seen to be still less so when translated into Italian as *Il Vagabondo*. But titles are not of the first importance, and though the periodical circulation of the journal was only about 500 copies (at 2d. a copy) it brought Johnson in about four guineas a week, gave him a reputation comparable to Addison's, and collected in volume form had a sale only exceeded by the bound volumes of the *Spectator*.*

Compared with the *Spectator*, it has not been read much in modern times. That Johnson had wit and humour is evident from Boswell's record of his conversation, and from such incidental flourishes as those in the Dictionary; but there is not much of this humour in the *Rambler*, and not much of the fictional element seen in Steele's *Tatler* letters and Addison's Coverley papers. Johnson took over, it is true, the letter convention, as Fielding did in the *Champion* and

* Its contemporary reputation is seen in Goldsmith's amusing essay *A Reverie*, where Johnson is supposed to be taking his place in the coach bound for the Temple of Fame: "He lifted a parcel of folios into the seat before him, but our inquisitorial coachman at once shoved them out again. 'What! not take in my Dictionary?' exclaimed the other in a rage. 'Be patient, Sir,' replied the coachman: 'I have drove a coach, man and boy, these two thousand years; but I do not remember to have carried above one dictionary during the whole time. That little book which I perceive peeping from one of your pockets, may I presume to ask what it contains?' 'A mere trifle,' replied the author; 'it is called *The Rambler*.' '*The Rambler*!' says the coachman; 'I beg, Sir, you'll take your place; I have heard our ladies in the court of Apollo frequently mention it with rapture '".

Cowper and others in the *Connoisseur*; and the letters supposedly written by "Cornelia" are a rather ponderous attempt at the lighter manner of Isaac Bickerstaff, Esq. There was little variety in the *Rambler*, and some readers complained that Johnson had used all the hard words he could find so as to make his Dictionary indispensable. In general it was the lay-sermons which the public came to like, as it liked those in the Saturday *Spectators*; and here Johnson, with his own journal and more elbow-room than in the *Gentleman's Magazine*, was in his element. His hard training had given him the required stamina—we must remember that the Dictionary was in progress all this while—and he had a fund of learning and experience to draw upon. He wrote all but four of the papers, which appeared regularly twice a week from March 1750 till his wife's death in March 1752; one of the four exceptions was written by Richardson, whom he introduced as "an author who has enlarged the knowledge of human nature and taught the passions to move at the command of virtue".

The conclusion of the essay on pedantry, which appeared during November 1751, is a good example of the *Rambler's* usual style:

> It is as possible to become pedantic by fear of pedantry as to be troublesome by ill-timed officiousness. There is no kind of impertinence more justly censurable than his who is always labouring to level his thoughts to intellects higher than his own, who apologises for every word which his own narrowness of converse inclines him to think unusual, keeps the exuberance of his faculties under visible restraint, is solicitous to anticipate enquiries by needless explanations, and endeavours to shade his own abilities lest weak eyes should be dazzled with their lustre.

The style, with its reliance on Latinised words and constructions, may seem at first sight rather pedantic itself—Boswell observed that "Sir Thomas Browne, whose *Life* Johnson wrote, was remarkably fond of Anglo-Latin diction; and to his example we are to ascribe Johnson's sometimes indulging himself in this kind of phraseology"—but a good test of the genuineness of a style in writing is to compare it, where possible, with the recorded conversation of the author; and Johnson can pass this test with ease. His conversational style, as recorded by Boswell and others, is so very like the style of the *Rambler* that no pedantry can be attributed to either. As he talked, so he wrote; and it has been as truly observed of Steele and Addison that their written style has the effect of good conversation, was in fact close to the actual talk of the coffee-house wits. If Johnson had written in any other style than he commonly used in serious conversation, he would have been guilty of pedantry in the way he himself described.

From 1753 he began to contribute to the *Adventurer*, edited by his friend Dr Hawkesworth; and from 1756 to the *Literary Magazine*. The same year he issued proposals for a new edition of Shakespeare, with notes, which was not, however, completed till 1765. His famous Preface to this edition can best be considered together with his other chief work of literary criticism, the *Lives of the Poets*. Here we must consider the two last works of the "middle period", the two important works between the publication of the Dictionary and the granting of the pension of £300 a year from the Crown.

There are some striking resemblances between most of the writings of these middle years of Johnson's life. It would not be fanciful to call them all by the generic name of "The Vanity of Human Wishes". The argument of that poem had been repeated in some papers of the *Rambler*; even the Preface to the Dictionary (and, of course, the letter to Chesterfield) had acknowledged Johnson's realisation of the disappointment attending on human hopes: "I have protracted my work till most of those whom I wished to please have sunk into the grave, and success and miscarriage are empty sounds". And now a similar argument was to inform some of the most impressive papers in his new journal, the *Idler*, and was to be the philosophy underlying that remarkable work *Rasselas*.

The "Idler" and "Rasselas"

The *Idler* was published from April 1758 to April 1760 as a supplement to a weekly newspaper called the *Universal*

Chronicle, and collected in volume form in 1761.* In one of the essays which give their name to the journal Johnson depicts himself, under the guise of Mr Sober, as an example of idleness:

> There are others to whom Idleness dictates another expedient by which life may be passed unprofitably away without the tediousness of many vacant hours. The art is to fill the day with petty business, to have always something in hand which may raise curiosity, but not solicitude, and keep the mind in a state of action, but not of labour.
>
> This art has for many years been practised by my old friend Sober, with wonderful success . . . I have often teased him with reproof, and he has often promised reformation; for no man is so much open to conviction as the Idler, but there is none on whom it operates so little. What will be the effect of this paper I know not . . . but my hope is that he will quit his trifles and betake himself to rational and useful diligence.

This grave humour—recalling the tone of some of Addison's essays—was apparently meant by Johnson as a serious reproof to himself. He actually seems to have thought, in some of the busiest years of his life, that he was inclined to laziness. He agreed with his friend Young's famous words in *Night Thoughts*:

> Procrastination is the thief of time;
> Year after year it steals, till all are fled . . .

---

* Johnson himself wrote almost all the essays. A few were contributed by friends, including three essays on art by Sir Joshua Reynolds. These, incidentally, together with their expansion in the famous *Discourses* to the students at the Royal Academy, gave Reynolds a reputation in literature at the time almost equal to his reputation in painting. To-day we can see a greater service to literature in his masterly portraits of many of the writers of his age. The Johnson and the Sterne in particular are most impressive studies, which seem to bring the men before us as they lived. Other fine examples are the Gibbon, the Goldsmith, the Boswell, and the Sheridan. We can best judge Reynolds's contribution in this field by reflecting how much we would give for similar portraits of the Elizabethan dramatists. Johnson's namesake we are fortunate in having in the impressive portrait by Honthorst, but there is no good authentic portrait of Shakespeare and no portrait at all of Marlowe, Tourneur, or Webster.

In his private meditations occurs the note: "This year I hope to learn diligence". It is true he was sometimes slow in starting a work, and the edition of Shakespeare was so long delayed that it called forth a squib from the satirical poet Churchill:

> He for subscribers baits his hook,
> And takes your cash; but where's the book?

But he was in general so much the reverse of idle that his conviction to the contrary can best be explained as part of his consciousness that his success in life had come too late to gratify those who had expected a brilliant career for him. His father had died before he had made anything of a start in life at all; his wife had died in the midst of his first success (and the £800 he had received from her to start his school no doubt weighed upon his conscience); and now, when he was becoming an established figure in the literary world, his mother died, in 1759, at the great age of ninety. Such an extension of the psalmist's span must have been as gratifying to him as it was, in a similar case, to Pope; but his natural sorrow seems to have been combined with a feeling of self-reproach. He seems to have felt that he had not made sufficient return for his parents' early care, though it is difficult to see what more he could have done than he actually did. He was as affectionate a son as Pope; had triumphed, as Pope had, over physical disabilities; and had won a place in literature and learning by his own unaided efforts. If his had been a slow growth, there are analogies in nature which show that a long incubation often produces the most lasting fruit.

No doubt he had, like Mr Sober, his idle periods, but we know that they were interspersed with bouts of almost incredible activity. Boswell records the speed with which the *Idler* was often produced:

> Many of these excellent essays were written as hastily as an ordinary letter. Mr Langton remembers Johnson, when on a visit at Oxford, asking him one evening how long it was till the post went out; and on being told about half an hour, he exclaimed, "then

> we shall do very well". He upon this instantly sat
> down and finished an *Idler*, which it was necessary
> should be in London the next day. Mr Langton having
> signified a wish to read it, "Sir," said he, "you shall
> not do more than I have done myself." He then
> folded it up, and sent it off.

The excellent *Rasselas* (1759) was an even more striking
instance of concentration. He wrote it in the evenings of a
single week—it is about the length of Dickens's *Christmas
Carol*—in order, says Boswell, "that with the profits he might
defray the expense of his mother's funeral, and pay some little
debts which she had left". That a work written under such
circumstances should have the appearance of being composed
at leisure, with great deliberation, is one of the wonders of
literature. The explanation is partly the hard training as
journalist he had gone through, but even more the relation
between the theme of *Rasselas* and the thoughts which were
disturbing him about this time and which had become inten-
sified on his mother's death. Probably he could not have
written on any other theme so speedily, if at all, during this
period of heart-searching reflection.

Rasselas—or *The Prince of Abyssinia*, to give it its original
title—is not, however, a depressing work. If a prose version
of *The Vanity of Human Wishes*, as it has been called,* it has
nevertheless, some admirable character sketches and some
shrewd touches of humour. The Prince himself is modelled
on the author's half-humorous view of his own character:

> As he passed through the fields, and saw the animals
> around him, "Ye," said he, "are happy, and need not
> envy me that walk thus among you, burdened with
> myself; nor do I, ye gentle beings, envy your felicity;
> for it is not the felicity of man. I have many distresses
> from which you are free; I fear pain when I do not feel
> it; I sometimes shrink at evils recollected, and some-
> times start at evils anticipated: surely the equity of

---

* The *Rambler* 204-5, which describe how an Abyssinian prince
sought happiness in vain, are presumably an earlier draft of the novel,
while the background of the first few chapters was probably provided
by the translation of Lobo.

> Providence has balanced peculiar sufferings with peculiar enjoyments."
>
> With observations like these the Prince amused himself as he returned, uttering them with a plaintive voice, yet with a look that discovered him to feel some complacence in his own perspicacity, and to receive some solace of the miseries of life from consciousness of the delicacy with which he felt and the eloquence with which he bewailed them.

Johnson shared Fielding's scorn at the comfortable doctrine that success is always distributed according to merit. (Even Richardson had come to see that Virtue is not always Rewarded.) He had written in the *Adventurer* in 1754 of

> the boast of some swelling moralists that every man's fortune was in his own power, that prudence supplied the place of all other divinities, and that happiness is the unfailing consequence of virtue. But, surely, the quiver of Omnipotence is stored with arrows, against which the shield of human virtue, however adamantine it has been boasted, is held up in vain: we do not always suffer by our crimes; we are not always protected by our innocence.*

The argument of *Rasselas* is an extension of this passage. The Prince and his sister search for happiness in vain throughout the world, finding their cloistered ideas of its prevalence rudely shattered by experience. Even the poet Imlac, "used to vicissitudes", has to remind them—by an analogy with Johnson's own life—that when he returned to his native land expecting "the caresses of my kinsmen and the congratulations of my friends" he found his father had been dead fourteen years and that "of my companions, the greater part was in the grave . . ."

Though written in the form of a novel, *Rasselas* has little of what we have come to expect from prose fiction. There is not much incident, and all the characters speak Johnsonese. In point of wit, it is inferior to Voltaire's *Candide*—which, strangely enough for a novel on a similar theme, came out the same year—and considered as an allegory it has not the

* Compare the passage in *Tom Jones* quoted above, p. 136.

dramatic life of the *Pilgrim's Progress*. Yet there is much to be said on the other side. We have observed that there is little in the *Rambler*, or the *Idler*, that can properly be compared with the more fictional philosophy of the *Spectator*. *Rasselas* supplies this deficiency. It stems, after all, from Johnson's meditations in essay-form and can best be considered an adjunct to them. Its fictional dress, in which no chapter is longer than an average *Rambler* or *Idler*, gives it a greater interest to the modern reader than the *Rambler* and *Idler* themselves, as the Coverley Papers are the best remembered work of Addison. If *The Vanity of Human Wishes* is by common consent Johnson's most considerable achievement in poetry, *Rasselas* is as truly the best prose work of his middle years.

Four years after came the pension from the Crown which relieved him for the rest of his life from the necessity of writing for bread. He was rather doubtful at first whether he should accept it,* but on being told that nothing of a "Laureate" nature was expected from him, and that the pension was to be considered as the country's acknowledgment of the work he had already performed, he gladly assented to the grant. He was fifty-three and had been writing for a living for over twenty years.

Johnson's Last Years: 1763-84

The characteristic of Mr Sober, quoted as epigraph to this chapter, was true of Johnson himself and was no doubt drawn from a study of his own life. For more than twenty years he had to subordinate his love of conversation to his need for writing, or else suffer the self-reproach of being idle. With the granting of the pension, he was no longer forced to write for a living and could have as much conversation as he pleased. Boswell's *Life* is sometimes criticised for its lack of balance: only a sixth of the work is given to the period from Johnson's

* He had defined "pension" in the Dictionary as "An allowance made to any one without an equivalent; in England it is generally understood to mean pay given to a State hireling for treason to his country".

birth to his pension, the rest dealing in great detail with his last years. This was not due entirely to the fact that Boswell first met Johnson in 1763. The written works of Johnson speak, after all, for themselves; and there were about ten chief works in the period before 1763, but only three in the period after. Boswell's *Life* is therefore chiefly notable for its record of Johnson's conversation in his last years, and though there are other records of that conversation—by Mrs Thrale, Fanny Burney, and others—without Boswell's vigilance the majority of it would have been lost.

In this conversation of his last years, as in the writings of his early journalism, the sheer bulk and variety are the things we notice first. Literature, it is true, forms the leading topic, but morality runs it close; and nearly everything that can be publicly discussed—in religion, in law, in politics, in social manners and customs—was eagerly discussed by Johnson and his friends. Most of these friends, it is important to observe, were distinguished men in various walks of life; and it was as much owing to their variety of occupation as to the wide range of Johnson's own mind that the conversations were so agreeably diverse. There were, among the more intimate circle, the actor-manager Garrick, the painter Reynolds, the statesman Burke, the poet Goldsmith, the dramatist and philanthropist Hannah More, the musician Burney and his novelist daughter Fanny, besides such lesser figures in their age as Boswell himself, who had been trained for the law, the Thrales, who were business people, and several aristocrats and clergymen and dons. When what was later known as the Literary Club was founded in 1764, among the first members were Reynolds, Johnson, Burke, and Goldsmith, later members including Garrick, Boswell, Gibbon, Sheridan, Burney, the critics Malone and the Wartons, the statesmen Fox and Wyndham, the dramatist Colman, the orientalist Jones, the naturalist Banks, the economist Smith, the theologian Douglas, Bishop of Salisbury, and the antiquarian Percy, Bishop of Dromore. Boswell, in fact, introduces us in the *Life*, not simply to Johnson himself, but to a remarkably wide section of eighteenth-century society.

Of the three publications of this last period of Johnson's life, two were literary—the edition of Shakespeare, with preface and notes (1765) and the *Lives of the Poets* (1779-81)—while the third was his *Journey to the Western Islands of Scotland* (1775), which, like its companion volume, Boswell's *Tour to the Hebrides*, can best be considered as adjuncts to the *Life*. It is interesting to compare Johnson's literary criticism in conversation with his criticism in print.

They have one thing in common, and that is their common sense. The common-sense approach to literature has its limitations, but compared with the Augustans' frequent reliance on the "rules" of French classicism, it comes as a relief. The Three Unities, for instance, had bogged down dramatic criticism for a hundred years—two hundred, if we count Sidney's view as typical of the more academic Elizabethan mind. Johnson demolishes the Unities in one fine sweep of the Shakespeare Preface:

> The objection arising from the impossibility of passing the first hour at Alexandria, and the next at Rome, supposes that, when the play opens, the spectator really imagines himself at Alexandria, and believes that his walk to the theatre has been a voyage to Egypt, and that he lives in the days of Antony and Cleopatra. Surely he that imagines this may imagine more . . . Delusion, if delusion be admitted, has no certain limitation . . . There is no reason why a mind thus wandering in ecstasy should count the clock, or why an hour should not be a century in that calenture of the brain that can make the stage a field.
>
> The truth is that the spectators are always in their senses, and know, from the first act to the last, that the stage is only a stage, and that the players are only players. They came to hear a certain number of lines recited with just gesture and elegant modulation. The lines relate to some action, and an action must be in some place; but the different actions that complete a story may be in places very remote from each other; and where is the absurdity of allowing that space to represent first Athens, and then Sicily, which was always known to be neither Sicily nor Athens, but a modern theatre?

This is a magnificent example of the value of the common-sense approach;* and if we see some limitations in Johnson's view of dramatic poetry—"a certain number of lines recited!"—we must in fairness allow it to have been a prevalent view of the age, and indicative not only of Johnson's own failure in the drama but of the general dramatic mediocrity of the eighteenth century. It is significant that Johnson thought Shakespeare's genius showed itself more in comedy than in tragedy, and comedies—from Congreve to Sheridan—were the only distinguished productions in the century's theatre.

The main difference between Johnson's written criticism and his criticism as recorded in conversation is, naturally enough, a difference in attitude to the writer or work criticised. In conversation, he reminds us of a brilliant barrister—as he confessed to Boswell, he sometimes was indifferent as to which side of an argument he took—but in written criticism, while the appeal is still to common sense,† he reminds us more of a

---

* Anticipated, of course, to some extent, by the dramatist Farquhar in his *Discourse upon Comedy* (1702). Replying to a critic armed with the very latest rules from Paris, Farquhar remarks that "if you are so inveterate against improbabilities, you must never come near the play-house at all; for there are several improbabilities, nay, impossibilities, that all the criticisms in Nature cannot correct . . .". For instance, we suppose that we are watching Alexander the Great, "yet the whole audience at the same time knows that this is Mr Betterton, who is strutting upon the stage, and tearing his lungs for a livelihood . . .". Farquhar goes on to criticise the Unities in much the same spirit, if not with the same weight, as Johnson was to do.

† For example, in dealing with Addison's Latin poems in the *Lives of the Poets*: "Three of his Latin poems are upon subjects on which perhaps he would not have ventured to have written in his own language: *The Battle of the Pigmies and Cranes*; *The Barometer*; and *A Bowling-green*. When the matter is low or scanty, a dead language, in which nothing is mean because nothing is familiar, affords great conveniences; and, by the sonorous magnificence of Roman syllables, the writer conceals penury of thought, and want of novelty, often from the reader, and often from himself". Though few modern readers would agree with Johnson about "low" or "mean" matters—we remember that he could "scarcely check his risibility" at the low metaphor "blanket of the dark" that occurs in *Macbeth*—this common-sense dismissal of poems too often taken at their face value was needed at the time. Johnson was not to know

judge, soberly weighing the evidence in as unprejudiced a manner as possible. His remarks in conversation about Swift and Fielding—quoted above, on p. 56 and p. 138 respectively—are not criticism at all; they tell us nothing more than that he happened to dislike these writers. Compare his written criticism of Gray in the *Lives of the Poets*. While expressing the reasons for his considering most of Gray's poems affected and obscure—"Gray thought his language more poetical as it was more remote from common use"—he nevertheless rejoices "to concur with the common reader" in praising highly the famous *Elegy*. If he had *written* of Fielding, he might well have adopted the same procedure. While still retaining his conviction of Richardson's superiority, and giving his reasons for it, he would have omitted such tavern expressions as "blockhead" and "barren rascal"—for which, if we had not known who Johnson was, we should have taken him for a fishmonger*—and might well have exempted from his general disparagement either *Joseph Andrews* (which he confessed he had not read) or *Amelia* (which he later confessed he was so interested in that he read it through without stopping). There is too much animosity in his recorded references to both Fielding and Swift for them to have the status of even the most hastily-composed of his written criticism.

He had always excelled in the writing of prefaces; he observed himself, with pardonable self-satisfaction, that this was one of the things he knew he could do well. The Preface to his edition of Shakespeare is, despite its limitations, a masterly work of judgment; and what are now known as the *Lives of the Poets* were originally prefaces "biographical and critical". Forty of the leading publishers of London had decided to bring out a fine uniform edition of the English poets, and Johnson agreed to write a preface to each poet.

that the naturalist Gilbert White, in his *Natural History and Antiquities of Selborne* (1789), was to include lines about a barometer—quoted above, p. 87—which in their false poetic diction would make Addison's "Roman syllables" comparatively refreshing.

* Richardson used to say, according to Johnson, "that had he not known who Fielding was, he should have believed he was an ostler".

It was only later that these prefaces were gathered together and published separately.

They constitute in all his most lengthy piece of criticism, and the most removed in attitude, as has been said, from the "snap judgments" of his conversational criticism. Even where prejudiced, as in the Gray or the Milton, he expresses himself, in general, so judiciously that he makes out a proper case to be answered. It is unfair, really, to talk of "prejudice" at all, for he simply gives us his opinion as straightforwardly, but also as carefully, as he can. Some of the biographies are models of compression; and while the majority of the criticism, after more than a hundred and fifty years, is mainly of interest as expressing at its best the eighteenth-century view, a minority is still highly relevant to the poets concerned. The *Lives* are probably—if we except the conversations in Boswell—the work of Johnson's still most widely read, and they were a fitting conclusion to his long career in English literature.

His personal character has been touched on in several pages of this chapter and can be read in detail in the *Life*. He was full, like Mr Sober, of self-reproaches; but few men, by all accounts, have had less to reproach themselves for. His affection for his relatives and friends inevitably reminds us of Pope's, and his charity exceeded even Fielding's. The civilisation of a people, he once remarked, is to be measured by their treatment of the poor. "No man loved the poor like Dr Johnson," observed Mrs Thrale; and out of his pension of £300 a year he is said to have spent less than a third upon himself. We have mentioned the variety of his public circle, whose conversation is recorded in the *Life*; but he had also a private circle. His house off Fleet Street was a home for five people, besides his negro servant,* who because of

* It is interesting to see that Johnson, who was opposed to the idea of self-government for the Americans, detested slavery as much as Cowper or Wilberforce; while Boswell, who supported the rights of the colonists, held the "Southern" view that slavery was not only justifiable but a pious institution (and the slave trade "a very important and necessary branch of commercial interest"). Boswell's opinion can perhaps be traced back to his upbringing in "feudal"

affliction or poverty had no home of their own.   There was an elderly blind lady, Mrs Williams, a friend of his late wife; the widowed daughter of his godfather Dr Swinfen, and her daughter; another destitute woman named Polly Carmichael; and a Mr Levett, who had been a doctor among the poor in the slums of the city.   It is fitting that Johnson's lines on the death of Levett, written in 1782, should be commonly regarded as the finest of his shorter poems.

Johnson and Boswell

After Johnson's own death, two years later, his friends competed with each other in producing lives and anecdotes. Boswell's *Tour to the Hebrides* appeared in 1785, the same year that Johnson's own *Prayers and Meditations* were published. Then came Mrs Thrale's *Anecdotes of the late Samuel Johnson* (1786); Sir John Hawkins's *Life of Samuel Johnson* (1787); Mrs Thrale's *Letters to and from the late Samuel Johnson* (1788); and Boswell's *Life of Samuel Johnson, Ll.D.* (1791).   Fanny Burney's diaries and letters, another source of information about the Johnson circle, were not published till fifty years later.

Boswell's biography, of course, is the supreme authority, both upon the man himself and his relation to the age.   Its familiarity has perhaps tended to obscure its original merits. No biographer before Boswell had given us so complete a picture of his subject: rather overbalanced as it is in favour of the later years, the *Life* enables us to see Johnson in the round, as no earlier literary figure had been seen.   Carlyle can even be excused, in a time of revaluation of the eighteenth century, for rating the biography above Johnson's own works: "All Johnson's own writings, laborious and in their kind genuine above most, stand on a quite inferior level to it; already, indeed, they are becoming obsolete for this generation; and for some future generation may be valuable

Scotland, while the apparent paradox in Johnson's was answered by himself when he wrote in his pamphlet *Taxation no Tyranny* (1775) "how is it that we hear the loudest *yelps* for liberty among the drivers of negroes?"

chiefly as prolegomena and expository scholia to this *Johnsoniad* of Boswell".*

Nevertheless, this extreme expression of the popular view must give us pause. Not only would it have shocked Boswell, who conceived his work as "valuable chiefly as prolegomena" to Johnson's own writings, it puts the conversation higher than the literature. Boswell is the chief source for this conversation, and there is no doubt that it is superbly recorded and that, as a whole, it deserves to rank as one of Johnson's chief contributions to literature and life. But to treat it as superior to *Rasselas* and the *Rambler* and the *Vanity of Human Wishes* and the *Lives of the Poets* is to place Johnson on the same literary level as those interesting eighteenth-century characters—such as Mary Montagu, Lord Hervey, Chesterfield, Horace Walpole, Anna Seward, Parson Woodforde, Richard Edgeworth, etc.—whose reputation rests almost entirely on their talk, letters, diaries, or eccentricities. We are displaying not the least scorn for such characters when we insist that Johnson, as a *writer*, is very much their superior.

But was not Boswell himself partly to blame for treating Johnson as a "character"? We have come so far from the nineteenth-century view that a recent critic has claimed that Boswell's Johnson is "a character almost as mythical as Sherlock Holmes". This is a healthy reaction from Carlyle and Lamb, especially if it leads to more reading of Johnson; but it is not very convincing. There is an easy test of Boswell's genuineness, which every reader can make for himself. If he reads Boswell first (as he probably will do), then reads Johnson's chief works, then goes back to Boswell and asks himself whether the biography gives him the picture of the man who could have written those works; the answer, to most readers, we believe, will be "on the whole, yes". Boswell is too careful a biographer to stray very far from his texts; and the picture he gives is, in general, borne out by other evidence and by the portrait of Johnson by Reynolds.

* Compare Hazlitt, recording the conversation of Lamb and his circle: "In general, we were hard upon the moderns. The author of the *Rambler* was only tolerated in Boswell's *Life* of him . . .". (*On the Conversation of Authors: II.*)

There is no doubt, though, that Boswell had some of the gifts of the novelist. His figure of Johnson, reasonably authentic as it probably is, is nevertheless often heightened by the novelist's art. The famous episode—far too long to quote in full—where Boswell arranges a meeting between Johnson and Jack Wilkes is a good example:

> Mr Wilkes placed himself next to Dr Johnson and behaved to him with so much attention and politeness that he gained upon him insensibly. No man ate more heartily than Johnson or loved better what was nice and delicate. Mr Wilkes was very assiduous in helping him to some fine veal. "Pray give me leave, Sir;—It is better here—A little of the brown—Some fat, Sir—A little of the stuffing—Some gravy—Let me have the pleasure of giving you some butter—Allow me to recommend a squeeze of this orange;—or the lemon, perhaps, may have more zest."—"Sir, Sir, I am obliged to you, Sir," cried Johnson, bowing and turning his head to him . . .

They were soon in easy conversation:

> JOHNSON: "You must know, Sir, I lately took my friend Boswell and showed him genuine civilised life in an English provincial town. I turned him loose at Lichfield, my native city, that he might see for once real civility: for you know he lives among savages in Scotland, and among rakes in London." WILKES: "Except when he is with grave, sober, decent people, like you and me." JOHNSON (smiling): "And we ashamed of him."

If the whole biography consisted of such amusing episodes, then the comparison with Sherlock Holmes would be more convincing. But Boswell is so careful to give all the facts of Johnson's life, and so zealous in describing his most serious works and conversation, that these more fictional anecdotes are merely the light touches to a fundamentally sober design (as the famous repartees to the discussions on morality). They form a necessary part of the book, and we are only in error if we stress them at the expense of the rest.

The *Tour to the Hebrides*, though written first, is best considered as an adjunct to the *Life*. In small compass, it gives us Boswell's usual merits of good construction and recording. Nothing else published by him during his lifetime is at all important—unless we make an exception of his contributions to the *London Magazine*—but the letters and journals discovered in recent years seem to place him next to Pepys as a frank commentator upon the life and manners of his time.*

Politics and Religion

The meeting between Johnson and Wilkes reflects in little the lack of fundamental hostility in the political controversies of the mid-eighteenth century—compared, at any rate, with those of the Augustan Age or the period of the French Revolution. There was certainly not much of permanent significance in the political literature of the age. When George III succeeded in 1760, he was determined from the first to be more of a king than his predecessors, and, getting rid of Chatham, he made his Scottish friend Lord Bute the head of the government. Smollett's government paper, the *Briton* (1762), was a poor attempt to defend Bute's policy; and it was answered by Wilkes's *North Briton* (1762-3), a

---

* These recently discovered letters and journals are still in process of being published. They appear to be of varying interest. *Boswell's London Journal: 1762-3* (1950) is of importance for the social rather than the literary history of the age. It reveals Boswell as a young man in London, spending his time between lofty speculations and the coarsest pursuits. The moralists who condemned *Tom Jones* would have been staggered by these revelations of the apparently ordinary conduct of a young man about town. Johnson's remark to Wilkes that Boswell lived among rakes in London was evidently not meant so humorously as the *Life* seems to suggest.

Generally speaking, this private *Journal* bears out the character of Boswell as read between the lines of the *Life*. His eagerness to mix with prominent people, for instance, is much confirmed—as it is in *Boswell's Column* (1951), the first collection in book form of his contributions to the *London Magazine* from 1777 to 1783. The reference to Captain Cook is typical: "Captain Cook, the celebrated circumnavigator, who is now for the fourth time surrounding the globe, and whose plain, candid, and judicious remarks I value very highly, gave me, in a conversation which I had with him at Sir John Pringle's table . . ." (etc.).

The unexpurgated *Life of Johnson*, which is being published soon, will probably be the chief item of literary importance in this recently discovered Boswelliana.

lively weekly which led to the editor's imprisonment and to his being acclaimed in England, France, and America as a martyr to liberty of speech. His scorn of the Scots, personified by the hated Bute, can be seen in this imaginary picture of the future, typical in its style of the *North Briton's* journalism:

> Some time since, died Mr John Bull, a very worthy plain honest old gentleman of Saxon descent. He was choked by inadvertently swallowing a thistle which he had placed by way of ornament on top of his salad.*

The satirist Charles Churchill wrote about half of this journal. Already celebrated for his *Rosciad* (1761), a satire upon the contemporary stage, he allied himself with Wilkes in the anti-Bute, anti-Scots campaign, not only in the *North Briton* but in his chief satirical poem, *The Prophecy of Famine* (1763). His work is vigorous enough, but has little of the genius of a Pope or a Dryden. Johnson said that it "had a temporary currency, only from its audacity of abuse", and that "being filled with living names, it would sink into oblivion".

After Wilkes and Churchill there was little of interest in political literature till the time of the Whig "Peter Pindar" and the Tory *Anti-Jacobin*. The one exception was the series of letters written by "Junius" which appeared in the *Public Advertiser* from 1769 to 1772. A strong Whig, "Junius" first assailed the ministers responsible for the prosecution of Wilkes, then attacked in more general terms both the Tory government and the King himself. His celebrated letter to George III led to the imprisonment of the publisher; but neither then nor afterwards was the identity of "Junius" revealed. It is commonly supposed he was Sir Philip Francis; but other names have been put forward, including that of the Rev. James Wilmot, a Warwickshire parson who is claimed to have been also the first critic to "prove" that Shakespeare's plays were really written by Bacon.

---

* Arbuthnot, a Scot, would not have agreed that John Bull was of pure Sassenach descent. To him, the figure of honest John had represented Great Britain, as opposed to the "cunning, sly, covetous" Nic. Frog.

Though "Junius" has something of Swift's pungency, and Wilkes and Churchill a little of the wit of Arbuthnot, the contrast is, nevertheless, immense between the political literature of the Age of Johnson and that of the Augustan Age. Johnson—and also Gray—wrote some political verse, but in general the literary genius of the age went into other fields. Between Swift and Fielding in the 'twenties and 'thirties and Burke and Paine in the late 'eighties and 'nineties there is little in political literature that is not of purely historical interest.

The religious literature of the age is much more interesting. With the decline of religious politics, it was natural that thoughtful men should turn their gaze inward and that some of the more fundamental issues of seventeenth-century religious thinking should be revived. William Law (1686-1761) was both a victim of religious politics and the man who did most to further an ideal of Christianity that was to make the Age of Johnson and Wesley so different from that of Swift and Addison. An ardent High-Churchman, and a supporter of the Stuarts, he had refused to take the oaths of allegiance to George I, and so had lost not only his Fellowship at Emmanuel College, Cambridge, but all prospect of further employment in the Church. He later became tutor and private chaplain to the father of Edward Gibbon, living until 1740 in the Gibbon household at Putney and leaving behind him, wrote the historian, "the reputation of a worthy and pious man, who believed all that he professed and practised all that he enjoined". It was probably at Putney that the *Serious Call* was written, a book as "puritan" in its moral attitude as the earlier pamphlet against the stage, but whose "imitation of Christ" was just the thing, by its very difficulty, to appeal to those young men, like Johnson and the Wesleys, who were dissatisfied with the easy-going Christianity taught in church and university. There had been little mysticism in the Augustan Age, but now Law and his friend John Byrom became deeply interested in the mystics of the seventeenth century, particularly in the writings of the German cobbler Jacob Boehme. Law's *Appeal to All that Doubt* (1740) and

Way to Divine Knowledge (1752) are the most important of his mystical works. Byrom, chiefly remembered for his hymn *Christians, awake*, also showed Boehme's influence in his posthumously-published *Private Journal*, as did Henry Brooke in a curious philosophical novel called *The Fool of Quality*. Wesley so admired Brooke's work that he edited a shortened version of it which was read by generations of devout Methodists.

"Methodism" was the eighteenth-century Oxford Movement. The title was originally applied as a nickname for the small group of young men who were so far from falling into step with the practice of their elders that they determined to take Christianity seriously, to follow the Church's rules of fasting and prayer, and to receive Holy Communion weekly. It differed, of course, from the Oxford Movement of the nineteenth century in that it passed from High Anglicanism to Evangelicalism, not—as with Newman—the other way about. (And where Newman and others finally landed up in the bosom of the Roman Church, the Methodists were eventually to become allied with the older forms of Dissent in the Free Church Federal Council.) Among the earliest members of this enthusiastic group of students were George Whitefield, son of an innkeeper, who was to become the most inspiring preacher of the age, and the brothers Wesley, sons of a country parson.

John Wesley (1703-91) was at first greatly influenced by Law, but there was little of the mystic in his religious composition. He was rather the born organiser, so determined to go his own way—or to follow his own inner light—that he separated from Whitefield in 1742 and eventually from the Church of England. This latter event was, of course, the natural result of his being refused the use of Church pulpits and having to take the Gospel to the fields and the mines. But it is interesting to observe that the hymn-writer Charles, who was less fanatical than his brother, was shocked by John's heresy in ordaining preachers and wrote the skittish verse:

> How easy now are Bishops made,
>   By man or woman's whim;
> Wesley his hands on Coke hath laid,
>   But who laid hands on him?

Wesley's *Journal* gives an intimate picture of the man and his works. For fifty years he rode about the country on horseback, preaching daily, largely in the open air, and often several times a day. He is said to have travelled 250,000 miles and to have preached 40,000 sermons. His influence on the poor, particularly on the miners of Wales and Cornwall, of the Midlands and Durham, was immense and lasting. There is a great deal of truth in the observation that Methodism in the early nineteenth century was one of the principal causes why the English poor, under the shadow of new industrial hardship, preferred constitutional methods to those of the French Revolution.

Charles Wesley (1707-88) was less of a leader than his brother but at least equally gifted in literature. His position as our leading hymn-writer is hardly disputable: not only was he splendidly prolific, writing more than 6,000 hymns, but his quality is shown in such famous examples as *Jesu, lover of my soul* and *Love divine, all loves excelling*. While some of the hymns are perhaps too full of bloody symbolism for a modern taste, they share that obsession with the sermons of John Wesley and with the extraordinary scenes that used to take place at Methodist conversions. The fanatical side was, of course, what made Methodism so disgusting to many contemporary observers; but it was the nobler, more rational side which lasted, to become one of the chief influences on English life and character in the nineteenth century.*

The various disputes in which the Methodists were engaged, both from outside and from within, produced many books and pamphlets but of no great importance in literature. (Wesley

---

* Blake was to write in his *Milton*:

He sent his two Servants, Whitefield and Wesley: were they Prophets,
Or were they Idiots or Madmen?—Show us Miracles!
Can you have greater Miracles than these? Men who devote
Their life's whole comfort to entire scorn and injury and death?
Awake! thou sleeper on the Rock of Eternity, Albion, awake!

himself wrote or edited over a hundred books, which proved so popular that he made £30,000 to spend on the poor.) A typical controversialist was Augustus Toplady, who attacked Wesley in *An Historic Proof of the Doctrinal Calvinism of the Church of England*. This is now a mere item in theological history, but the same man wrote *Psalms and Hymns for Public and Private Worship* (1776), a collection which contained the famous *Rock of ages, cleft for me*.

Religion and Philosophy

It was the general indifference to spiritual matters that the Methodist Movement chiefly attacked. There was little conscious scepticism among the body of the people until the turn of the century, but, as Wesley pointed out in his *Further Appeal to Men of Reason and Religion*, the indolence of the clergy was leading to some contempt for the Church as a whole. Among the "gentlemen-philosophers" the position had altered from the vague Deism of the Augustan Age to the more thorough-going criticism of such men as Hume and Gibbon. The Deist controversy in these circles—though Wesley was to claim that he had found Deists even among the ploughmen—had been more or less ended by the publication in 1736 of a remarkable book called *The Analogy of Religion, Natural and Revealed, to the Constitution and Course of Nature*, by Joseph Butler, later Bishop of Durham. Butler set out to show that there are no difficulties in the doctrines of religion not paralleled by those in the course of nature, and that the element of revelation in Christianity was inherently probable, even if not capable of logical proof. Such was the dignified moderation of the book that the one controversy that had threatened to disturb the Augustan religious peace was admitted to be closed in a thoroughly Augustan manner.

With the critical philosophy of David Hume (1711-76) we are in a world more familiar to the modern mind. As Johnson used common sense to destroy some of the academic theories of Augustan literary criticism, so Hume claimed that his philosophy was no more than the correction and systemisation of "reflections of common life". So far from setting up a philosophical system in the academic sense, the main purpose of his writings was to dispose of the inflated claims of his predecessors. Not only the metaphysicians, but the rationalist philosophers, were subjects of his sceptical approach; for he held that, in regard to such matters as the origin of the world and the existence of God, we have no knowledge and can have none; but if we want to know how to behave, we must consult our feelings. For Butler's "inherently probable" Christianity, Hume in his *Treatise on Human Nature* (1739-40) substituted the ingenious "orthodoxy" of desiring to "confound those dangerous friends or disguised enemies to the Christian religion who have undertaken to defend it by the principles of human reason. Our most holy religion is founded on faith, not on reason". Johnson remarked that Hume's style of writing was French—he had studied in France from 1734-7—and the tone of this "disguised enmity" is certainly like that of Voltaire.

Johnson's dislike of Hume is very natural. The two men shared a common-sense criticism of the more optimistic traits in Augustan philosophy—see, for example, the closing paragraphs of Chapter XXII of *Rasselas*—but where Hume adopted a fundamentally sceptical approach to religion, Johnson was always reverent and inclined to mysticism. Hume, too, like Gibbon, was an historian—his *History of Great Britain* (1754-61) was the first large-scale work of its kind—and between the mystical view of religion and the historical there is little common ground. In his essay on miracles, contained in *An Enquiry concerning Human Understanding* (1758), he argued that it was more probable that witnesses should lie, or be mistaken, than that miracles should actually have occurred. Johnson added that Hume was right in theory, but that "the Christian revelation is not proved by the miracles alone, but as connected with prophecies, and with the doctrines in confirmation of which the miracles were wrought".

The positive side of Hume's teaching is seen most clearly in his reflections upon the problem of comprehension. His stress upon feeling was part of that psychological approach which was to have so great an influence upon German philosophy—

though it was his contemporary David Hartley's *Observations on Man* (1749) which had the greater influence on Coleridge. In political thought, Hume has been called the Father of the Utilitarians; and in theology, however unsatisfactory some of his ideas may now seem, he at any rate cleared away misunderstandings about such controversial terms as Free Will and opened up more definite lines of enquiry. His chief critics in his own day were his fellow-Scotsmen Thomas Reid and James Beattie. A poet as well as a philosopher, Beattie and his work were much admired by Johnson.

CHAPTER VII

GRAY, COWPER, AND THE COUNTRY CHURCHYARD
1742-1785

> Night, sable Goddess! from her ebon throne,
> In rayless majesty, now stretches forth
> Her leaden sceptre o'er a slumb'ring world.
> > YOUNG: *Night Thoughts.*

> The Curfew tolls the knell of parting day,
> > The lowing herd wind slowly o'er the lea,
> The ploughman homeward plods his weary way,
> > And leaves the world to darkness and to me.
> > > GRAY: *Elegy.*

The Country Churchyard

There is a peculiar fitness in the fact that Gray's *Elegy* is the best remembered poem of the mid-eighteenth century. For not only is it a great poem in itself, it is representative of as much in the Age of Johnson as Pope's *Moral Essays* in the Augustan Age. Johnson's own *Vanity of Human Wishes,* we observed, has something of the dignified melancholy of this poem, and two widely-read minor works of tho 'forties— Young's *Night Thoughts* and Blair's *Grave*—prove how popular was the idea of a poet reflecting on mortality, "far from the madding crowd's ignoble strife". The Augustan Age was pre-eminently the age of the Town, satire on public affairs being perhaps the most typical literature; now in the 'forties begins the age of private meditation, not on contemporary men and events but on the universal themes of life and death. Augustan satire at its best could be universal, too, of course; and is chiefly valued now for that reason. But the fact remains that such typical pieces of Augustan literature as the *Dunciad* and the *Moral Essays* are packed with contemporary allusions, whereas in the *Elegy* and *Rasselas* and *Night Thoughts* it is the general rather than the particular, the universal rather than the contemporary, which engages the writer's attention. London was still the centre of the literary world, but in the 'forties we have the beginning of that conception of a poet as a recluse living in the country—and meditating in the churchyard after dusk—which was to gather strength after the Wordsworthian Revolution.

We should avoid, of course, making clear-cut distinctions. Pope's *Elegy to the Memory of an Unfortunate Lady* appears more typical of the Age of Johnson than of the Augustan Age; and Young and Blair were contemporaries of Pope who wrote the poems by which they are remembered in their closing years. The single decade 1742-51 saw the publication of the fourth book of the *Dunciad*, *Night Thoughts*, *The Grave*, the *Odes* of Collins, Thomson's *Castle of Indolence*, *The Vanity of Human Wishes*, and Gray's *Elegy*. The most we can say is that the *Dunciad* appears typical of the age that was closing, and the *Odes* and the *Elegy* of the age that was coming to birth.

Collins's ode on the death of Thomson, published in 1749, reminds us of the part played by the poet of *The Seasons* in this departure from the typical Augustan. Thomson meant more to the age of Gray and Collins than either Pope or Young. The idea of the poet as a "Druid", playing on his "airy harp" (see the quotation from Collins, p. 90 above), was not one likely to appeal to the coffee-house public. Wherever we mark the change, and we should remember that Thomson owed much to Pope and that both acknowledged the influence of Spenser, the change in the conception of the poet—from the Wit to the Druid, from the patron of the London coffee-house to the recluse meditating among the country tombs—was definite and lasting. (*The Recluse* was the original title of Wordsworth's unfinished philosophical poem, of which some gigantic fragments remain under the names of *The Prelude* and *The Excursion*.) Johnson was certainly a townsman, but most of his poetry belongs to his early years; he wrote little in verse after 1749.

The reference to "Druid" in Collins's poem is also an indication of that feeling for the British past which led to the work of Bishop Percy and Gilbert White, to Gothic Romance and Scott. The Augustans had been generally content to form their civilisation on what they conceived to be classical standards; there was little interesting to them between the old Rome and the new. Now begins a literary interest in the writers' country as a whole, in both time and space, an interest based on personal experience or antiquarian research. That it led to some foolish fashions may be granted, but the Augustan attitude to the past was sometimes equally foolish.

We have called this chapter after the most famous and the most representative poem of the age. We shall be considering, in turn, first Gray himself, then Collins and Cowper, besides minor poets such as Shenstone and Akenside. Young's *Night Thoughts* and Blair's *Grave* introduce the period, but, in contrast with Gray's *Elegy* and some of the poems of Collins and Cowper, they cannot be said to have more than historical interest now. *The Complaint; or Night Thoughts on Life, Death, and Immortality*—to give Young's poem its full title— was very popular for many years after its first appearance between 1742 and 1745, but it makes gloomy reading to-day. The blank verse, sprinkled with exclamation marks—

> A part how small of the terraqueous globe
> Is tenanted by Man! the rest a waste,
> Rocks, deserts, frozen seas, and burning sands!
> Wild haunts of monsters, poisons, stings, and death.
> Such is earth's melancholy map!

—is melodramatic rather than dramatic, having neither the metaphorical life of the Elizabethans nor the power of Milton. Johnson said that there are "very fine things" in *Night Thoughts*, and we have quoted (p. 162 above) the opening of the famous passage on procrastination which was probably one of those he had in mind; but the search for these things through the melancholy waste of moral commonplaces is a cure for the insomnia which the poet complains of at the opening of Night One.

The poem was occasioned by the death of Young's wife, and of the two children by her former marriage, within a short time of each other in 1741. But the cast of the poet's mind had been taken earlier, for in one of his first poems he speaks of his Muse as the Melancholy Maid,

> whom dismal scenes delight,
> Frequent at tombs, and in the realms of night.

He used to spend many hours walking among the graves in the churchyard at Welwyn, in Hertfordshire, where he was rector;* and used to have a lamp in his study made of a human skull with a candle stuck into it.

Robert Blair seems to have been a more lively figure, though his chief poem *The Grave* (1743) has a similar theme, expressed in similarly exclamation-marked blank verse. There is the same dismal relish as that of Young in the opening of his poem:

> the task be mine
> To paint the gloomy horrors of the tomb . . .

but occasionally we come across a more "Elizabethan" passage: for instance, the lines about "the petty tyrant":

> Now tame and humble, like a child that's whipp'd,
> Shakes hands with dust and calls the worm his kinsman;
> Nor pleads his rank and birthright. Under ground
> Precedency's a jest; vassal and lord,
> Grossly familiar, side by side consume.

Both of these productions of reflective melancholy continued to be read for more than fifty years; Blake engraved *Night Thoughts* for the edition of 1797 and *The Grave* for the edition of 1808.

Gray and the "Elegy"

Thomas Gray (1716-71) was born in London, and was educated at Eton and Peterhouse, Cambridge. In 1739 he started on a tour of France and Italy with his school-friend Horace Walpole, returning to London in 1741. The death of his father that year narrowed the family fortunes, and, giving

---

* Compare his younger contemporary James Hervey, whose *Meditations Among the Tombs* (1746) and *Contemplations on the Night* (1747) were inspired by similar rectorial musings among "the rude forefathers" in Northamptonshire.

up his intention to study the law, Gray passed some time with his mother at Stoke Poges, Buckinghamshire—the scene of the *Elegy*—afterwards returning to Cambridge, first to his old college and then to Pembroke. At Cambridge he remained for the rest of his life—varied by occasional visits to Stoke and several tours in England, notably in the Lake District—and in 1768 was made Professor of Modern History.

His first poems appeared anonymously in Dodsley's *Miscellany* in 1748. Two years later he sent the manuscript of the *Elegy* to Walpole, who seems to have circulated it so freely that some magazines got hold of it, and Gray was forced to send it to Dodsley for authorised printing. His first collection was the six pieces published in 1753 with designs by Richard Bentley, son of the scholar. Walpole issued the two "Pindaric Odes"—*The Progress of Poesy* and *The Bard*—from his private press at Strawberry Hill in 1757. Cibber had died the same year, and Gray was offered the Laureateship, which he declined; it was then bestowed on the minor poet and dramatist William Whitehead. A complete collection of Gray's poems did not appear till 1775.

It was in the early 'forties that he appears to have first applied himself seriously to poetry, producing in those years the *Ode to Spring*, the *Sonnet on the Death of Richard West*, the *Hymn to Adversity*, and the famous *Ode on a Distant Prospect of Eton College*. The *Sonnet on West* gained a somewhat undeserved notoriety when Wordsworth quoted it as an example of false poetic diction. We can agree with most of Wordsworth's general strictures, while claiming that Gray, even in this early poem, is comparatively free of the worst features of his age. It is much to his credit that he can refer, twice, to "the birds", not "the feather'd tribe" which was the eighteenth-century synonym.

The reaction of Wordsworth and Coleridge was necessary for the life of English poetry, and indeed it is surprising that it came so late, and that Wordsworth's early poems should have been written in the diction he was later to condemn. But a poetic style has to be judged by its successes, rather than by the average product of its practitioners. The

Elizabethan drama is not judged by *Titus Andronicus*, nor Augustan satire by the average product of Prior or the early Young. Johnson's *Vanity of Human Wishes* is one great poem written in the diction that produced so much verbiage; and Gray's *Elegy* is an even greater instance of a poet in command of a style that so frequently commanded him and others. Some of the favourite poetical expressions of the age—"mould'ring heap", "hoary-headed swain", "genial current", "sequester'd vale"—are not missing from the *Elegy*; but, in contrast with similar expressions in most other contemporary poems, they do not call attention to themselves, seeming here perfectly subordinated to the impressive theme. Poetry-writing was so popular in the eighteenth-century— perhaps partly due to the teaching of Latin verse at the grammar-schools—that many poems were written without any inner pressure at all. Gray here was evidently deep in his theme, so that he could write at leisure—the poem was begun some years before its completion in 1750—lines that give the impression of being composed on the spot. Its movement, furthermore, is so easy, so "inevitable", that modern readers, learning it at school perhaps forty years since, find many passages still in their memory. Such poems are rare enough in all periods, and are particularly rare in the eighteenth century because of the artificiality of the current diction.

The famous conclusion in Johnson's estimate of Gray's poetry is all the more impressive for the rigorous criticism that has gone before it:

> In the character of his *Elegy* I rejoice to concur with the common reader; for by the common sense of readers uncorrupted with literary prejudices, after all the refinements of subtlety and the dogmatism of learning, must be finally decided all claim to poetical honours. The *Churchyard* abounds with images which find a mirror in every mind, and with sentiments to which every bosom returns an echo . . . . Had Gray written often thus, it had been vain to blame, and useless to praise him.

Johnson singled out four stanzas near the close as being particularly original: "I have never seen the notions in any

other place; yet he that reads them here, persuades himself
that he has always felt them"—a phrase that can be applied
to all great poetry:

> Yet ev'n these bones from insult to protect
>   Some frail memorial still erected nigh,
> With uncouth rhymes and shapeless sculpture deck'd,
>   Implores the passing tribute of a sigh.
>
> Their name, their years, spelt by th' unletter'd muse,
>   The place of fame and elegy supply;
> And many a holy text around she strews,
>   That teach the rustic moralist to die.
>
> For who to dumb Forgetfulness a prey,
>   This pleasing anxious being e'er resign'd,
> Left the warm precincts of the cheerful day,
>   Nor cast one longing ling'ring look behind?
>
> On some fond breast the parting soul relies,
>   Some pious drops the closing eye requires;
> E'en from the tomb the voice of Nature cries,
>   E'en in our Ashes live their wonted Fires.

The power of the *Elegy* is at once the justification of the
churchyard musings of the age and of the poetic diction in
which so often they were embodied.   A poem of this stature
could support any number of lesser things, as Wordsworth's
Tintern Abbey his Goody Blakes and Harry Gills.

The Pindaric Odes

Gray's other poems have never enjoyed the same popularity.   The burlesque *Ode on the Death of a Favourite Cat*
has, of course, always been a favourite, but about the merits of
the later serious poems—particularly of the so-called
"Pindaric Odes"—there was controversy from the moment
they were published.   Johnson's is typical of one opinion:

> In 1757 he published *The Progress of Poesy* and
> *The Bard*, two compositions at which the readers of
> poetry were at first content to gaze in mute amazement.
> Some that tried them confessed their inability to under-
> stand them, though Warburton said that they were
> understood as well as the works of Milton and Shake-
> speare . . . Some hardy champions undertook to rescue

> them from neglect, and in a short time many were con-
> tent to be shown beauties which they could not see.*

The contrary opinion lays stress on Gray's originality here, pointing out that the heroic-couplet form was getting a little worn and that the admitted artificiality of these poems is countered by their magnificent rhetoric. The abrupt opening of *The Bard*—

> "Ruin seize thee, ruthless King!
> Confusion on thy banners wait . . ."

—was much admired by some contemporary readers; but Johnson observed that "technical beauties can give praise only to the inventor. It is in the power of any man to rush abruptly upon his subject, that has read the ballad of *Johnny Armstrong* . . .". He had made the same criticism, and the same comparison, in conversation in 1763, but had added that the next two lines in the ode—

> "Though fanned by Conquest's crimson wing
> They mock the air with idle state . . ."

—were "very good". Gray himself would have agreed with this criticism, for so far from considering himself an "inventor" he wished to bring back into poetry some of the virtues of the traditional songs and ballads. There had been a touch of patronage in the Augustan attitude to traditional literature, and Gray, who had studied Norse and Welsh poems and was to paraphrase some of them, was anxious to show that such things were worth taking quite seriously. The machinery of *The Bard* is admittedly too much in evidence, and in general Gray's eighteenth-century diction was not a suitable partner for his intended simplicity; but the common notion of him as in some sort the precursor of the romantic poets of the early nineteenth century is true, at any rate, of certain of his objectives, if his one supremely great poem is as typical of the Age of Johnson as Johnson himself.

* Compare Hazlitt, writing forty years later: "Gray's Pindaric Odes are, I believe, generally given up at present: they are stately and pedantic, a kind of methodical borrowed frenzy". (*Lectures on the English Poets.*)

It was Matthew Arnold who wrote that "Gray, a born poet, fell upon an age of prose . . . Gray, with the qualities of mind and soul of a genuine poet, was isolated in his century". This was part of Arnold's attempt to divide poetry composed in the wits, like Dryden's and Pope's, from "genuine poetry—conceived and composed in the soul". The distinction has not really the value which Arnold placed upon it; he must, furthermore, have realised that Gray's greatest achievement was the *Elegy* and that this poem, so far from falling on stony ground, had been received with acclamation from the start, being praised in the highest terms by Gray's severest critic. A poet cannot be considered isolated if his greatest poem is praised on all sides by his contemporaries—Wordsworth for the first forty years of his life was far more isolated—and even the offering of the Laureateship is some indication of the esteem in which Gray was held. Arnold, then, could not choose the *Elegy* as witness to his argument; he chose instead *The Progress of Poesy*, whose "evolution", he wrote, "must be accounted not less noble and sound than its style".

He probably had Johnson's disparagement in mind when choosing this poem as illustration, but he seems to have missed the point that Johnson was defending his own opinion against the praise that the Pindaric Odes had received from others. Warburton, the friend and editor of Pope, had admired them; Boswell and Mrs Thrale had expressed their disagreement from Johnson in this respect; and Cowper was to think Gray "the only poet since Shakespeare entitled to the character of sublime". So Arnold was in the somewhat paradoxical position of seeking to defend a poet whose works, including the one he singled out, had pleased some of the most representative figures of the age. His opinion of the style of *The Progress of Poesy* as "noble and sound" would have met with the approval of these representatives of "an age of prose". Few poems of Gray's have, in fact, more "eighteenth-century diction"; and the reminiscences of Milton—for instance,

Till the sad Nine in Greece's evil hour
Left their Parnassus for the Latin plains—

are common to a good deal of the minor poetry of the period.

Gray, furthermore, looked to Dryden as his master: "If there is any excellence in my numbers," he acknowledged, "I have learnt it wholly from that great poet." The utmost we can say in agreement with Arnold is that Gray, though severely criticised by Wordsworth, did anticipate some aspects of the Wordsworthian Revolution: he sought to get away from the influence of the heroic couplet (it was probably Dryden's other poems, especially *Alexander's Feast*, which he particularly admired); he had an appreciation of the easier movement of the traditional ballads; and his reaction from the satirical poetry of the coffee-house—his position in the country churchyard, to put it symbolically—was a precursor of Wordsworth among his native mountains and the shy Tennyson hiding in the Isle of Wight. We can still speak of "eighteenth-century poetic diction", but there had grown up a different conception of the poet to that prevailing in the Augustan Age, a conception which was to wait till Wordsworth and Coleridge for definition in theory and for more suitable expression in practice.*

The Poetry of Collins

There is a grim jest in the fact that the eighteenth century, often considered the Age of Reason, saw no less than three great writers—Swift, Collins, Cowper—who lost their reason at some stage of their lives; another great writer, Johnson, who suffered from melancholy and was in constant dread of

* Gray, of course, as his letters make plain, was a man of more varied interests than could be imagined from most of his poems. That he could have written of public affairs in the spirit of Churchill, if not of Pope, can be seen from his fragment against Lord Holland (father of Fox) which contains the lines:

Ah, said the sighing Peer, had Bute been true,
　　Nor Murray's, Rigby's, Bedford's friendship vain,
Far better scenes than these had bless'd our view,
　　And realised the beauties which we feign.
Purg'd by the sword, and purified by fire,
　　Then had we seen proud London's hated walls.
Owls would have hooted in St Peter's choir,
　　And foxes stunk and litter'd in St Paul's.

The energy of those lines can hardly be matched in Churchill, and perhaps throws a new light on Gray's acknowledgment to Dryden.

becoming insane; besides a minor poet, Christopher Smart, who wrote his best verse in an asylum; a Scottish poet, Fergusson, who died in a similar institution; and one of the greatest of poets, Blake, who was thought mad by some of the worldly-wise but was only mad north-north-west and knew a Michael Angelo from a Reynolds. Whereas the early nineteenth century, the romantic era when it became the fashion for poets to be a little delirious, saw few of such melancholy cases.

William Collins (1721-59) was born at Chichester, educated at Winchester and Oxford, and—surprisingly enough, for a poet whom we associate with country themes—led for some years a precarious literary existence in London. According to his friend Gilbert White, he "commenced a man of the town, spending his time in all the dissipation of Ranelagh, Vauxhall, and the playhouses; and was romantic enough to suppose that his superior abilities would draw the attention of the great world, by means of whom he was to make his fortune". But he was less successful in this ambition than his master Thomson, lacking perhaps the ease in society that seems to have been the inborn gift of so many eighteenth-century Scotsmen. His *Persian Eclogues* came out in 1742, followed by his chief work, *Odes on several Descriptive and Allegoric Subjects*, in 1747. Two years later came the *Ode occasioned by the Death of Mr Thomson*, part of which we quoted at the close of our chapter on Augustan Poetry.

There has been little controversy over the relative merits of his not very extensive output. The *Eclogues*, which he himself did not much admire, contain some interesting passages, but so immersed in the dullest of eighteenth-century verbiage that they hardly repay the labour of searching for them. It is the *Odes* on which his reputation rests, and particularly perhaps the *Ode to Evening*, the *Ode on Thomson*, and the short *Ode written in the beginning of the year 1746*:

> How sleep the Brave, who sink to Rest,
> By all their Country's Wishes blest!
> When Spring, with dewy Fingers cold,
> Returns to deck their hallow'd Mould,

> She there shall dress a sweeter Sod
> Than Fancy's Feet have ever trod.
>
> By Fairy Hands their knell is rung,
> By Forms unseen their Dirge is sung;
> There Honour comes, a Pilgrim grey,
> To bless the Turf that wraps their Clay,
> And Freedom shall awhile repair,
> To dwell a weeping Hermit there!

This poem was occasioned by the battle of Fontenoy, where the French in 1745 defeated a combined force of British and Dutch. It is remarkable chiefly for the delicate, individual feeling which Collins has brought to what is so often a subject treated in a dull, formal manner. He uses, we observe, some of the stock imagery of the period, but in so fresh a way that the poem is hardly more affected by it than is Gray's much greater elegy. Collins's *Dirge in Cymbeline* has something of the same quality.

The reference to "fairy hands" in *How sleep the Brave*, as to "Druid", "harp", and "fairy valleys" in the *Ode on Thomson*, is part of that aspect of Collins which annoyed some contemporary observers but which found greater favour in the Victorian Age. ("He loved fairies, genii, giants, and monsters," wrote Johnson in his sympathetic *Life*; "the grandeur of wildness, and the novelty of extravagance, were always desired by him, but not always attained.") It comes mainly from the imitation of Spenser, which Gilbert West had originated, for Thomson, Collins, and also Shenstone, to follow; and is, of course, allied to the general feeling for our older literature which produced the enthusiasm for the traditional ballads. Sometimes in Collins it is absurdly artificial, as in the line "To hear a British shell" in the *Ode to Pity*. This "shell" is not of the military kind, but is an antiquarianism for "music" or "poetry", the word being roughly synonymous with "lyre". The excessive alliteration, which Johnson found a defect in Gray, is really more true of Collins; even in the *Ode to Evening*, commonly considered his best poem, we have the "short shrill shriek" of the "weak-ey'd bat", three "s"s of great charge which might perhaps be defended on onomatopoeic grounds. "Warbled wand'rings", "future feet", "hermit heart", "mingled murmurs", "servile scene", all occur, paradoxically enough, in the *Ode to Simplicity*. Alliteration was, of course, a feature of the old ballads, and is common in Elizabethan drama, but in verse meant to be *read*—not sung or spoken aloud—it becomes less effective the more it is used.

"Nymphs" occur frequently in the *Odes*, chiefly as personifications of the subject in hand. The "nymph reserv'd" of the *Ode to Evening* is the most attractive example, recalling to the modern reader some of the symbols in Blake's *Poetical Sketches*:

> If aught of Oaten Stop, or Pastoral Song,
> May hope, O pensive Eve, to soothe thine Ear,
>   Like thy own solemn springs,
>   Thy Springs, and dying Gales,
>
> O Nymph reserv'd, while now the bright-hair'd Sun
> Sits in yon western Tent, whose cloudy Skirts,
>   With Brede ethereal wove,
>   O'erhang his wavy Bed . . .

It is a charming movement, in both the original and the modern meaning of the word "charm"; "oaten stop" is a typical Collins Spenserianism for "flute" or "pipe", but it does not especially hold us up as we surrender to the "pastoral song". What is remarkable is that Collins manages to evoke this willing surrender without the aid of rhyme, this being one of the few lyrics in English—Blake's *Seasons* and Tennyson's *Tears, Idle Tears* are others—which dispense with rhyme altogether. The alliteration, therefore, has to be more subtle than in the *Ode to Simplicity*, so as to maintain the rhythm; and in general this is so, though "rudely rends thy robes", in the penultimate verse, is an unfortunate exception.

Considering the superiority of the *Odes* to the *Eclogues*, Collins might well have achieved greater things had he not become insane at the age of thirty, to die eight years afterwards. Almost as with Keats, we have to judge him by what would normally have been his "juvenile" work. Keats wrote his best poems in the few years before he died at the age of twenty-five; Collins wrote most of his *Odes* at the age of twenty-five or twenty-six. It was no doubt a consciousness of this, as much as his sympathy with the poet's insanity and the memories of friendship, that led Johnson to give so kindly a portrait of Collins in the *Lives of the Poets*.

Minor Poets of the Period

The minor poets contemporary with Gray and Cowper can be read in the collection to which Johnson wrote his famous prefaces or in the volumes of Dodsley's *Miscellany*. Several mainly self-educated poets—the farm-labourer Stephen Duck, the sailor William Falconer, Robert Dodsley himself—exist side by side in these collections, or others, with aristocrats like Chesterfield and Lyttelton. The "democracy" which we noted in the Johnson circle, public and private, was thus well maintained on the lower slopes of the contemporary Parnassus.

The imitations of Spenser produced by Gilbert West were praised by Johnson for "the excellence of the sentiments", but the critic observed that works of this kind can never claim the merit of original genius, "because their effect is local and temporary; they appeal not to reason but to memory, and presuppose an accidental or artificial state of mind. An imitation of Spenser is nothing to a reader, however acute, by whom Spenser has never been perused". Johnson might have added that Spenser's style was archaic when he wrote it, and was criticised for its "old rustic language" by his friend Sidney and for its obsolete nature by Johnson's namesake Ben. So the eighteenth-century imitations of Spenser are really imitations of imitations, old poetry at two removes.

Nevertheless, the Spenserian stanza was Spenser's own invention, and in an age when the heroic couplet was getting rather worn, and when few poets could manage blank verse with more than moderate ability, its revival was well worth while. It was to have its successes with Keats, and though nothing Spenserian in the eighteenth century can quite equal the romantic charm of *The Eve of St Agnes*, Thomson's *Castle of Indolence* and Shenstone's *Schoolmistress* are poems better worth reading than the minor heroic couplets of the period. Their chief weakness is the uncertainty of the poets as to how seriously their acknowledged imitations were to be taken. In the advertisement to *The Castle of Indolence*, Thomson writes: "This poem being writ in the manner of Spenser, the obsolete words, and a simplicity of diction in some of the lines, which borders on the ludicrous, were necessary to make the imitation more perfect". Thomson had little idea of true simplicity in language, but his poem has some of Spenser's minor virtues, if the vigour of *The Fairie Queene* was beyond his power.

William Shenstone (1714-63) began *The Schoolmistress* merely as a parody, and the complete version—usually quoted from the extended second edition of 1748—still bears traces of the author's uncertainty of intention. The archaic language—"I ween", "y-gazing", "thilk wight", "sorely shent"—is laid on with a trowel, but has its entertaining qualities, as in the passage where the village schoolmistress, having birched one unruly boy, treats the class to "sugared cates" and "ginger-bread y-rare":

> See to their seats they hye with merry glee,
> And in beseemly order sitten there;
> All but the wight of bum y-galled, he
> Abhorreth bench, and stool, and fourm, and chair . . .

Johnson's general criticism remains, however, sound; and we should remember that Keats, the most original of the later users of the Spenserian stanza, became dissatisfied with it. For certain purposes—chiefly the narration of a romantic story—the Spenserian stanza is the best; and judging by the merits of *The Eve of St Agnes* it is better for a poet to treat it seriously—with whatever later reservations—than with the half-parody of Thomson and Shenstone.

Shenstone's poem is further limited by the discrepancy between his archaic language and his contemporary subject. (It is perhaps significant that Goldsmith's lines about the village schoolmaster have always been more popular.) *The Castle of Indolence* and *The Eve of St Agnes* take place in the Never-Never-Land of Gothic Romance; but for Shenstone to tackle a contemporary theme and an everyday character in an idiom (even in the country) more than half obsolete was surely an initial mistake from which the poem hardly recovers. There is sufficient of Goldsmith's observation in *The School-mistress* for us to wish that Shenstone had been brave enough to tackle a "low" subject in a straightforward manner.

It was a natural error of nineteenth-century criticism to look mainly in the eighteenth century for precursors of the Romantic Revival. When taken as far as Arnold sometimes took it, this was tantamount to a rejection of much of the century's poetry altogether, or at best a classing of it as inferior poetry "conceived and composed in the wits". A more satisfactory view is to recognise the diversity of a reader's moods, to consider Pope, for instance, as equally great in his own field as Shakespeare and Wordsworth in others. Nevertheless, there is something in Gray, we observed, that leads on to Wordsworth, and no admirer of *Tintern Abbey* and *The Prelude* can fail to notice the Wordsworthian quality—the "emotion recollected in tranquillity"—of these lines from Mark Akenside's *Pleasures of the Imagination*:

> O ye Northumbrian shades, which overlook
> The rocky pavement and the mossy falls
> Of solitary Wensbeck's limpid stream;
> How gladly I recall your well-known seats
> Beloved of old, and that delightful time
> When all alone, for many a summer's day,
> I wander'd through your calm recesses, led
> In silence by some powerful hand unseen.
>   Nor will I e'er forget you; nor shall e'er
> The graver tasks of manhood, or the advice
> Of vulgar wisdom, move me to disclaim
> Those studies which possess'd me in the dawn
> Of life, and fix'd the colour of my mind
> For every future year . . .

The resemblance to Wordsworth is extraordinary, both in some of the actual phrases—"the graver tasks of manhood . . ."—and in the general movement of the verse. It is just possible that Wordsworth was unacquainted with Akenside's work, but more likely that it was among the influential reading of his youth. Akenside was a fellow-northerner, born in

1721, the son of a Newcastle butcher, and dying in the year of Wordsworth's birth, 1770. His chief poem is the one quoted, a lengthy work first published in 1744 and revised in 1757. It has not the sustained interest of *The Prelude*, but, considering the period when it was written, it is remarkably free from that poetic verbiage which Wordsworth and Coleridge were to condemn.

Boswell records the following conversation between Johnson and the musician Dr Burney:

> BURNEY: "How does poor Smart do, Sir; is he likely to recover?" JOHNSON: "It seems as if his mind had ceased to struggle with the disease; for he grows fat upon it." BURNEY: "Perhaps, Sir, that may be from want of exercise." JOHNSON: "No, Sir; he has partly as much exercise as he used to have, for he digs in the garden. Indeed, before his confinement, he used for exercise to walk to the alehouse; but he was *carried* back again. I did not think he ought to be shut up. His infirmities were not noxious to society. He insisted on people praying with him; and I'd as lief pray with Kit Smart as anyone else . . ."

The subject of this conversation—Christopher Smart (1722-91)—was sincerely pitied for his affliction by Johnson and others, but few of his contemporaries had any use for his poetry. Johnson, indeed, on being questioned by the Shakespearian critic Morgann as to whether he reckoned Derrick or Smart the better poet, replied that "there is no settling the point of precedency between a louse and a flea". The poetry of Samuel Derrick, an early friend of Johnson's in his journalistic years in London, is now forgotten and may well have been as "lousy" as Johnson claimed; but Smart's poetry, particularly that written after his confinement in 1756, is now often considered among the best of the minor verse of the period.

A Song to David and *Rejoice in the Lamb* were the principal poems composed in the asylum. Undoubtedly Johnson was right in his conviction that the poet ought not to have been shut up, for these poems appear to be proof that Smart's 'madness" was no more than a moderate attack of what the irreligious world calls religious mania. The Bible was his chief reading, and the language of the Authorised Version is fortunately the same as that of Shakespeare. Though Smart in these poems is recognisably eighteenth century, he has a vocabulary and an idiom that sometimes suggest the Elizabethan rather than the Augustan. There is, of course, a comic touch about these poems, and Mason can be excused for writing to Gray: "I have seen his *Song to David* and thence concluded him as mad as ever". (Southey came to much the same conclusion over Blake.) But consider, not only the comic aspect, but the remarkable imagery, and the economy of expression, of these typical stanzas from the *Song*:

> Strong is the lion—like a coal
> His eyeball—like a bastion's mole
>   His chest against the foes:
> Strong the gier-eagle on his sail,
> Strong against tide, th' enormous whale
>   Emerges, as he goes.
>
> But stronger still, in earth and air,
> And in the sea, the man of pray'r:
>   And far beneath the tide;
> And in the seat to faith assign'd,
> Where ask is have, where seek is find,
>   Where knock is open wide.

William Cowper

Born in 1731, the year that Johnson left Oxford, Cowper lived to the last year of the eighteenth century, his poetry belonging mainly to the 'seventies and 'eighties. His personal life resembles in its misfortune both Collins's and Smart's; his poetry is among the last of any merit, in which a writer of original if not striking genius expressed himself in a vein of Johnsonian reflection, if not in conventional eighteenth-century diction.

His sorrows seem to have come, from the very first, not in single spies but in battalions. The son of a Hertfordshire clergyman, he lost his mother at the age of six* and was

* She was, it is interesting to observe, a descendant of the poet Donne, and from her family is descended the great Dorsetshire novelist Mr T. F. Powys.

shortly afterwards so bullied at the first boarding-school he was sent to that he had to be taken away. He appears to have dwelt with more than normal sensitivity on these troubles which he refers to in his poems and letters in later life—for instance, in *Tirocinium*, where he attacks the brutality of boarding-schools, and in the poem *On the Receipt of my Mother's Picture out of Norfolk*:

> My mother! when I learnt that thou wast dead,
> Say, wast thou conscious of the tears I shed?
> Hover'd thy spirit o'er thy sorrowing son,
> Wretch even then, life's journey just begun?
> I heard the bell toll'd on thy burial day,
> I saw the hearse that bore thee slow away,
> And, turning from my nursery window, drew
> A long, long sigh, and wept a last adieu!

After spending a slightly happier eight years at Westminster School, he was articled to an attorney in London, being called to the Bar in 1754. He had spent much time at his uncle's house in the Strand, in the company of his two cousins Harriet and Theodora; but when he asked his uncle's consent to his engagement to Theodora, permission was refused and the cousins were no longer allowed to meet nor even to correspond.

About this time he lost his father, and his best friend was drowned while bathing in the Thames. His spirits appear to have been totally depressed by this three-fold loss, and when he was required to appear before the House of Lords—a mere formality necessary to secure a post there as Clerk of the Journals—he felt himself incapable of standing the examination, attempted in a fit of despair to commit suicide, and had to be confined for a time in an asylum at St Albans. His "madness" was no doubt mere depression at first, caused by a series of misfortunes coming on top of one another; and two years later he was normal enough to settle at Huntingdon in the care of a retired clergyman, Morley Unwin, and his wife Mary. On Unwin's death, Cowper and Mrs Unwin went to live in the nearby village of Olney, where their friend John Newton was vicar; they remained there nearly twenty years, subsequently moving to another village close by until Mrs Unwin's death in 1796.*

At St Albans, Cowper seems to have undergone a kind of religious conversion. At first fancying himself, by a species of Calvinistic doctrine, to be among the wretches for whom nothing was to be hoped either in this world or the next, he seems to have moved out of that slough of despond into a somewhat airier region where he was able to take comfort from the assurances of the New Testament. His happier life at Huntingdon confirmed him in this view; but the influence of the extraordinary preacher Newton—a former slave-trader, converted to the most intense form of Evangelicalism—cast him back again on his old Calvinistic doubts. The disadvantage—to speak mildly—of the strict Genevan creed is that the less sensitive souls, such as Burns's "Holy Willie", become convinced of their election, while the ultra sensitive, like Bunyan and Cowper, are liable to consider themselves damned from the creation of the world to all eternity. Newton no doubt thought himself saved, without the trial of the desert island suffered by his fictional counterpart Crusoe, but Cowper still had the idea that his early misfortunes had been the result of his sins. In 1773 he sank again into insanity.

The association with Newton, however, led to their collaboration in the *Olney Hymns* (1779), one of the classics of Evangelical literature. Newton's contributions include *How sweet the name of Jesus sounds* and *Glorious things of thee are spoken*; Cowper's include *Hark, my soul, it is the Lord* and —most poignant of the hymns—

> God moves in a mysterious way
> His wonders to perform;
> He plants His footsteps in the sea,
> And rides upon the storm . . .

---

* Characteristically, Cowper blamed himself for her fatal illness:

> Thy spirits have a fainter glow,
> I see thee daily weaker grow;
> 'Twas my distress that brought thee low,
>   My Mary!

These hymns have the impressive simplicity of Charles Wesley's; and in general, though much of it was ephemeral, the literature of the eighteenth-century Evangelicals was no less admirable in its way than their propaganda against the slave-trade.

Much of the space in Cowper's *Poems* (1782) is given to eight satires: *The Progress of Error, Truth, Table Talk, Expostulation, Hope, Charity, Conversation,* and *Retirement.* The comparison between Voltaire and the humble cottager is typical of their style:

> O happy peasant! O unhappy bard!
> His the mere tinsel, hers the rich reward;
> He praised, perhaps, for ages yet to come,
> She never heard of half a mile from home:
> He lost in errors his vain heart prefers,
> She safe in the simplicity of hers.

Such "satire" needs the qualifying inverted commas. Cowper's very virtues inhibited him from the satirical; he was incapable of feeling a greater anger against Voltaire than that common to the most ordinary tract-writer. (Contrast the zest of Blake's epigrams against Voltaire and Rousseau.) The mild genius which makes so genuinely moving some of the *Olney Hymns* was a disqualification here. Cowper had humour—witness his letters and the ballad of *John Gilpin*—but in a purely Pickwickian sense; he had no scorn in his composition, not even the righteous scorn of a Goldsmith or a Dickens. He had no gift for the epigram, nor for the sudden flash of wit that illumines the dullest stretches of his friend Churchill. Compared with Pope—where every word, every cadence, tells—both his language and his movement are slack and unenterprising. It is significant that, though Hazlitt called his satire "excellent", he has not usually been regarded as a satirical poet at all. Perhaps his nearest approach to the satirical is in some parts of *The Task*; for instance in *The Garden*, lines 133-54.

To Lady Austen, a friend of Cowper's at Olney, we owe the original conception of both *John Gilpin* and *The Task.* She told him the Gilpin story one evening, to rouse him out of one of his recurring fits of melancholy, and he put it into verse the following morning; and on his complaining that he could not find a subject for the blank-verse poem she had urged him to write, she exclaimed—perhaps with recollections of Crébillon—"Oh, you can write upon anything: write a poem upon this sofa". Cowper took her at her word—as his mother's descendant T. F. Powys was to take a very similar exclamation by his brother Llewelyn—and the first part of *The Task* to which she had set him was duly called *The Sofa*, in which he meditates on the effect of luxury and the increase of wealth rather in the style, though not with the force, of Goldsmith in *The Deserted Village*. From *The Sofa* he turned to *The Timepiece*, and thence to *The Garden*, *The Winter Evening*, *The Winter Morning Walk*, and *The Winter Walk at Noon*. *The Timepiece* contains the famous lines: "England, with all thy faults, I love thee still . . ."; *The Garden* has the comparison between himself and the stricken deer:

> I was a stricken deer that left the herd
> Long since; with many an arrow deep infixed
> My panting side was charged, when I withdrew
> To seek a tranquil death in distant shades.
> There was I found by One who had Himself
> Been hurt by the archers. In His side He bore,
> And in His hands and feet, the cruel scars.
> With gentle force soliciting the darts,
> He drew them forth, and healed and bade me live.
> Since then, with few associates, in remote
> And silent woods I wander, far from those
> My former partners of the peopled scene . . .

and also the defence of his altruism against the worldly-wise philosopher:

> What's the world to you?
> Much. I was born of woman, and drew milk,
> As sweet as charity, from human breasts.
> I think, articulate, I laugh and weep,
> And exercise all functions of a man.
> How then should I and any man that lives
> Be strangers to each other?

Such passages are the most eloquent in Cowper, and there is no doubt that *The Task*—published in 1785, together with

Gilpin and *Tirocinium*—is much the best of his lengthier works. It bears an obvious relation, in its dignified melancholy and didactic mood, to the central theme of this chapter, but Cowper—as some tearful quotations have already shown— also has a connection with the contemporary cult of sensibility. In Jane Austen's *Sense and Sensibility*, Cowper's poetry is among the favourite reading of Marianne Dashwood, a girl of seventeen to whom ruined castles and falling leaves are provocative of the most tender emotions. That the meditations in the country churchyard should have led, among other things, to a "passion for dead leaves"—as Elinor Dashwood describes her sister's sensations—is not very surprising; and part of Cowper's historical importance is that he was one of the chief links between the two.

We end this chapter with the year of his last important publication, that of 1785. In the remaining fifteen years of his life, he produced some interesting shorter poems—among them two of his best, *Yardley Oak* and *The Castaway*—as well as a translation of Homer. The "destined wretch" of *The Castaway* is less Alexander Selkirk than Cowper himself; and this persistence on the personal is one of the reasons why he is as much a poet of romantic sentiment as of Johnsonian reflection.

CHAPTER VIII

SENSE AND SENSIBILITY

1759-1796

> "In the meantime, we will philosophise and senti-
> mentalise—the last word is a bright insertion of the
> moment, which was written for yours and Dr Johnson's
> service—and you shall sit in my study and take a peep
> into the world as into a showbox and amuse yourself
> as I present the pictures to your imagination. Thus
> will I teach you to love its follies, to pity its errors and
> detest its injustice—and I will introduce you among
> the rest to some tender-hearted damsel on whose cheeks
> some bitter affliction has placed a tear, and having heard
> her story you shall take a white handkerchief from your
> pocket and wipe the moisture from her eyes and your
> own."
>
> <div align="right">STERNE: <i>Letters.</i></div>

Sentiment in the Age of Reason

It would be interesting to know whether the sale of pocket
handkerchiefs greatly increased about the middle of the
eighteenth century. There were tears in literature before,
of course, but not until the 'forties and 'fifties of the so-called
Age of Reason was there any deliberate cult of sentimentality,
of luxuriating in emotion for emotion's sake. There were
touches of sentiment in the time of the Augustans, in the
comedies of Steele, for example, and in some of the Coverley
Papers; but the overriding impulse of the Augustans was
away from such emotional enthusiasm and towards classical
decorum in every aspect of life and literature.

Richardson is often called the "inventor" of Sensibility
with a capital S; and certainly the amount of tears shed by
readers of *Clarissa*, both here and on the Continent, was greater
than that provoked by any previous work of literature. The
book that was to send the next generation fumbling in their
pockets, Rousseau's *Nouvelle Héloise*, was frankly imitated

from *Clarissa*, which also influenced, we observed, the cult of romantic fiction in Germany. But no one writer, obviously, could have "invented" such an emotion; it was in the air, quite as much as were the churchyard meditations which, in some degree, led on to it. If we seek an "inventor" of the most deliberate, most calculated, form of sentimental indulgence, we can more accurately point to Sterne than to Richardson; and this chapter, for want of any more precise indication, is dated from the year of composition of the first volumes of *Tristram Shandy*.

We should remember that Augustan Reason could tolerate a good deal of political corruption and a penal code that was as harsh as it was unreasonable; and that, among the clauses of that Treaty of Utrecht which Swift and Prior were so proud of, was the infamous Asiento agreement, whereby England obtained a thirty years' monopoly of the slave trade to Spanish America. However foolish some of the aspects of sensibility may have been, it often went along with a genuine desire for social reform, at home and abroad. If *Shandy* is one side of the sentimental coin, the prison reforms of Howard and the propaganda against the slave trade, by Cowper and Wilberforce and their colleagues, are the reverse.

Sterne and "Tristram Shandy"

The literary career of Laurence Sterne, like that of Richardson twenty years before, occupied only the last decade of an uneventful life. Born in 1713, and dying of consumption in 1768, his literary activity was confined to the volumes of *Tristram Shandy* (1760-7) and its smaller companion *A Sentimental Journey* (1768), besides several volumes of sermons (1760 onward) and the posthumously-published letters. Some of the sermons and letters antedate this decade, and for a full understanding of the Shandean sensibility some knowledge of the earlier life is probably necessary.

Sterne's ancestry, as we should be inclined to guess from a reading of *Tristram*, was both military and clerical. His father, a lieutenant in an infantry regiment, was one of the grandsons of Richard Sterne, Archbishop of York in the reign of James II. The lieutenant, who seems to have been the double model for Mr Shandy and My Uncle Toby, had married the daughter of a suttler—a man responsible for regimental provisions—and Laurence Sterne was born at his mother's Irish home and spent the first ten years of his life in various barracks. He entered holy orders in 1736, held several livings in Yorkshire, and up to the age of forty-seven led the typical life of an eighteenth-century country parson. "Books, painting, fiddling, and shooting," he wrote, "were my amusements."

The publication of the first two volumes of *Tristram Shandy*, on the first of January 1760, brought a complete change in his circumstances. The oddity of the book caused a great sensation in London, and when Sterne made a personal appearance and it was found that the author was no less odd, his reputation for eccentricity was established. There is no doubt that he traded on this reputation, particularly in his relations with lady admirers; and that he was determined to keep it on the boil by issuing the various parts of *Tristram* in small instalments through the years. The first two volumes quickly went into a second edition; he announced a collection of *Sermons of Mr Yorick*; and by the end of January 1761 two more volumes of *Tristram* were ready, the author again following his manuscript to London and sharing personally in the applause. Other volumes appeared regularly, till the first collected edition of 1767. Its minor companion, *A Sentimental Journey through France and Italy by Mr Yorick*, was the outcome of a tour he had vainly taken for his health; it came out three weeks before he died. The final volumes of the *Sermons* were issued to a mourning public the year after.

The full title of *Tristram* is *The Life and Opinions of Tristram Shandy, Gent.*, and it has been observed that this is Sterne's initial jest, since the book mostly concerns the life of the gent's uncle and the opinions of the gent's father. The jest would, admittedly, have been characteristic; but it is more likely that Sterne originally had the determination to write a book on the scale of the old romances, and to spin it out he began, not as Dickens was to do in *Copperfield* with the hero's birth, but with his conception, nine months before. Tristram remains unborn during the greater part of the book as we have it, and this delay, while affording Sterne openings for a good deal of bawdy humour, also gives him the opportunity to develop at length the characters of Mr Shandy and My Uncle Toby.

The technique of the book reminds a modern reader of Joyce's *Ulysses* (as it would have reminded an Elizabethan reader of Nashe's *Pierce Penilesse*). Joyce is more subtle, but Sterne's eccentric typography, his dashes and asterisks and blank spaces, bear a close relation to the unpunctuated dialogue and other technical devices used and misused in *Ulysses*. The legend of the books' massive size is also similar. Sterne probably intended to write a work of great length, but *Tristram* as we have it, in spite of its being originally issued in nine volumes, is only a moderately-sized novel. (In the *Everyman* edition, it occupies one volume, to *Amelia's* two and *Clarissa's* four.) The typographical eccentricities make it seem much longer than it really is, as they do *Ulysses*, which is not so long as an average novel by Dickens. To support the legend of *Ulysses'* formidable length, it was printed in the same style as popular annuals for boys, as *Tristram* was originally published with excessively wide margins. These were no doubt useful for making notes, as the gross shape of *Ulysses* used to make it possible to slip the banned book past His Majesty's Customs disguised as the Bible appointed to be read in churches.

To ban any book is doubtful tactics, but from the strictly moral point of view *Ulysses* was less deserving of official damnation than *Tristram*. Sterne's indecency has found few defenders; from the first it was recognised as too pervasive and prurient to stand comparison with the occasional and frank bawdiness of a Chaucer or a Fielding. His reply to the lady who told him she had heard that there were some things in his books not fit for women to read—that there was nothing more to it than the antics of her child playing on the carpet and innocently showing more than is usually shown—was an extremely poor defence. His indecency is the reverse of innocent, the effect being carefully calculated in advance.

His famous sensibility, though equally calculated, is not so much to be condemned. The modern reader is inclined to feel, as with similar passages in Dickens, that Sterne has simply spoilt his tenderness by insisting too much on it. The celebrated passage in *Tristram*, about the death of the old soldier Le Fever, has been carefully prepared by a number of previous incidents: for example, My Uncle Toby's proverbial characteristic of not being able to hurt a fly:

> Go—says he, one day at dinner, to an overgrown one which had buzzed about his nose, and tormented him cruelly all dinner-time,—and which after infinite attempts, he had caught at last, as it flew by him;—I'll not hurt thee, says my uncle Toby, rising from his chair, and going across the room, with the fly in his hand,—I'll not hurt a hair of thy head:—Go, says he, lifting up the sash, and opening his hand as he spoke, to let it escape;—go, poor devil, get thee gone, why should I hurt thee? This world surely is wide enough to hold both thee and me.

There is observation and humour in this passage as well as calculated sentiment. When Sterne goes on—"I was but ten years old when this happened . . ."—the probability of the incident having been based on personal experience is increased. He had spent his childhood in barracks, and though it seems comical for professional soldiers to be so tender in their feelings that they would not willingly hurt a fly, such paradoxes have been known in real life.

The actual death of Le Fever, like that of Poor Joe in Dickens's *Bleak House* ("Dead, your Majesty. Dead, my lords and gentlemen . . .") is, as we say, rather spoilt in its effect by the author's excess of sentimentality. Only a little less striving for tears would have made the scene more genuinely affecting. It is not one of Sterne's complete failures; it is rather one of his near misses:

> You shall go home directly, Le Fever, said my uncle Toby, to my house,—and we'll send for a doctor to see what's the matter,—and we'll have an apothecary,—

and the corporal shall be your nurse;—and I'll be your servant, Le Fever.

There was a frankness in my uncle Toby,—not the effect of familiarity,—but the cause of it,—which let you at once into his soul, and showed you the goodness of his nature; to this, there was something in his looks, and voice, and manner, superadded, which eternally backoned to the unfortunate to come and take shelter under him; so that before my uncle Toby had half finished the kind offers he was making to the father, had the son insensibly pressed up close to his knees, and had taken hold of the breast of his coat, and was pulling it towards him.—The blood and spirits of Le Fever, which were waxing cold and slow within him, and were retreating to their last citadel, the heart—rallied back,— the film forsook his eyes for a moment,—he looked up wishfully in my uncle Toby's face,—then cast a look upon his boy,—and that ligament, fine as it was,—was never broken.—

Nature instantly ebbed again,—the film returned to its place,—the pulse fluttered—stopped—went on— throbbed—stopped again—moved—stopped—shall I go on?—No.

Compared with the economy of sentiment in Shakespeare— for instance, in *Henry V*, where Mistress Quickly describes the death of Falstaff—and with the more genuine of the sentimental passages in Dickens, the sensibility of Sterne is bound to seem affected. There is an evident forcedness about it, in such passages as the above from *Tristram*, and even more obviously in the sentimentality about the old cab and the funeral of the donkey in the *Sentimental Journey*. As Canning was to put it, satirising "Sweet Sensibility" in the *Anti-Jacobin*:

> Mark her fair votaries, prodigal of grief,
> With cureless pangs, and woes that mock relief,
> Droop in soft sorrow o'er a faded flower;
> O'er a dead jack-ass pour the pearly shower . . .

But if there was nothing else in Sterne but sentimentality, interspersed with bawdiness and typographical eccentricities, he would not have won the admiration of such diverse men of genius as Dickens and D. H. Lawrence. Both his indecency and his sentiment are admitted to be contrived; in what, then, lies his more genuine strength, his unforced ability?

We should notice, first, that all his writings—the letters and the sermons as well as *Tristram* and the *Journey*—give exactly the same impression. And the outstanding characteristic is similar to that of his Corporal Trim: he loved to hear himself talk; "set his tongue a-going—you had no hold of him—he was voluble". He was half-Irish, we remember, and the eloquence of Irishmen is proverbial. If anyone could talk the hind leg off a donkey—and we can imagine Sterne's crocodile tears over an ass thus amputated—it would be a man with either Irish or Welsh blood in his veins. The celebrated digressions are partly a contrivance to keep the reader guessing, but partly also the natural genius of Sterne for anecdote, for being constantly reminded of something or other too good to be missed out. Most critics have agreed that he is not among the great humorists, not a humorist of the stature of Chaucer or Shakespeare or Dickens, but several of his characters, notably My Uncle Toby, are among the humorous masterpieces of the eighteenth century, and perhaps the most original of them. He was notoriously a borrower of other men's styles, but his chief characters were the product of his own observation. No novelist before him had had that intimate experience of regimental life, as no novelist before Smollett had had personal experience of the British Navy. Though so sentimentally conceived, My Uncle Toby seems as life-like as Parson Adams or Squire Western; limited as he is, in the same way as Ben Jonson's and Dickens's characters, he yet shares with them some of that poetical quality which gives such figures more reality than we can easily point to.

For the rest, Sterne can be called, if not a great humorist, "a fellow of infinite jest", like his own borrowed Yorick. He must have been an unusual clergyman, even in a period of eccentric clerics. "Have you read his Sermons," enquired Gray, "with his own comic figure, from a painting by Reynolds, at the head of them? They are in the style I think most proper for the pulpit, and show a strong imagination and a sensible heart; but you see him often tottering on the verge of laughter, and ready to throw his periwig in the face of the audience."

"Congregation" would have been a more suitable word, but "audience" has a fine poetic truth about it. For Sterne, in spirit, was always on the stage; his natural eccentricities, even of face and figure, were deliberately exaggerated to catch the public eye. He was always personal, in the pulpit as elsewhere. Compare with the passage from Addison's lay-sermon, quoted on p. 29 above, this typical passage from the *Sermons of Mr Yorick*:

> Let the torpid monk seek Heaven comfortless and alone. God speed him! For my own part, I fear I should never so find the way: let me be wise and religious, but let me be Man; wherever thy Providence places me, or whatever be the road I take to Thee, give me some companion in my journey, be it only to remark to, "How our shadows lengthen as our sun goes down;"— to whom I may say, "How fresh is the face of nature! how sweet the flowers of the field; how delicious are these fruits!"

One admirable quality about Sterne's sensibility, even at its most sentimental, is that it is usually directed—as here—to living things. There is scarcely a trace in him of that sentiment for dead leaves and mouldering ruins that was so characteristic a feature of eighteenth-century sensibility. He was, indeed, sensuous, both in his private correspondence—later made public to a scandalised world by his beloved daughter, who should have known better—and in his literature. The relation of man to man, and man to woman, meant more to him than thoughts of mortality. We can more easily picture him riding to a convivial dinner than meditating among his village tombs, like Young and Hervey. However gross we find some of his deliberate appeals to sentimentality, this distaste for the mouldering must be counted in him as a sign of health.

He was too eccentric a novelist to be a founder of any school of writing, but the kind of sensibility which he was the first to exploit in fiction had some influence on two minor novels which had a great success in their day: Henry Brooke's *The Fool of Quality* (1766), which has been mentioned for its religious aspect, and Henry Mackenzie's *The Man of Feeling* (1771).

Scott called Mackenzie "the northern Addison", and the epithet describes, at any rate, his Cato-like leadership of Edinburgh literary society, as well as his editorship of the *Mirror* (1779-80) and the *Lounger* (1785-7), two periodicals founded on the model of the *Spectator*. He is an interesting combination of sense and sensibility, many of his views being those of Augustan reason, while his novel, in its style and in its very title, was the embodiment of that kind of sentiment which both Scott and Jane Austen, in their very different ways, sought to counter.*

Goldsmith and "The Deserted Village"

A more notable example of sense and sensibility than the half-forgotten Mackenzie or the totally-forgotten Brooke is the author of *The Vicar of Wakefield* and *The Deserted Village*, of *The Citizen of the World* and *She Stoops to Conquer*, a man who almost rivals Johnson himself in the variety of his literary output and the general high level of it. If we knew him only by *The Vicar*, we might conclude him to be one example of eighteenth-century sensibility, more humorous than Mackenzie, less eccentric than Sterne. But *The Deserted Village*, particularly, reveals a writer not so easily summed up. Full of nostalgia and private sentiment as this poem is, it has a public purpose behind it and a social philosophy which has gained in application as the years have passed.

Much of his work is autobiographical. His father, "passing rich with forty pounds a year", was the main model, not only

* According to Scott's *Journal*, he was also something of a mixture in real life. "No man is less known from his writings," Scott noted. "We would suppose a retired, modest, somewhat affected man, with a white handkerchief, and a sigh ready for every sentiment. No such thing: H.M. is alert as a contracting tailor's needle in every sort of business . . . and is the life of the company with anecdote and fun." On his death, Scott briefly observed: "He has long maintained a niche in Scottish literature—gayest of the gay, though most sensitive of the sentimental".

for the parson of *The Deserted Village*, but for Dr Primrose, the Vicar of Wakefield. And the "seats of my youth" in

> Sweet Auburn! loveliest village of the plain,
> Where health and plenty cheered the labouring swain . . .

was a reminiscence of Lissoy, in County Westmeath, where his early life had been passed. He was born in the neighbouring county of Longford in 1728, and, after receiving his early education from the village schoolmaster, was able in 1744 to enter Trinity College, Dublin, as a sizar—that is, as a student who, in return for part of his board and tuition, had to do some of the servants' work in the college. His family wished him to enter the Church, but he was refused ordination and after a year of tutoring he decided to take up medicine, studying first at Edinburgh and then at Leyden. He seems to have acquired the degree of M.B., but the next we hear of him is when he had left Leyden and was making a kind of "grand tour" on foot through Flanders, France, Germany, Switzerland, and Italy, supporting himself by singing and playing on the flute and by taking part in disputations at universities. In 1756 he landed at Dover almost penniless, walked to London, and for some years led a life of toil and poverty, first as teacher, then in a druggist's shop, then as corrector for the press, and finally as a similar kind of literary man-of-all-work to Johnson twenty years before.

Their early career had much in common: they were both plants that flowered late (as Johnson actually said of Goldsmith); both were seemingly idle in youth, while storing up impressions of life and literature that were to serve them in good stead in later life; both achieved literary success largely by their own efforts. Goldsmith, of course, died comparatively young—at forty-six—and so was not enabled to achieve the massive distinction of Johnson. Their temperament, too, was widely different, Johnson being of a melancholy cast of mind, Goldsmith of a more ebullient nature. This difference is reflected in their works, Johnson's being the more profound, Goldsmith's the more varied and the more immediately attractive. We cannot imagine Goldsmith with the learning necessary to compile a dictionary, or with the literary judgment that went into the *Lives of the Poets*—though some of his scattered remarks upon contemporary writers, such as his attack upon Sterne in *The Citizen of the World*, show something of Johnson's penetration. Neither can we imagine Johnson writing *The Vicar of Wakefield* or having the stage sense revealed in *She Stoops to Conquer*.

Goldsmith's first work appeared in the *Monthly Review* in 1757, and two years later he published *An Enquiry into the Present State of Polite Learning in Europe*, based partly upon his own observations in the countries through which he had travelled. This book attracted some attention, as did his essays in a short-lived periodical called *The Bee* (October-November 1759) which he founded on the model of the *Gentleman's Magazine*. But it was not till his *Chinese Letters* appeared—first in the *Public Ledger* during 1760-1, then collected under the new title of *The Citizen of the World* (1762) —that his work became at all widely known. This remains one of his most readable books, the scheme—no doubt taken from Montesquieu's *Lettres Persanes*—of a philosophical Chinaman writing letters home from London, giving Goldsmith the opportunity of expressing his own mind upon the society and literature of the day. In his essay-style, he owes more to Addison than to Johnson, his flair for the fictional representation of typical figures giving us such characters as the shabby-genteel pretender Beau Tibbs.

During 1761-2 he wrote *The Vicar of Wakefield*, which was not, however, published till 1766. His first great success was *The Traveller* (1764), which went through nine editions in ten years. Johnson, who contributed a few lines near the end—notably the characteristic couplet,

> Still to ourselves in every place consigned,
> Our own felicity we make or find—

considered that "There has not been so fine a poem since Pope's time". Certainly it shares with Johnson's own *Vanity of Human Wishes* the merit of being one of the few lengthy poems written in mid-century which can bear comparison with Pope. The diction is often reminiscent of the early Pope of the *Pastorals*:

> No vernal blooms their torpid rocks array,
> But winter ling'ring chills the lap of May . . .

but occasionally there is a more muscular line, as when Goldsmith well describes Holland as the country

> Where the broad ocean leans against the land . . .

and, in general, the argument of the poem, and its working out, are much more serious than anything in the *Pastorals* and approach near the Pope of the later works and the Johnson of *The Vanity of Human Wishes*.

Goldsmith's attempt to show how the very genius of a race can lead to misgovernment is, however, only moderately successful here. Though he knew the countries he described, Europe was too big a subject altogether for his theme, and it is significant that he is at his best when treating of England and of his prevailing political philosophy,

> honour sinks where commerce long prevails.

The Deserted Village (1770) is a more impressive statement of this theme. It is, of course, open to the objection which has been raised against it, that in combining in one picture the consequences of Irish eviction and English enclosures Goldsmith had created a situation which did not in fact exist. But it is more to the point to recognise that the poet was in advance of the conscience of his age in seeing the grave social drawbacks of the agricultural revolution. At a time when Cobbett was a small boy, scaring the crows, Goldsmith was uttering the fundamental truth which, whatever factual qualifications need to be made, remains an urgent reminder:

> Ill fares the land, to hastening ills a prey,
> Where wealth accumulates, and men decay:
> Princes and lords may flourish, or may fade;
> A breath can make them, as a breath has made;
> But a bold peasantry, their country's pride,
> When once destroyed, can never be supplied.

Goldsmith's warning about the nation's wealth is in the spirit, not only of Cobbett's later and more detailed polemic, but of some passages that Pope had written in the *Moral Essays*:

Ye friends to truth, ye statesmen, who survey
The rich man's joys increase, the poor's decay,
'Tis yours to judge, how wide the limits stand
Between a splendid and a happy land.
Proud swells the tide with loads of freighted ore,
And shouting folly hails them from the shore;
Hoards, even beyond the miser's wish abound,
And rich men flock from all the world around.
Yet count our gains. This wealth is but a name
That leaves our useful products still the same.
Not so the loss. The man of wealth and pride
Takes up a space that many poor supplied;
Space for his lake, his park's extended bounds,
Space for his horses, equipage, and hounds;
The robe that wraps his limbs in silken sloth
Has robbed the neighbouring fields of half their growth,
His seat, where solitary sports are seen,
Indignant spurns the cottage from the green . . .

Where Goldsmith is deeply moved, we observe, his rhythm is easy and his language free from the falsities of "poetic diction". Crabbe was to correct, in certain respects, his picture of rural society; but *The Deserted Village* remains a most impressive poem and probably the best of all Goldsmith's varied work.

We have mentioned that *The Vicar of Wakefield*, completed in 1762, was not published till four years later. Its success was not immediate, either, but it slowly made its way at home and abroad—Goethe called it "one of the best novels that have ever been written"—and eventually it was to become the most widely-read of all eighteenth-century novels with the exception of *Crusoe* and *Gulliver*.

"The hero of this piece," Goldsmith writes in the Preface, "unites in himself the three greatest characters upon earth—he is a Priest, a Husbandman, and the Father of a family; he is drawn as ready to teach and ready to obey, as simple in affluence and majestic in adversity." The main intention is to set before the reader an example of virtue in distress, and to this end the good Vicar and his family are plunged into every kind of misery—until, even more improbably, they are made completely happy and prosperous in the last chapter. "It now only remained," the Vicar concludes, "that my gratitude in good fortune should exceed my former submission in adversity."

The weaknesses are chiefly in the plot, and in the rather dubious morality in the treatment of Olivia's marriage, which recalls that of Pamela; the strength is in the humorous episodes, in the scenes of family life, and most of all in Dr Primrose himself, as dutiful and unaffectedly simple in the debtor's prison as round his own fireside. *Pickwick* owes much to *The Vicar*, which is mentioned by Dickens as among his earliest reading. It is interesting to speculate on what further novels Goldsmith might have written had he not died, in middle age, in 1774. For he had the dramatic sense that seems to be a necessity for humorous fiction, and in fact he followed his novel by two stage comedies, one of which is among the very few eighteenth-century plays to have maintained their popularity down to modern times.

Sheridan and the Georgian Drama

The general development by which the tradition of English humour passed from the stage to the novel during the eighteenth century showed two exceptions in the 'seventies— exceptions, alas, which were but to prove the rule. Both Goldsmith and Sheridan were among the Johnson circle, and both to some extent were defenders of sense against the false sensibility of the theatre. After Fielding, the drama was not in a position to withstand the growing taste for sentimentality, and such dramatists as Hugh Kelly and Richard Cumberland gave the stage the pathos of Sterne allied to a complication of plot which makes *The Vicar of Wakefield* seem realistic. The efforts of these two dramatists led to the reaction of *The Clandestine Marriage*, in which Garrick and the elder Colman collaborated. The success of this more traditional comedy encouraged Goldsmith to write in 1767 *The Good Natured Man*, which had a fair run at the time but has not often been revived. With his second and last play, *She Stoops to Conquer* (1773), he scored a deserved success that has been repeated some thousands of times, the comedy of the man who is shy among his social equals, but becomes a swaggering young fellow when he mistakes his host's house for an inn, having something so fundamentally true about it that the play has become a favourite with both professional and amateur companies. Though partly written as a counterblast to Cumberland's sentimental melodrama *The West Indian*, it has been accused by a modern critic of being itself full of sentimentality. Unfortunately for this accusation the critic has based his opinion on a speech torn out of its context—the famous speech by Mr Hardcastle in the opening scene: "I love everything that's old: old friends, old times, old manners, old books, old wine; and I believe, Dorothy, you'll own I have been pretty fond of an old wife". Apart from the fact that Mrs Hardcastle replies, in effect, "Not so much of the old!", this speech is not the "smug sentiment" that the critic supposes. It is part of the contrast between the speakers, and is sufficiently in character—like Shallow's sentimentality about the good old days in *Henry IV* —for the dramatist's own views not to be mistaken for it. Goldsmith, of course, like Sheridan, seems sentimental beside Wycherley and Congreve; but it was something to write a comedy that has the freshness of *Tom Jones* rather than the cynicism of Congreve or the sentimentality of Sterne.

The history of the English drama seems to be one of fits and starts. Even the great period, the Elizabethan-Jacobean, lasted only about twenty years. It was followed by a period, first of gradual decline, then of almost complete suppression by the government; and afterwards we had about twenty to thirty years of "heroic" drama and "Restoration" comedy, culminating in a further period of decline into sentimental commonplaces. The reaction of the 'seventies was briefest of all: four plays which have lasted in themselves—*She Stoops to Conquer*, *The Rivals*, *The School for Scandal*, and *The Critic*—and then the flood of sentimentality and bombast that endured this time for more than a hundred years. If it had not been for the growing appreciation of Shakespeare during this period, it could be held, with a good deal of truth, that the English drama hibernated with the death of Goldsmith and when Sheridan forsook the theatre for the House of Commons.

Richard Brinsley Sheridan (1751-1816) was born in Dublin, the grandson of Swift's friend and collaborator and the son of Mrs Frances Sheridan, later one of the best-known novelists of the time. Educated at Harrow, he had an early career which, if put on the stage, would be dismissed as too romantic for real life. Rescuing the beautiful daughter of the musician Linley from the attentions of an unwelcome admirer, he subsequently married the lady and fought two duels on her behalf. Setting up house in the most fashionable quarter of London, he found his expenses exceeding his means and turned to writing for the stage to support his extravagant existence. His first play, *The Rivals* (1775), made a bad start, having to be withdrawn for further revision; but then it had a great success and has frequently been revived. At the end of the same year he wrote an opera *The Duenna* in collaboration with his father-in-law, and this was even more successful at the time, though it has not had the lasting stage-career of *The Rivals*. Like Congreve, eighty years before, everything seems to have gone well with Sheridan during this early part of his life. *The Rivals* and *The Duenna* had made him so rich that when Garrick retired from Drury Lane he bought his share in the theatre for £35,000 and took over the management. He was then only twenty-six. Early the next year, 1777, he produced at the Lane his own best comedy, *The School for Scandal*, which like *The Rivals* has always held the stage. It was written in his usual hurried manner, the last act being delivered only five days before the first performance. With his next play, *The Critic* (1779), the stage-manager had to lock him in a room at the theatre in order that the last scene might be written and the actors complete their rehearsal.

The explanation is that Sheridan, like Congreve and unlike Shakespeare, took the business of play-writing and theatre-managing far less seriously than the "business" of high society. He was not merely frivolous, however, for he valued his position in society as a step to a political career. He was a failure as a theatre manager, but from 1780, when he was elected to Parliament, until thirty-five years later, he was recognised as one of the finest orators in the Commons, his speeches at the trial of Warren Hastings in 1789 being particularly notable. His political career does not concern us here, the significant feature of his later life being that fortune, which had so smiled on him during his youth, showed the reverse side of her nature in his middle age: his wife died of consumption, his theatre was burnt down, and he himself died heavily in debt, with the bailiffs at the door. As a kind of *Vicar of Wakefield* in reverse, his life-story must be one of the most extraordinary in our literature.

His dramatic fame rests on his three comedies, written in such haste during his 'twenties. "Restoration Comedy without the smut" they have been called, and this is a fair description. We observed that dramatists like Steele and Cibber, wanting to achieve such a combination, comparatively failed because they had not a quarter of the wit of the indecent comedies they condemned. Even Fielding never really succeeded in writing a stage comedy of lasting merit, and it was left to Sheridan to show the eighteenth century that immorality is not an essential ingredient of comic drama.

Compared with the comic masterpieces of Shakespeare and Jonson, Sheridan's comedy, of course, is concerned with the mere surfaces of life. There is no Falstaff or Epicure Mammon in his plays, still less a Caliban or a Volpone; instead, we have stock characters like Mrs Malaprop in *The Rivals* and Sir Oliver Surface in *The School for Scandal*. Though "the man of feeling", Joseph Surface, is deliberately made the villain of the latter piece, there is a touch of sentiment in the scene where the scapegrace brother Charles, in disposing of the family portraits to his disguised uncle, refuses to part with his uncle's picture. Congreve would have made the young buck entirely oblivious of such natural affection, but whether this is more true to real life depends on the amount of cynicism in the individual spectator.

Sheridan's satire does not pretend to dig very deep. Mrs Malaprop's affectations, Joseph Surface's hypocrisy, are lightly scorned. In *The Critic*, which is the most successful of those plays which provide a rehearsal of a satirised piece, the object of scorn is the sentimental drama of the age, Richard Cumberland being the model for Sir Fretful Plagiary. There is nothing particularly original in Sheridan's own plots or characters; his originality resides rather in his freshness of dialogue and in the very way he accepts his limitations. In some of Fielding's plays, we are conscious of an ambition not fully realised, of a constant striving after effect; Sheridan, by remaining satisfied with what he knows he can do, is much more natural and has kept the stage for more than a hundred and fifty years.

Apart from Goldsmith and Sheridan, there is not much of interest in the Georgian drama after Fielding. It was, in fact, the start of a long period in which the actor predominated over the dramatist. John Home, of course, on the strength or fretful plagiarisms of his *Douglas* (1756), was for years considered by patriotic Scotsmen "the modern Shakespeare"; and Hannah More's *Percy* was being greeted with thunderous applause at Covent Garden while *The School for Scandal* was running at Drury Lane. The attempt by the Johnson quartet—Garrick, Colman, Goldsmith, Sheridan—to stem the tide of sentimentality and melodrama was not very successful. Goldsmith and Sheridan found no real successors till the close of the Victorian Age, while the successors of Kelly and Cumberland, of Home and Murphy, and of Garrick in his interpretative capacity, made the nineteenth-century theatre the most unoriginal in our history.

Crabbe and the Pastoral Tradition

A younger friend of Johnson who expressed the reaction of common sense against one of the most foolish of poetic conventions was George Crabbe, whose poem *The Village* (1783) was revised by him in manuscript, "its sentiments as to the false notions of rustic happiness and rustic virtue" being, says Boswell, "quite congenial with his own". The

pastoral tradition had, of course, been ridiculed by Gay in
The Shepherd's Week; and John Langhorne, in *The Country
Justice* (1774-5), had insisted that there was as much in need
of reform in the country as in the town. Yet the dominant
attitude was still that represented by Cowper's conviction
that God had made the country, man the town, and by Goldsmith's contrast of the honest peasant and the man of commerce. Goldsmith had seen the social drawbacks of the
agricultural revolution, but had been inclined to idealise the
villager, not indeed in the conventional idiom of Corydons and
Phillidas, but enough under that influence to be able to write
of "swains" and "bowers". There were truly parsons like
the one in *The Deserted Village*, who went about doing good
on a paltry forty pounds a year—which they eked out by
husbandry, like their neighbours—but, as Crabbe deliberately
reminds us in *The Village*, there were also parsons of a different
sort, "holy strangers" to the afflicted in the poor-house, for
instance, where they were most needed:

> And doth not he, the pious man, appear,
> He, "passing rich with forty pounds a year"?
> Ah, no, a shepherd of a different stock,
> And far unlike him, feeds this little flock;
> A jovial youth, who thinks his Sunday's task
> As much as God or man can fairly ask;
> The rest he gives to loves and labours light,
> To fields the morning and to feasts the night . . .*

Part of the reason for the perseverance of pastoral conventions was, of course, that poets, whether resident in town or
country, were usually cut off from the more sordid realities of
village life, whereas those of London had become notorious.
As Crabbe put it:

> Save honest Duck, what son of verse could share
> The poet's rapture and the peasant's care?
> Or the great labours of the field degrade
> With the new peril of a poorer trade?

---

* The probability is that most eighteenth-century country parsons
were somewhere between Goldsmith's practical saint and Crabbe's
cheerful sinner. See, for example, *The Diary of a Country Parson,
1758-1802*, by James Woodforde.

Crabbe himself was the son of poor parents, born in 1754 at Aldeburgh on the Suffolk coast, where his father was a warehouse-keeper. He was apprenticed to an apothecary, and set up on his own at Aldeburgh in 1775; but four years later gave up medicine altogether and sought "the new peril of a poorer trade" in London. He failed to make any sort of a living by literature, and was only saved from absolute destitution by the kindness of Burke, who liked the poems he had shown him but wisely advised him not to trust to writing for a livelihood and helped him to enter the Church. He became ordained in 1781, was for a time chaplain to the Duke of Rutland, and later held various livings, finally becoming vicar of Trowbridge, Wiltshire, from 1814 to his death in 1832.

The Library, published during the year he was ordained, is his first work of any maturity, but it was *The Village*, published two years later, which made the literary public aware of a new poet of individual views and character. His deliberate intention to satirise the stock conventions of the pastoral poem is made plain from the beginning:

> Fled are those times, if e'er such times were seen,
> When rustic poets prais'd their native green;
> No shepherds now in smooth alternate verse,
> Their country's beauty or their nymphs' rehearse;
> Yet still for these we frame the tender strain,
> Still in our lays fond Corydons complain,
> And shepherds' boys their amorous pains reveal,
> The only pains, alas! they never feel.

He mocks at the fashionable pretence that the villager's life is one of healthy labour and good living:

> Go then! and see them rising with the sun,
> Through a long course of daily toil to run;
> Like him to make the plenteous harvest grow,
> And yet not share the plenty they bestow . . .

and, like Mark Rutherford a hundred years later, he contrasts the "humble cot" of romantic painting and fiction with the reality:

> Go! if the peaceful cot your praises share,
> Go look within, and ask if peace be there:
> If peace be his—that drooping weary sire,

> Or theirs, that offspring round their feeble fire,
> Or hers, that matron pale, whose trembling hand
> Turns on the wretched hearth th' expiring brand.*

The old and infirm, the blind and the idiot, "forsaken wives and mothers never wed":

> Theirs is yon house that holds the parish poor,
> Whose walls of mud scarce bear the broken door . . .

They suffer the quackery and the insults of the parish doctor, and the neglect of the sporting parson, until death comes and relieves them:

> Up yonder hill, behold how sadly slow
> The bier moves winding from the vale below;
> There lie the happy dead, from trouble free,
> And the glad parish pays the frugal fee;
> No more, O Death, thy victim starts to hear
> Churchwarden stern, or kingly overseer;
> No more the farmer gets his humble bow,
> Thou art his lord, the best of tyrants thou!

Goldsmith and Crabbe agree in pointing out the growing difference in fortune between the various classes. "The wealth around them makes them doubly poor," says Crabbe of his labourers; compare *The Deserted Village*, lines beginning

> Where then, ah where, shall poverty reside,
> To 'scape the pressure of contiguous pride? . . .

and also the lines in Chatterton's satire *Resignation* (1770):

> For 'tis a maxim with the guiding wise,
> Just as the commons sink, the rich arise . . .

The last line of Goldsmith quoted is also interesting from the technical point of view. Eighteenth-century diction is commonly ornate—for example, "the finny tribe" for "fish"—but "contiguous pride" is a fine instance of economy, where the Latinised adjective and the personification give in two

---

* Despite his more sentimental approach, Cowper has some lines very much like these in *The Task*:

> Warm'd, while it lasts, by labour all day long
> They brave the season, and yet find at eve,
> Ill-clad and fed but sparely, time to cool.
> The frugal housewife trembles when she lights
> Her scanty stock of brushwood, blazing clear,
> But dying soon, like all terrestrial joys . . .

words what would take a whole phrase in ordinary English. Other instances, which justify much of this usage, can be found in Gray's *Elegy* and Johnson's *Vanity of Human Wishes*, as well as in the volumes of narrative poems which Crabbe published late in life.   Technically, indeed, besides his main-tenance of the common-sense tradition, Crabbe was the last poet to be successful in the manner of Johnson.

Tendencies in the Novel : 1759-96

The development of fiction in the earlier part of the century, up to the time of Sterne and Walpole, seems straight-forward in comparison with the complications that those two authors, among others, ushered in.   Early Georgian fiction was dominated by three great novelists—Defoe, Richardson, Fielding—the distinctions between whom have been discussed in relation to journalism and the stage.   Smollett was the main successor of Fielding, and Sterne developed one side of Richardson; but, in general, the novel in the late eighteenth century was complicated by conflicting tendencies, to which a host of minor novelists gave support.   It was perhaps natural that there should have been a certain decline in quality, if not quantity, between the great period of Richardson and Fielding, and the next great period of Jane Austen and Scott.   The groundwork had been prepared by the former novelists and Defoe, and it was inevitable that minor novelists should rush in where the angels had trodden, and that the various senti-ments and philosophies that were in the air should find fictional form.   Many of these minor novelists were women, from Sarah Fielding and Mrs Haywood to Mrs Sheridan and Mrs Lennox; and it is rather surprising to find Fanny Burney's step-mother still so convinced that novel-writing was hardly decent for a woman that she persuaded the future author of *Evelina* to burn all her early manuscripts.   Mrs Burney had in mind, of course, the impropriety of the Restoration novels of Aphra Behn, and perhaps also the fact that Charlotte Lennox, whose *Female Quixote* was praised by Johnson, had died in poor circumstances.   She was not to guess the impressive achievement in the novel of Jane Austen and the

Brontës and George Eliot; nor to imagine that Fanny Burney, by her *Evelina* (1778), *Cecilia* (1782), and *Camilla* (1796), was to play a pioneer role in that achievement. Yet so we can call it, for these novels, written in the letter-form which Richardson had made popular, were the main link between him and Jane Austen (whose own early attempts were letter-novels). Fanny Burney seems slight enough beside her successors, but she was able to maintain the tradition set by Richardson, of ordinary domestic life instead of Defoe's life in the under-world and extraordinary adventures, without Richardson's long-windedness. And she has, particularly in *Evelina*, that touch of humour which Richardson so sorely needed.

It is largely by nineteenth-century standards, of course, that we are able to talk of such a thing as "the novel proper", and to see Defoe and Fielding, Richardson and Fanny Burney, as among its ancestors. *Tristram Shandy* is an "improper novel" in more than one sense; it is one of our eccentric novels, perhaps the only one of its period to retain some of its original popularity—neither Thomas Amory's *John Buncle* nor William Beckford's *Vathek* (originally written in French) being much read to-day. Richard Graves's *Spiritual Quixote* is even less known, while the children's novels of the period, including such former favourites as Robert Paltock's *Peter Wilkins* and Thomas Day's *Sandford and Merton*, have not maintained the popularity of those earlier and later books—*Crusoe, Ivanhoe*, etc.—that were not expressly written for children.

Horace Walpole's *Castle of Otranto* began the fashion for the tales of mystery and historical romance which eventually were to lead to the achievement of Scott. This will be a part concern of our next chapter, and in our general chapter on The Age of Revolution we shall be discussing briefly those novels of the 'eighties and 'nineties, such as Godwin's *Caleb Williams*, which are "improper novels" in the sense of being fiction with a social and political purpose. Perhaps even *Amelia* suffers to a certain extent from Fielding's concern with propaganda; but Fielding at his best is a great humorous artist, and there is little of artistry or humour in the novels of revolution or the tales of terror.

CHAPTER IX

CLASSIC HISTORY AND GOTHIC ROMANCE
1764-1800

"It was at Rome, on the 15th of October, 1764, as I sat musing amidst the ruins of the Capitol, while the barefooted friars were singing vespers in the Temple of Jupiter, that the idea of writing the decline and fall of the city first started to my mind."

GIBBON: *Autobiography.*

"The favourable manner in which this little piece has been received by the public, calls upon the author to explain the grounds on which he composed it . . . It was an attempt to blend the two kinds of Romance, the ancient and the modern . . . Desirous of leaving the powers of fancy at liberty to expatiate through the boundless realms of invention . . . he wished to conduct the mortal agents in his drama according to the rules of probability; in short, to make them think, speak, and act, as it might be supposed mere men and women would do in extraordinary positions."

WALPOLE: Preface to the Second Edition of
The Castle of Otranto.

Mediaevalists in the Age of Classicism

The co-existence of an age of reason with an age of sensibility, which we discussed in the previous chapter, is not more curious that the fact that the year 1764 witnessed both the conception of *The Decline and Fall of the Roman Empire* and the writing of *The Castle of Otranto*. The history was a fitting culmination to a period of classical education; the story ushered in a period of so-called "Gothic Romance" which had many absurdities but was eventually to be transformed by the genius of Scott.

The two contemporary attitudes had each an historical justification. The Augustan Age, we observed, had been consciously classical, looking upon itself as the new Rome and regarding the thousand years between the fall of the city and the enlightenment as an age of darkness and superstition. The revival of interest in Shakespeare and Spenser was one sign of the changed outlook that made itself felt as early as the 'forties; another was the attention given to the old ballads by such poets and antiquarians as Gray and Percy in the 'fifties and 'sixties. Quite how this increasing respect for the more immediate and more national past* was connected with the cult of sensibility is not an easy question to answer. What is evident, at any rate, is that the age of strict classicism in England soon found itself challenged by different assumptions, as the age of reason steadily gave ground before the advocates of sensibility. Johnson and Sterne were contemporary instances of two contrasting attitudes of mind, as Gibbon and Walpole were of others.

To Scott, the classical style of Gibbon was distasteful; but, though he had an equal dislike of some of the cruder aspects of Gothic Romance, he found he was able to build upon it. In much the same way, Wordsworth felt he had as little in common with the poet of the *Elegy* as with Pope and Johnson; but the poetry of the "country churchyard", of Gray and Collins and Cowper, seems to have as definite a connection with *Tintern Abbey* and *The Prelude* as Percy's *Reliques* with *The Ancient Mariner*. By the time Gibbon had completed his *Decline and Fall*, the native "Roman Empire" had begun to decline, too. The emphasis on the classics in English educated life was turning to a broader—if often more sentimental—interest in the past as a whole.

* More "northern" past, we might almost say, in view of the Augustan concentration on Mediterranean culture and the researches of Gray into Norse, Mallet into Danish, and Percy into Scottish traditions. The reaction from the exclusively classical is also seen in the popularity in the mid-eighteenth century of oriental literature: Percy's first publication was *Hau Kiou Choaun* (1761), a Chinese novel translated from the Portuguese; in the 'seventies William Jones published a Persian grammar and some translations of Arabic poems. Johnson's *Rasselas* has some connection with this revival of interest in the East.

Gibbon and the " Decline and Fall "

Johnson wrote in the *Idler* that every man's life is best written by himself. We may dispute this in regard to politicians, but in regard to literary men it is more just. The actions of public men may be variously construed, by themselves and others; but the development of an author's mind can be known only to himself. The value of such letters as those of Gray and Cowper is that they give us glimpses of such development; but the value is immensely enhanced when the author writes his own biography with the definite intention of tracing the evolution of his work. There are not many instances, and perhaps the best is the *Autobiography* of Edward Gibbon.

Compared with Johnson's, Gibbon's early life was easy, and he acknowledges his sense of having been placed in a social position particularly suitable for his work and temperament: that is, in a middling state, without the temptations of riches or the cares of poverty. His father had inherited a profitable drapery business, and at the time of the historian's birth in 1737 was Member of Parliament for Petersfield in Hampshire, near which the family estate was situated. (The evolution of tradespeople into landed proprietors, and aristocrats into trade, was one of the distinctive features of English society.) The chief event of his brief life at Oxford—and the most ironical, in view of his later opinions—was his conversion in 1753 to the Catholic faith.

He was only sixteen at this time, and his father resolved to try the effect of contrast, sending him to Lausanne into the household of a Calvinist minister. He was soon reconverted to Protestantism, and, more important for his future work, had exchanged the sleepy provincialism of Oxford for a self-education* in both the classics and modern European literature.

But he was again to displease his father by contemplating an engagement to the daughter of a Protestant pastor—who later became the wife of the French statesman Necker and

* "Every man who rises above the common level", he observes, "has received two educations: the first from his teachers; the second, more personal and important, from himself".

the mother of Mme de Stael. Upon his father vetoing the proposal, "I sighed as a lover, I obeyed as a son". In 1758, he returned home, more European than English, with his first work, *Essai sur L'Etude de la Littérature*, half completed; it was published in its original French in 1761.

He had long meditated the writing of a history; and, like Milton with his epic scheme, made and abandoned several projects before his visit to Rome in 1764 finally decided the subject of his ambition. Volume One of *The Decline and Fall of the Roman Empire* was published in 1776, and was a great success; further volumes followed regularly, till the completion of the published work in 1788. He had now retired to Lausanne, and a famous passage of the *Autobiography* records the ending of his labours:

> It was on the day, or rather night, of the 27th of June, 1787, between the hours of eleven and twelve, that I wrote the last lines of the last page, in a summer-house in my garden. After laying down my pen, I took several turns in a *berceau*, or covered walk of acacias, which commands a prospect of the country, the lake, and the mountains . . . I will not dissemble the first emotions of joy on recovery of my freedom, and, perhaps, the establishment of my fame. But my pride was soon humbled, and a sober melancholy was spread over my mind, by the idea that I had taken an everlasting leave of an old and agreeable companion, and that whatsoever might be the future date of my *History*, the life of the historian must be short and precarious.

Gibbon was, unfortunately, a true prophet. He survived the publication of his last volumes only six years, dying in 1794 at the age of fifty-six.

As with dictionaries before Johnson's, English men of letters had long been dissatisfied with our achievements in history, compared with the French. This was not altogether a sound judgment, for the historical works of Clarendon and North, of Burnet and Strype, of Collier and Bolingbroke—not to mention the antiquarian studies of Hearne and his successors—were not an achievement to be lightly dismissed. But the contemporary dissatisfaction was abated with the publication of Hume's *History of Great Britain* (1754-61) and with the works of his fellow-Scotsman, William Robertson: *History of Scotland* (1759), *History of Charles V* (1769), and *History of America* (1771). Both Hume and Robertson praised the work of Gibbon, though his own modesty could not altogether concur with the general judgment which placed him on a level with his admired elders. "I will freely own," he wrote, "that my pride is elated as often as I find myself ranked in the triumvirate of British Historians of the present age, and though I feel myself the Lepidus, I contemplate with pleasure the superiority of my colleagues."

Hume and Robertson are still read, but the modern view is the opposite of Gibbon's. Though later research has caused some of his statements to be questioned—and though there will always be controversy over his treatment of the rise of Christianity—he is seen as the Augustus of Georgian history, the classic instance of an historian whose prejudices are so obvious that they do not greatly interfere with the lasting merits of his work. He was truly "Augustan" in his impatience with the long, troubled period of blood and theology that separated the civilisation of the Roman Empire from the civilisation of the Roman Church. Much of his criticism of the Jewish religion, and of the conflicting attitudes in early Christianity, is fundamentally sound, but he seems not to have asked himself the question whether the achievements of Greek and Roman civilisation might not have perished altogether without the rise of Christianity and Islam. He was, after all, no less than Hume and Robertson, a child of the Gothic North, and if the Moslem influence was perhaps the greater on the late-mediaeval culture of the Mediterranean, the Gothic North owed almost everything to Christianity. Only if the Gothic invasions had not actually occurred could Gibbon's regret for the counter-invasion of the Roman Church have been logically justified.

These famous fifteenth and sixteenth chapters, dealing with the rise of the Church to the reign of Constantine, met with a good deal of criticism at the time of publication, though he had flattered himself, he tells us, "that an age of light and

liberty would receive, without scandal, an inquiry into the
human causes of the progress and establishment of Christianity". So, indeed, it might have done, had his attitude
been more strictly impartial; but the irony of this passage,
for instance, from the close of the fifteenth chapter, was too
evidently relished by the author to appeal to even a broad-
minded Christian reader:

> But how shall we excuse the supine inattention of
> the Pagan and philosophic world to those evidences
> which were presented by the hand of Omnipotence, not
> to their reason, but to their senses? During the age of
> Christ, of his apostles, and of their first disciples, the
> doctrine which they preached was confirmed by innumer-
> able prodigies. The lame walked, the blind saw, the
> sick were healed, the dead were raised, demons were
> expelled, and the laws of Nature were frequently sus-
> pended for the benefit of the church. But the sages
> of Greece and Rome turned aside from the awful
> spectacle, and, pursuing the ordinary occupations of
> life and study, appeared unconscious of any alterations
> in the moral or physical government of the world.
> Under the reign of Tiberius, the whole earth, or at least
> a celebrated province of the Roman empire, was in-
> volved in a preternatural darkness of three hours.
> Even this miraculous event, which ought to have excited
> the wonder, the curiosity, and the devotion of mankind,
> passed without notice in an age of science and history.

Most of the attacks of the orthodox, Anglican and
Methodist, were, however, too weak to affect the general
popularity of the work;* and from the time of publication it
was recognised by the less bigoted that the outstanding merits of

* Gibbon's most abusive antagonist was Archdeacon Travis, only
remembered to-day because he was the subject of the *Letters to Travis*
(1788-9) of the Cambridge scholar Richard Porson. "The wretched
Travis", observes Gibbon in the *Autobiography*, "still smarts under
the lash of the merciless Porson. I consider Mr Porson's answer to
Archdeacon Travis as the most acute and accurate piece of criticism
which has appeared since the days of Bentley . . ." And on a later
page: "I am less flattered by Mr Porson's high encomium on the
style and spirit of my history than I am satisfied with his honourable
testimony to my attention, diligence, and accuracy; those humble
virtues, which religious zeal had most audaciously denied. The
sweetness of his praise," adds Gibbon, "is tempered by a reasonable

the history—the mastery over the materials, the easy flow of the narrative, the power in design—far outweigh the occasions on which the historian falls short of his own ideal of impartiality.

What he would have next attempted, had he lived, is not precisely known. He suggested to William Mitford his *History of Greece*, but seems to have contemplated for himself an excursion into more modern history, writing to Sheffield of a "scheme of biographical writing: the lives, or rather the characters, of the most eminent persons in arts and arms, in Church and State, who have flourished in Britain from the reign of Henry VIII to the present age". This book would have been of a totally different nature from the *Decline and Fall*, and it is interesting to speculate whether Gibbon's powers would have been so successfully extended in modern as in ancient history.

Walpole and the "Gothic" Novel

The cult of sensibility, we observed, was associated with a feeling for the past—not the classical (and "early Gothic") past of Gibbon, but the half-understood past of the later Middle Ages. It was at first a half-ashamed feeling, too, as we can see by Walpole's device in the first edition of *The Castle of Otranto* of pretending that his novel was a translation from the Italian. The original title-page (printed as in 1765, but the book was actually published in December 1764) runs as follows: "The Castle of Otranto. A Story. Translated by William Marshal, Gent. From the Original Italian of Onuphrio Muralto, Canon of the Church of St Nicholas at Otranto". In the original Preface, Walpole apologises for the miraculous element in the story in a manner that is still uneasily half-Augustan:

> If this air of the miraculous is excused, the reader will find nothing else unworthy of his perusal. Allow the possibility of the facts, and all the actors comport themselves as persons would do in their situation . . .

---

mixture of acid"—as when Porson remarks: "Nor does his humanity ever slumber, unless when women are ravished or the Christians persecuted."

Terror, the author's principal engine, prevents the story from ever languishing; and it is so often contrasted by pity that the mind is kept up in a constant vicissitude of interesting passions.

Sterne, too, was desirous of arousing "interesting passions", and the connection between the two writers is seen further in the Sonnet to Lady Mary Coke, prefixed to the second edition of Walpole's novel, which opens:

> The gentle Maid, whose hapless tale
> These melancholy pages speak;
> Say, gracious Lady, shall she fail
> To draw the tear adown thy cheek?

When we add that *The Castle of Otranto* had an even more favourable reception than *Tristram Shandy*—and, incidentally, a European fame only exceeded by *Clarissa Harlowe*—the appeal of the two kinds of fiction to the same kind of reader will be apparent.

Walpole himself must have been agreeably surprised by the immediate popularity of his story. In his Preface to the second edition, he acknowledged the authorship, apologised for his deception, and tried to justify his blending of the "two kinds of romance, the ancient and the modern", by an appeal to one of the Augustan verities—"My rule was Nature"—and by the example of Shakespeare. There is no doubt that this was sincerely meant, though to a modern reader the story seems the reverse of natural and the relation to Shakespeare somewhat of a burlesque kind. Walpole's characters are stagey rather than dramatic, and they speak a language more akin to that of Home's *Douglas* than to Shakespeare's. The frequent supernatural incidents have not maintained their original effect;* some of them, indeed, can more easily be read as comic relief:

> "Audacious rebel!" said Manfred, endeavouring to conceal the awe with which the friar's words inspired him; "dost thou presume to threaten thy lawful prince?"

---

* "I have received the C. of O., and return you my thanks for it. It engages our attention here, makes some of us cry a little, and all in general afraid to go to bed o' nights." (Gray to Walpole.)

"Thou art no lawful prince," said Jerome; "thou art no prince. Go, discuss thy claim with Frederick; and when that is done—"

"It is done," replied Manfred: "Frederick accepts Matilda's hand, and is content to waive his claim, unless I have no male issue—"

As he spoke these words, three drops of blood fell from the nose of Alfonso's statue.

It is difficult, of course, to know quite how seriously Walpole took his story—or, indeed, his general attitude to the Middle Ages which led him to convert his house at Strawberry Hill into a "Gothic castle". Certainly there was more than a trace of affectation in his attitude to the past, a kind of self-indulgence in the mysterious and the supernatural, a fitting hobby perhaps for a leisured gentleman who regarded professional men of letters like Johnson as beneath his notice. Yet his massive correspondence—the latest edition is in more than twenty volumes—reveals a more interesting mind that is apparent from either *The Castle of Otranto* or the castle at Strawberry Hill. There is much in it, it is true, of his mediaeval fads and "upholsterer's catalogues";* but his birth and position make him a good commentator on some sides of Georgian politics and high society. In a sense, his letters, or a selection from them, make up a better novel than his "Gothic" story, and in recent years they have been more widely read.

The importance of *The Castle of Otranto* is, then, almost entirely historical. Its influence upon German romantic literature was immense, and even in this more reasonable island it was the parent of a host of novels—ridiculed by Jane Austen in *Northanger Abbey*—which are of interest because they form part of the background to the achievement of Scott. Strictly speaking, Walpole had failed in his intention of combining ancient with modern romance, because his

* Scott observes in his *Journal* that "Horace Walpole, with all his talents, makes a silly figure when he gives an upholsterer's catalogue of his goods and chattels at Strawberry Hill". Pope and Swift died too soon to be able to satirise his mania for collecting— which, an object of scorn to the Augustans, was now becoming fashionable.

imagination was of the most primitive kind and his characters were figures of wood. Clara Reeve in *The Old English Baron* (1777) and Ann Radcliffe in *The Mysteries of Udolpho* (1794) were more successful; and in *The Monk* (1796) Matthew Lewis added notoriety to the usual tale of persecuted heroines in mysterious castles by indulging in a more than Sternian indecency. Scott had a contempt for most of his "Gothic" predecessors, but at the same time was able to transform the species into literature by the greater seriousness of his mind and by the circumstances of his birth and upbringing.

Neither Walpole nor his "Gothic" followers knew very much about the feudal society they depicted; in England, it was too much in the past for anyone but a professional historian to comprehend. But feudalism had lingered long in Scotland, and Scott was born just early enough—in 1771— to know by personal experience, and by the tales of his elders, some of the virtues of the order that was rapidly passing away. His first attempt at romantic fiction—written about 1800— was in the Walpole vein, but the best of the Waverley Novels give us a combination of personal experience and historical imagination that is almost comparable to Shakespeare's. It may seem extraordinary that *The Castle of Otranto* should be the parent, not only of *The Monk*, but of *The Heart of Mid-Lothian* and *Old Mortality*; but Kyd's *Spanish Tragedy* was the parent, not only of *Titus Andronicus*, but of *Hamlet* and *King Lear*.

Percy and the Old Ballads

The last phrase in Walpole's Preface, quoted in the epigraph to this chapter, is reminiscent to a modern reader of Coleridge's words about the *Lyrical Ballads* in his *Biographia Literaria*. Speaking of his own part in the project, he observed that "the incidents and agents were to be, in part at least, supernatural; and the excellence aimed at was to consist in the interesting of the affections by the dramatic truth of such emotions as would naturally accompany such situations, supposing them real".

"Dramatic truth" was the aim of both *The Castle of Otranto* and *The Ancient Mariner*; yet the one was almost a

complete artistic failure, the other one of the greatest achievements in English literature.   The difference is not attributable
entirely to the much greater genius of Coleridge.   Walpole,
after all, built his *Castle* on an extremely flimsy foundation;
he knew pretty well what he wanted to do, and his immediate
success was of course tremendous, but he had little behind
him save a vague feeling for the mysterious, while behind
Coleridge was the body of work on the old ballads accomplished by eighteenth-century scholars and—more important
—the collections of these ballads themselves. *The Ancient
Mariner* is, in fact, one of the very few modern examples of
the old ballad form which can bear comparison with the
originals.

The originals belong mostly to the fifteenth century, and
the collection of them which had most influence on Coleridge
and Wordsworth, and upon the nineteenth-century romantic
movement in general, was that entitled *Reliques of Ancient
English Poetry*, published in 1765. The editor was Thomas
Percy, a friend of Johnson's, who became Bishop of Dromore
in 1782.   Though his collection was much the more influential,*
he was stimulated by the contemporary success of James
Macpherson, who had published in 1760 *Fragments of Ancient
Poetry collected in the Highlands of Scotland*.

The controversy over the genuineness of Macpherson's
epics, *Fingal* (1762) and *Temora* (1762-3), claimed to be
translations from the third-century Gaelic bard Ossian, is
not of much importance now.   As Macpherson declined to

---

* Scott read it first about the age of thirteen, *c.* 1784. Speaking
of the literature he was reading at this period, he observes: "Above
all, I then first became acquainted with Bishop Percy's *Reliques of
Ancient Poetry*. As I had been from infancy devoted to legendary
lore of this nature . . . it may be imagined . . . with what delight
I saw pieces of the same kind which had amused my childhood . . .
considered as the subject of sober research . . . Nor do I believe I
ever read a book half so frequently, or with half the enthusiasm."
Compare Wordsworth's tribute, in 1815: "For our own country, its
poetry has been absolutely redeemed by it. I do not think that there
is an able writer in verse of the present day who would not be proud
to acknowledge his obligations to the *Reliques*; I know that it is so
with my friends; and, for myself, I am happy on this occasion to
make a public avowal of my own."

produce his "originals", though requested to do so by the enthusiastic Gray and the sceptical Johnson, the presumption is that these epics were original poetry disguised as translations. They had an immense success, temporary in England, more lasting in Europe. Macpherson is a very minor poet, but he had been born in the Highlands and really knew more about their poetry than most of his critics. His influence upon Percy (and, alas, upon Blake) is more interesting than the Ossianic Cult in Europe and the extravagant praise of Goethe and Napoleon. Scott ridiculed the epics in *The Antiquary*, and Wordsworth wrote that "from my very childhood I have felt the falsehood that pervades the volumes imposed upon the world under the name of Ossian".

Macpherson is little read now either in England or Scotland, though he still retains some of his original reputation in France. It might be thought that Percy shares his eclipse, since few people to-day have seen a copy of the *Reliques*. But Percy's influence has, as a matter of fact, been lasting; and though modern editions of the original collection are not numerous (there is one in *Everyman*) most of the contents are known to everybody through later anthologies.

Some of them were known to the eighteenth century. Addison had written a commentary upon the famous ballad of *Chevy Chase*, for instance, but he had taken for his text a corrupt modern version, whereas Percy was able to print, from the manuscripts he had discovered, a version at least as old as the reign of Henry VII. The version that Addison used, observed Scott, was "a composition bearing only a general resemblance to the original—expressing the same events and sentiments in much smoother language, and more flowing and easy versification; but losing in poetical fire and energy, and in the vigour and pithiness of the expression, a great deal more than it has gained in suavity of diction". It was, of course, that "vigour and pithiness" which so impressed the younger generation, who had grown tired of the "gaudiness and inane phraseology"—as Wordsworth was to call it—of contemporary poetic language.

The earlier collections of D'Urfey and others, particularly the Scottish collections of Watson and Ramsay, would have been known to some readers, but the *Reliques* contained ballads like *Sir Patrick Spens, The Nut-Brown Maid, The Brave Lord Willoughby, Child Waters, The Bailiff's Daughter, The King and the Miller of Mansfield, Barbara Allen,* and *Waly Waly*, which were certainly not much known at the time and may never have regained their former popularity without Percy's efforts. And though the modern imitations of the old ballads were not to be very successful, we should probably not have had, without the influence of Percy's collection, either Coleridge's *Mariner* or Scott's *Proud Maisie*.*

Chatterton and the "Rowley" Poems

The tragic figure of Thomas Chatterton must be mentioned before we conclude this chapter with some discussion of the revolution in literary criticism which accompanied the mediaeval revival.

Chatterton was born at Bristol in 1752, son of a poor schoolmaster and grandson of the sexton of the church of St Mary Redcliffe. From a child he seems to have been fascinated by the past, becoming familiar with the ancient documents he found in the muniment room of St Mary's. He later composed poems which he claimed as the work of Thomas Rowley, an imaginary monk of the fifteenth century, and his success in imposing these productions on his Bristol friends encouraged him to send specimens to Walpole. But Walpole, who admitted that he did not understand "the Saxon language", was advised by more learned men that the specimens were forgeries. So Chatterton was denied the assistance that Walpole might have given him.

He then turned to modern themes and began contributing political articles and satires—one of which, *Resignation*, we

* One thing Percy had in common with Walpole was his uneasy feeling that his work might be thought unworthy of the public's attention. His explanation for having "bestowed attention on a parcel of old ballads" can be compared with the apology in Walpole's original preface.

quoted in our last chapter—to various periodicals. He went to London in 1770, but, despairing of success, poisoned himself the same year. His tragic story, and the remarkable quality of his youthful work, deeply affected the romantic movement. The early Coleridge saw him as one of the pioneers of liberty, addressing him in 1794 as a suitable person to share a "Pantisocratic" existence on the banks of the Susquehana:

> O Chatterton! that thou wert yet alive,
> Sure thou wouldst spread the canvas to the gale;
> And love with us the tinkling team to drive
> O'er peaceful Freedom's undivided dale . . .

Keats inscribed *Endymion* to his memory and wrote a sonnet beginning "O Chatterton! how very sad thy fate!" Wordsworth referred to him in *Resolution and Independence* as

> the marvellous Boy,
> The sleepless Soul that perished in his pride.

Some of the more extravagant praise given him by contemporary critics and their successors cannot bear a moment's reflection. Malone considered him "the greatest genius that England has produced since the days of Shakespeare"; another critic wrote that "he must rank, as a universal genius, above Dryden, and perhaps only second to Shakespeare"; a third compared him with Milton; a fourth with Homer. And Hazlitt's judgment—"I cannot find in Chatterton's works anything so extraordinary as the age at which they were written"—was so ill taken by his hearers that he had to devote the first part of his next lecture to clarifying his position.

But there is not much doubt that the opinion of Hazlitt* is substantially correct. It is the precocity of Chatterton, both in the *Rowley* poems and the political satires, which is so memorable. His "Mediaeval" pieces may have owed something to the example of Ossian, but he was a better poet than Macpherson; there is probably nothing in the Scotsman's

---

* Compare Johnson's remark to Boswell: "This is the most extraordinary young man that has encountered my knowledge. It is wonderful how the whelp has written such things."

epics so good as the *Minstrel's Song*, from the *Rowley* poems, which opens:

> O! synge untoe my roundelaie,
> O! droppe the brynie teare wythe mee,
> Daunce ne moe atte hallie daie,
> Lycke a rennynge ryver bee.
> > Mie love ys dedde,
> > Gonne to hys deathe-bedde,
> > Al under the wyllowe-tree.
>
> Black hys cryne as the wyntere nyght,
> Whyte hys rode as the sommer snowe,
> Rodde hys face as the mornynge lyghte
> Cale he lyes ynne the grave belowe.
> > Mie love ys dedde,
> > Gonne to hys deathe-bedde,
> > Al under the wyllowe-tree.

The Academic Revolt

The first critic to expose the *Rowley* poems was Thomas Warton, Professor of Poetry at Oxford from 1757 to 1767 and from 1785 to his death in 1790 Professor of History and Poet Laureate. His verse, like that of all other eighteenth-century Laureates, is not very interesting; he is remembered as one of the leaders of the revolution in literary criticism which accompanied the mediaeval revival.

As early as 1756, his brother Joseph Warton, Headmaster of Winchester, had startled the orthodox by placing Spenser above Pope;* and Richard Hurd, Bishop of Worcester, in his *Letters on Chivalry and Romance* (1762) had referred to Spenser and Milton as "the two greatest of our poets". The title of Hurd's book shows plainly the connection between the mediaeval revival and this questioning of the position of Augustan poetry; and, in fact, the Wartons had come to

---

* He had written in *An Essay on the Genius and Writings of Pope*: "We do not, it should seem, sufficiently attend to the difference there is between a Man of Wit, a Man of Sense, and a true Poet. Donne and Swift were undoubtedly men of wit, and men of sense: but what traces have they of pure poetry? . . . The sublime and the pathetic are the two chief nerves of all genuine poesy. What is there transcendently sublime or pathetic in Pope?"

their interest in Spenser and mediaeval literature through their appreciation of Gothic architecture, which had been fostered by their father, Thomas Warton the elder, Professor of Poetry at Oxford in the 'forties.

As with Walpole and Percy, however, their literary revolution was at first rather tentative. It is said that Joseph Warton's "heresy" gave so much offence that he did not venture to bring out his second volume on Pope till 1782; and Hurd added to his statement quoted above the qualification: "at least the two which an English reader is most fond to compare with Homer". It was not until Thomas Warton produced his *History of English Poetry* (1774-81) that the revaluation became at all established—though, of course, the controversy over Pope continued well into the nineteenth century, for instance in the reaction of Byron and Campbell to William Bowles's observation that Pope lacked imagination. As a kind of complement to the *History*, another Oxford man, Thomas Tyrwhitt, produced an *Essay on the Language and Versification of Chaucer* and an *Introductory Discourse to the Canterbury Tales*, in which he restored the metrical scheme of the poet who had been thought by Dryden and Pope to be a rough and unlearned genius. Both had admired Chaucer, but it was not till now that his full stature began to be recognised.

This academic revolution was as important in its way as the more famous poetic revolution of Wordsworth and Coleridge in the closing years of the century. The one did not altogether follow from the other, but the eventual success of what is usually called the Romantic Revival could hardly have occurred without some earlier reaction from the Augustan. The Wartons were no frivolous mediaevalists; unlike Walpole, they really knew something about Gothic architecture, and Joseph could see the ridiculous side of the "Gothic" cult—for instance, in his *Epistle from Thomas Hearne*—as Thomas could expose the pseudo-mediaeval language of Chatterton. They were friends of Johnson, the last of the classical critics, and the foundation of their "heresy" was simply that they took a broader view of English literature. Johnson, we observed, could challenge some of the Augustan assumptions, both in literature and life, by the sheer weight of common sense and experience; but he was still sufficiently under the Augustan influence to write that "The English nation, in the time of Shakespeare, was yet struggling to emerge from barbarity . . . The public was gross and dark . . ." (etc.). Thomas Warton was not nearly so great a critic, but when he expressed his belief that the Elizabethan Age was the greatest period of our poetry, he was pointing, however vaguely, towards the modern view that something valuable was lost at the Restoration.

It was not, of course, in the Wartons to affect this revolution in taste without some qualifying exceptions. They saw the glory of the Elizabethans in Spenser rather than in Shakespeare; and their emphasis on the fanciful side of Spenser and Milton tended both to obscure other sides of these poets and to propagate a dislike of the didactic and the witty that was to lead to the Victorian judgment that satire was not a proper vehicle for poetry. There is actually, of course, a good deal of satire in Spenser, as in Chaucer, and the didactic was the method of Milton as well as Pope; but the concern of the late eighteenth century for sentiment and romance was to become eventually Arnold's concern for poetry of the soul as distinguished from poetry of the intellect. Only those who still agree with Arnold that Gray was an isolated poet in an age of prose will regard this development from the Wartons' revolution with entire approval.

CHAPTER X

THE AGE OF REVOLUTION
1776-1804

Bliss was it in that dawn to be alive,
But to be young was very heaven!
WORDSWORTH: *The Prelude*.

The Return to Politics

As far as literature is concerned, the mid-eighteenth century, we observed, was a tranquil period between two ages when writers divided themselves into opposing political groups. We know that Johnson and Fielding opposed Walpole, and that later Wilkes and Churchill were among the principal opponents of George III's personal government, the government of "the King's friends", as it was called. But from the point of view of literature, these events are very much in the background, though they did lead in some degree to the succeeding Age of Revolution, when once again, as in the Augustan Age, some of the most representative writers of the time found themselves in opposing political camps.

We say "political", because of the events which give their name to the period; but it might be held, with a good deal of truth, that it was the mid-eighteenth century which was the period of *politics*, pure and simple, while the ages coming before and after were periods of fundamental change, when politics were only one aspect of the revolutions going forward. The periods, in fact, when literature is most connected with politics are those when politics are much more than a professional interest, when men find it difficult not to be on one side or the other. When we recall that even Pope and Blake took more than a superficial interest in the politics of their time, we begin to understand that "politics" in such ages of fundamental change cover a multitude of things which are not normally political. We have seen how close was the connection between politics and religion in the Augustan Age; at the end of the century, we find as close a relation between political events and that slow revolution in English society which was the result of new methods in agriculture and industry.

It was thus an Age of Revolution in several different ways, which nevertheless came to be connected. The effect on England of the American Revolution of 1776, and the French Revolution of 1789, was as profound as had been the effect on America and France of the English Revolution of 1688. We cannot say altogether that the American and French Revolutions were the result of the English, for many other causes contributed; but the political philosophy of Locke was behind that of Jefferson and Mirabeau, and the less admirable side of the English Revolution, the overwhelming power given to the richer classes, came to be seen as a positive evil when the domestic revolutions in agriculture and industry further separated one class from another. It was natural that Englishmen like Godwin and the young Wordsworth should see in the democratic aspirations of America and France an example which might relieve their own country of the injustice and corruption they saw around them. Their optimism in regard to France was similar to that of Voltaire and Montesquieu in regard to England; and both were inclined to forget the differences which separated England from the Continent. The very fact that the English Revolution had been bloodless, while the French Revolution developed from constitutional debates into the Reign of Terror, proves how false was the reasoning that, on the one hand, prophesied a peaceful shift of power in France, and, on the other, a violent revolution in England. Gibbon and Burke saw the likelihood of a Napoleon arising, but neither the Conservative fear of a violent revolution at home nor the Radical hope of a democratic government in France was destined to be realised. Only a few observers like Cobbett were shrewd enough to see that the English people would never follow the French, that France and England would work out their different problems by very different ways.

"Conservative" and "Radical" are new terms for this book, and, in fact, they only came into common use during the nineteenth century. Disraeli may be said to have founded the modern Conservative party, but the impulse that leads many Conservatives to-day to look back to Burke as their real ancestor has much justification. Burke was a Whig, prominent in the opposition to George III's American policy, who became more and more conservative under the stress of events in France and England. The Radicals were not at this time a parliamentary party at all, though Fox, Sheridan, and a small group of "New Whigs", who opposed Pitt's policy of intervention in France—which Burke and the "Old Whigs" supported—were perhaps among the ancestors of the "Left Wing" of the Liberal party who were not satisfied with the Reform Bill of 1832. In the late eighteenth century, "radical" was simply the loose name given to any sympathiser with the original aims of the French Revolution, or, indeed, to any advocate of parliamentary reform at home. Naturally, the name covered a good many people of widely differing beliefs, including a fair proportion of cranks, but the main tradition of Radicalism was eventually seen to be that of Paine and Cobbett. To understand the political struggle in England at the close of the century, it is best, perhaps, to concentrate on Burke and Paine, who not only wrote the two most widely-read political works of their time but who were representative of the merits and shortcomings of each side.

Burke and the French Revolution

We have already come across the name of Edmund Burke in our discussion of the Johnson circle and in our mentioning of him as the statesman to whom Crabbe turned in his distress. He was among the few original members of the Literary Club who survived to the period of the French Revolution, being at the time of the fall of the Bastille about sixty years old.

The exact date of his birth is uncertain—probably 1729—but we know that he was born in Dublin and was a contemporary of Goldsmith at Trinity College. Though he took up his father's profession of law, his main interests lay in literature and politics. In 1756 he published an ironical reply to the philosophy of Bolingbroke called *A Vindication of Natural Society*, and also an essay on aesthetics, *A Philosophic Enquiry into the Origin of Our Ideas of the Sublime and Beautiful*, which had a great influence on German thought. Three years later he began to edit for Dodsley an *Annual Register* of current events, the series of which was continued till 1788.

He was first elected to Parliament in 1765, at once making a name for himself by two speeches defending the rights of the American colonists. He became the leading spirit in the Whig Opposition, fighting for the freedom of the Commons against the interests of "the King's friends" and no less vigorously supporting the freedom of the Americans against the government's policy of taxation. His *Thoughts on the Causes of the Present Discontents* (1770), a pamphlet defending the principles of the English Revolution against both the personal government of the King and what seemed to him the equally unconstitutional behaviour of the Radicals, was followed by the two famous speeches on American policy during the critical years 1774-5. There is no doubt that had his views on America been supported by the House, the conflict would either have been avoided altogether or quickly come to an honourable peace. But he was without power, and the American Declaration of Independence in 1776 put an end to any compromise.

The difference between Burke's views on America (and on Ireland) and his views on the French Revolution has led to his being accused of inconsistency. But he considered himself entirely consistent, and it seemed natural to him to defend the English constitution against what he conceived to be the revolutionary policy of the Radicals, as he had defended the English tradition of freedom against George III. He was perhaps more interested in the effects of the French Revolution on England than in the Revolution itself, and in fact his *Reflections on the Revolution in France* (1790) was provoked by a sermon by a Unitarian minister named Richard Price.

Price was a member of a mainly Dissenting body called the Revolution Society, a body existing to commemorate the

English Revolution of 1688.   Its president was Earl Stanhope,
and its leading philosopher the great chemist and preacher
Dr Priestley.   Burke had, of course, his own conception of the
English Revolution, and though he was very much out in his
supposition that Price wanted another, and a violent, revolution in England,* he had no difficulty in showing that some of
Price's remarks upon the 1688 Revolution were false and that
the Society were confusing that constitution with the events
of the Puritan Rebellion and with the contemporary revolution
in France:

> These gentlemen [he pointed out] in all their
> reasonings on the Revolution of 1688, have a Revolution
> which happened in England about forty years before,
> and the late French Revolution, so much before their
> eyes, and in their hearts, that they are constantly con-
> founding all the three together.   It is necessary that we
> should separate what they confound . . .

Burke proceeded to do so, at great length and with
judicial thoroughness; but it was not his constitutional
arguments that made his book so influential, it was the
evolution of the French Revolution from aspiring democracy
to actual tyranny.   Burke came to be revered as a prophet,
because the way events actually went in France justified his
pessimism and seemed also to justify his criticism of Price
and the Revolution Society.   But his pretence that England
was in no need of radical reform may have deceived himself,
but could hardly deceive those who were aware of the abuses
that had been calling for reform for many years.   His ingenious
remarks upon parliamentary representation, for instance,
could hardly convince those Englishmen who were ashamed
of the existence of "pocket boroughs"—that is, a seat in
Parliament owned by a noble family—when industrial centres
like Birmingham and Manchester were without representation

* Price had, in fact, written that one of the distinctive features
of this country was "being in possession of the forms of an excellent
constitution of government, any changes or improvements necessary
to correct abuses and to give perfect liberty may be grafted upon
them without tumult or danger"—a statement proved true by the
Reform Bill of 1832 and by many later measures.

at all. The perpetuation of "pocket boroughs" and "rotten boroughs"—such as that of Old Sarum, whose non-existent voting population returned two members—could not be justified by Burke's airy talk about the benefits of the English constitution, any more than his defence of the established Church could defend such evils as "pocket benefices" (where there was neither church nor congregation, but nevertheless a substantial income for the parson) and the glaring contrast between hard-working rectors, "passing rich with forty pounds a year", and bishops like Watson of Llandaff, who lived almost all his life in Westmorland, yet held a chair of divinity at Cambridge and no less than fourteen livings in Huntingdonshire, Leicestershire, and Shropshire. If Burke was a more accurate prophet than Price over the outcome of the French Revolution, none the less by his rigid conservatism in this influential book he was one of the reasons—the chief of which was the war with France—why reform in England was put off for thirty or forty years.

Paine and the Radicals

Burke's *Reflections* provoked several answers, among them *A Vindication of the Rights of Men* by Mary Wollstonecraft, later the wife of Godwin, and *Vindiciae Gallicae* by the Whig historian, James Mackintosh. After the Reign of Terror, Mackintosh changed his views and his apparent "apostasy" was the subject of an epigram by Lamb, as that of Southey, Coleridge, and Wordsworth provoked the irony of Byron. No real apostasy, of course, existed; even more than with the Russian Revolution in recent years, there was a vast difference between supporting the original democratic aspirations and in defending the tyranny that followed. Few Englishmen, in fact, did defend the Terror, certainly not the veteran reformer Thomas Paine, who was to suffer under it, and whose reply to Burke, *The Rights of Man*, was even more widely read than the *Reflections*.

Tom Paine, as he is usually called, had one of the most extraordinary careers in our literary or political history. Born in 1737, the son of a Norfolk stay-maker, he was largely self-educated, though he acknowledged he owed much throughout his life to the moral instruction of his Quaker parents. After a short period as sailor on a privateer, he settled in London in his father's trade, studying in the evenings. His early life was one of almost continuous failure, and at the age of thirty-seven, despairing of finding a suitable position in England—he had tried teaching and tobacco-manufacture, and had spent some years as an exciseman—he emigrated to Pennsylvania, with a letter of recommendation from Benjamin Franklin, then in London as the colony's agent.

He settled in Philadelphia, and became editor of the *Pennsylvania Magazine*. His articles in this paper aroused great interest, his attacks on negro slavery leading to the first Anti-Slavery Society to be founded in America. But this agitation was destined to influence the future rather than the present, the interests of most Americans at this time being taken up with the approaching break with England.

Though so recent an arrival, Paine immediately identified himself with the colonists' cause, his pamphlet *Common-Sense* (1776) having a huge circulation and being among the chief reasons for the American determination for absolute independence. He joined Washington's army as a private, writing at evening, by the light of camp fires, the series of pamphlets later published under the title of *The American Crisis*. Afterwards he became Foreign Secretary to Congress, and the state of New York rewarded his services by granting him a small property. But he declined to settle down to an inactive life, and in 1787 returned to England to begin the second stage in his public career.*

In England, he soon became prominent among the men of reform, among such Radicals as Godwin, Holcroft, Horne Tooke, and Major Cartwright. He became a member of a club called the London Corresponding Society, which had been

* His motive was partly personal, for he wished to pursue his researches into applied science. He became the inventor of many mechanical appliances and was the constructor of the first iron bridge, made at Wearmouth after his designs. His combination of mechanical with literary and political ability makes him one of the most versatile men of the age.

founded by a shoemaker Thomas Hardy and which numbered some 30,000 members, mostly tradesmen, mechanics, and shopkeepers. His name was known in Europe as much as in England, and on the Fall of the Bastille in 1789 the key was presented to him as a present from a free France to a free America. He was, in fact, the one link between the two revolutions, and when Burke published his *Reflections* it was natural that Paine should attempt a reply.

The reply, *The Rights of Man*, published in two parts during 1791-2, was as well written as the provocation. We have observed that Burke considered himself quite consistent in his different attitudes to the two revolutions, and Paine can be judged equally consistent when he followed his agitation for entire independence for America by reminding Burke of the many things he had forgotten at home:

> When, in countries that are called civilised, we see age going to the workhouse and youth going to the gallows, something must be wrong in the system of Government. It would seem, by the exterior appearances of such countries, that all was happiness; but there lies hidden from the eye of common observation, a mass of wretchedness that has scarcely any other chance than to expire in poverty or infamy. Its entrance into life is marked with the presage of its fate; and until this is remedied, it is in vain to punish.
>
> Civil Government does not consist in executions; but in making that provision for the instruction of youth and the support of age, as to exclude as much as possible profligacy from the one and despair from the other.

There is no doubt that Paine convicted Burke of certain disingenuities, as Burke had convicted Price of certain falsities of fact. The argument of the *Reflections* had been too legal altogether; Paine was able to point to the injustices that actually existed behind "the exterior appearances", injustices that had eventually led to violent revolution in France and which could lead to another "glorious revolution" in England. The history of reform in Victorian England was to be the justification of his arguments, as Burke was more immediately justified by the outcome of the French Revolution.

Both books had enormous influence on the literature and social struggles of the future. Some of the talk of the reformers had, indeed, been full of wind; and Burke was able to remind his readers that tradition was a living thing, to be tampered with at a country's peril. To his influence we owe much of the wisdom of Scott and the later Coleridge, and probably, too, some of the more conservative ideas in the later reformers themselves. Paine's influence is as clearly traceable in the original Chartists and in the Victorian reformers and trade-unionists. It did not produce so much literature, but was behind most of the social struggles from 1815 onward. A combination of the wisdom of Burke and Paine may be said to have prevented a violent revolution in England, as the folly of each produced the figures of the hardened reactionary on the one hand and the woolly idealist on the other.

The immediate fortunes of the two books were as different as their arguments. Burke received the gratitude of all the crowned heads of Europe; Paine's book was denounced by the government and booksellers prosecuted for selling it. Despite this, it sold enough copies to make a thousand pounds for the author—who, with typical disinterestedness, gave the whole sum to the Corresponding Society. (As he had earlier given the profits of *Common-Sense* to Washington's army.) In 1792 Pitt accepted Burke's opinion that the author should be tried for high treason; but, acting on a prophetic hint from his friend William Blake, Paine escaped across the Channel and was condemned to death in his absence.

This was part of "the English Terror" which events in France and the influence of Burke's book had imposed upon the country. Radicals were imprisoned or transported to Botany Bay for having *The Rights of Man* in their possession, and in 1794 the Habeas Corpus Act, which had safeguarded suspected persons from being detained in prison without trial, was repealed by Parliament. The same year Hardy, Horne Tooke, Holcroft, and others were arrested for an alleged plot to overthrow the government—an absurd charge which Godwin attacked in one of the most powerful political pamphlets ever written. "An association for Parliamentary reform," he wrote, "may desert its object and become guilty of High Treason. True; so may a card club, a bench of justice, or even a Cabinet Council." The nation, of course, from 1792 to 1815, with a short interval in 1802-3, was at war with France, radical opinions being often regarded as treasonable in themselves. With the rise of Napoleon, most democratic hopes for France were destroyed; Wordsworth and many others recanted their earlier opinions when Napoleon invaded Switzerland in 1798, and when the victorious general was made Emperor of France in 1804 the Age of Revolution in England was virtually at an end.

Meanwhile Paine had arrived at Calais to find himself elected its deputy to the National Convention in Paris. He became prominent in urging the abolition of the monarchy, but when he urged with equal conviction that the King's life should be spared, he was imprisoned for a year while the execution of the King was proceeded with and only by a lucky chance escaped the guillotine himself.

While in prison he began *The Age of Reason*, which was published in 1793. No book of his has been more reviled, particularly by those who have never read it. In England it was burned by the common hangman,* and America proved herself so ungrateful for his former services that his last years in retirement there were embittered by petty persecution. The tradition lasted as long as the present century, when an American President referred to him as "a dirty little Atheist". If the President had condescended to open the book he condemned, he would have discovered it to be a defence of Deism—the creed of Franklin and Jefferson—against both

---

* The connection between radical opinions in politics and in religion had led to a remarkable change in the religious outlook of the governing classes. The old aristocratic scepticism was either recanted or covered up, the Methodists were encouraged instead of vilified, and every opportunity was taken to impress upon the public that reform in politics meant atheism in religion. This came to have a good side, when the Church of England in the first quarter of the nineteenth century corrected its outstanding abuses, and when the Methodist influence on the Trade Unions stood for moderation in place of violence, but in the time of Paine it was little else but hypocrisy.

atheism and orthodox Christianity. It was originally written, in fact, to counteract the atheist tendencies in the Jacobins. Some of Paine's arguments against orthodoxy are now so widely accepted that they form part of the reasoning of modernist bishops; but at the time, of course, they were received with horror and books were written in defence of the orthodox position. The most famous of these was *A View of the Evidences of Christianity* (1794) by William Paley, an archdeacon who was also a mathematician, and whose power of marshalling his arguments clearly and concisely led to his book being considered by the orthodox the perfect answer, not only to Paine, but to Hume and Gibbon.

Godwin and the "Anti-Jacobin"

Among the committee which undertook the publication of *The Rights of Man* were the philosopher William Godwin and the dramatist and novelist Thomas Holcroft. Godwin's own *Political Justice* only escaped the fate of Paine's book because Pitt considered that a work published at three guineas could not do much harm among those who had not three shillings to spare. He forgot the existence of working-men's clubs, which bought the book by subscription; and, more important, he forgot that it was the middle classes who were running the revolution in France and who were also in England the chief public for revolutionary philosophy. The immediate effect of Godwin's book has been well described by Hazlitt: "No work in our time gave such a blow to the philosophical mind of the country as the celebrated *Enquiry concerning Political Justice*. Tom Paine was considered for the time as a Tom Fool to him, Paley an old woman, Edmund Burke a flashy sophist. Truth, moral truth, it was supposed, had here taken up its abode; and these were the oracles of thought".

The early life of Godwin had been almost as obscure as that of Paine. Born in 1756, the son of a Calvinist minister, he was educated at the Dissenting Academy of Hoxton and became himself a minister for some years before taking to literature as a profession. He met Holcroft in 1786, and from the first the two men influenced each other greatly. The older man had risen from stable-boy and cobbler to become a successful dramatist, so was in himself an embodiment of the force of the human will in adverse circumstances that was to become a chief article in the Godwinian philosophy. They were well matched, the one having as wide an experience in life as the other in books, and at the outbreak of the French Revolution both were among the leaders of the English sympathisers.

It was in 1791 that Godwin began to write his *Political Justice*, which was not completed and published till 1793. His starting-point was that "the happiness of the human species is the most desirable object of human science to promote". Only by introducing universal political justice can that happiness be the common lot; and only by the abandonment of government, which perpetuates injustice and inequality, can universal justice be attained. Thus baldly summarised, the argument seems more foolish than it really is, the book being in fact a curious mixture of genuine insight and logical absurdity. No more than Swift—whose coldly noble Houyhnhnms are similar to the ideal man of *Political Justice*—could Godwin resist following a line of thought to its ultimate, if wildly impracticable, conclusion. This strained logic may not matter in a satirist, but in a philosopher it leads to confused thinking among his disciples and to easy rejoinder among his opponents. For instance, Godwin's seeming denial of the virtue of gratitude—actually a belief in the superiority of universal benevolence to private affection—made him the butt of common-sense Tory critics, such as those in the *Anti-Jacobin Review*.

This paper, founded in 1797 by George Canning and George Ellis, and edited by William Gifford, was for some years an effective counterblast to the revolutionary literature of Paine and Godwin, of the early Coleridge and Southey. Its attack on the Godwinian philosophy, entitled *Dialogue in the Shades*, appeared in 1799; the following passage is characteristic:

> NEODIDACTUS: Family attachments we regard as silly,
> and even criminal when they tend to bias our
> opinions; and as to promises, our master has written

a long chapter to prove that they are great evils, and are only to be observed when we find it convenient.

LUCIAN: Did it never occur to you that this system might produce more evil than good in the world? and that you have been recommending a plan, which, instead of perfecting man, and improving society, must be destructive of every estimable quality in his breast, and must drive him again into savage solitude? . . . But, come, that we may part in good humour, I will treat you with a sentiment which I derive from a dear friend of Swift. "We are for a just partition of the world, for every man has a right to enjoy life . . . A covetous fellow, like a jackdaw, steals what he was never made to enjoy, for the sake of hiding it. These are the robbers of mankind, for money was made for the free-hearted and generous; and where is the injury of taking from another what he has not the heart to make use of?" What is your opinion of this?

NEODIDACTUS: It is admirably expressed in the true spirit of our philosophy and of impartial justice. Indeed, our master has said something very like it. Pray, in what divine work is this great truth to be found?

LUCIAN: In the *Beggar's Opera*; it expresses the sentiments of a gang of highwaymen, an institution which approaches nearer to your idea of perfect society than any other with which I am acquainted.*

Godwin produced a second edition of his book in 1796 and a third in 1799, and it is interesting to observe how he gradually

---

* Who wrote this *Dialogue* is not precisely known. It may have been Canning, the future Prime Minister; or the ex-shoemaker's-apprentice Gifford, who had effectively satirised the "Della Cruscan" school of poetasters in *The Baviad* (1794) and was to be the first editor of the *Quarterly Review*; or Ellis, scholar in early poetry and friend of Scott, who had formerly been a Whig and collaborated in *The Rolliad*, a skit on the "King's friends"; or lastly, the future diplomatist J. H. Frere, who wrote *The Loves of the Triangles*, a parody of Erasmus Darwin's *Loves of the Plants*, and collaborated with Canning in another of the *Anti-Jacobin's* most witty productions, *The Needy Knife-grinder*, a parody of Southey. In its combination of political and literary criticism, the *Anti-Jacobin* did some useful service in the cause of Sense against Sensibility.

toned down some of his earlier statements, while still keeping his leading ideas. Thus, the attack on marriage and family affection was much modified after the experience of his own happy union with Mary Wollstonecraft. He had met her in 1796, had lived with her at first without benefit of clergy—according to their rigid principles—and then had married her in 1797, for the sake of their coming child. But she did not long survive the birth of her daughter Mary, the future wife of Shelley. Godwin's brief happiness with her, and his sorrow at her early death, had a great influence upon his mind. Not only in the later editions of *Political Justice*, but in his later work in general, we see a warmer Godwin than the original "Houyhnhnm" philosopher.

Some of this later work was in fiction. The fame which *Political Justice* had brought him had led to a desire to propagate his beliefs in more immediately attractive form. His friend Holcroft had written his most successful moral melodrama, *The Road to Ruin*, in 1792, and two "novels with a purpose", *Anna St Ives* and *Hugh Trevor*. *Things as they are; or The Adventures of Caleb Williams* (1794) was Godwin's first attempt in the same field, and it proved much the best of the "revolutionary novels", superior to Holcroft's and Mrs Inchbald's as well as to his own later fiction. The only novel of the same period and class which can be compared with it, in power and sincerity, is *Hermsprong; or Man as he is not* (1796) by a paper-maker, Robert Bage, whose work has been praised by Scott.

St Leon (1799) is the next best of Godwin's novels. It was followed by *Fleetwood* and *Mandeville: A Tale of the Seventeenth Century*. More important were his "Reflections on Education" called *The Enquirer* (1797) and the memoir of his wife (1798). Mary Wollstonecraft's chief work had been her pioneer *Vindication of the Rights of Woman* (1792), and Godwin's volume of reminiscences was called *Memoirs of the Author of the Rights of Woman*. It was attacked by the *Anti-Jacobin* in a satire *The Vision of Liberty*, in which the freedom of women, and the relationship of Godwin and his wife, were made the subject of coarse allusions.

New Paths in Philosophy

Two important events occurred in the year 1776: the American colonists declared their legal independence of Britain, and in his first published work, the *Fragment on Government*, Jeremy Bentham declared his legal independence of Blackstone.

Two other important events occurred in 1789: the French Revolution broke out, and in his *Introduction to the Principles of Morals and Legislation* Bentham expressed the essence of the Utilitarian philosophy, that the object of all legislation should be "the greatest happiness of the greatest number".

At first glance, it seems absurd to compare the philosophical conclusions of an unworldly recluse with two of the greatest events in modern history. Yet the effect of these political revolutions on England was more immediate than lasting, while Bentham's "revolution" was behind nearly all the legislative reforms of the early Victorian Age. That his doctrine of *laissez-faire* was mainly responsible for the opposition to other needed reforms, notably the Factory Acts, is also true, as is the fact that behind the detested new Poor Law of 1834 lurked that deficiency of imagination which Dickens was to criticise in his disciples. Both for good and evil, his influence was as long-lasting as it was wide-reaching and made itself felt on generations of Englishmen to whom the revolutions in America and France were just items in a history book.

As Adam Smith had held in his *Wealth of Nations* (1776) that every trader was the best judge of his own profit, so Bentham held that every man was the best judge of his own happiness. He had no truck with the Godwinian theory of "natural rights". Rights, he insisted, are created by law: "*Natural rights* is simple nonsense: *natural and imprescriptible rights*, rhetorical nonsense—nonsense upon stilts". He proceeded to attack all laws interfering with the free expression of religious belief or political opinion; he advocated the legalising of trade unions, the abolition of savage punishments, the reform of the Parliamentary franchise. In his very first book, he boldly criticised the *Commentaries on the Laws of*

England (1765-9) of Sir William Blackstone, volumes then regarded almost as sacrosanct as the laws they learnedly defended. In his next book, he took over from Priestley the famous saying, "the greatest happiness of the greatest number is the measure of right and wrong" and gave it currency as the criterion of a whole doctrine of thought and practice. Even more than Godwin, he was behind the Reform Bill of 1832, though none of his works had the popular success of *Political Justice*. His influence was on statesmen and legislators rather than on poets; also to some extent on the farmers and landlords of the agricultural revolution. Some of his articles appeared in Arthur Young's *Annals of Agriculture,* founded in 1784 as an organ to promote the new methods of farming.

Another philosopher to have an extended influence—and whose theories have cropped up again in the post-war world— was T. R. Malthus, a clergyman who wrote a reply to Godwin's *Political Justice* entitled *An Essay on the Principle of Population as it affects the future improvements of society*. The first edition (1798) was followed by a storm of controversy among the followers and opponents of Godwin; Malthus pondered the matter further, and produced a second edition, replying to his critics, in 1803. The controversy continued into the Victorian Age, Malthus being one of the inspirers of Darwin's theory of Evolution. The Darwinian phrase, "the struggle for existence", was actually part of Malthus's original argument.

He maintained, to put it briefly, that Godwin's doctrine of the perfectibility of man had overlooked a very important consideration: namely, that in the natural course of events population would expand beyond the means of subsistence, and the inevitable result would be inequality and misery. Every species, including man, he pointed out, increases in geometrical ratio, for the same reason that everyone has two parents, four grandparents, and so on; but the production of food can increase only in arithmetical ratio. To-day, when the rapid increase of the world's population—even after two world wars—contrasts alarmingly with its dwindling food-supply, and threatens to upset the degree of Godwinian

perfection to which we have laboriously attained, thinkers are
turning back to Malthus, if not agreeing with all his conclusions.   At the time, he was chiefly valuable in putting some
needed caution in the more extravagant visions of human
perfectibility.   As Burke sounded a note of conservatism
among the political philosophers, so Malthus among the
philosophers of social progress.

Cobbett and the Domestic Revolution

The Malthusian doctrine was once ridiculed by William
Cobbett in a farce that was played to a delighted country
audience.   But we do not commonly think of him among the
philosophical controversies of the age; rather do we regard it
as a relief to turn from the men of books to the man who was
as much a practical farmer as a political pamphleteer, the
man whom we immediately think of when anyone mentions
the time of transition between the agricultural age and the
industrial—that revolution in the domestic affairs of England
that was ultimately so much more important than any
political revolution.

The two, of course, were connected; and Cobbett is the
main link.   We feel with him, despite his greater genius, that
we are face to face with what the ordinary man, particularly
the ordinary countryman, was actually thinking during this
time of social change.   The theories of Godwin and Malthus,
of Smith and Bentham, even of Paine, seem at some points
irrelevant to the practical issues; Cobbett held no theories at
all, and throughout his stormy career had always the virtues—
and the limitations—of the common-sense approach.

He was born in 1762 at Farnham in Surrey, the son of a
small farmer and innkeeper.   "With respect to my ancestors,"
he tells us, "I shall go no further back than my grandfather,
and for this very plain reason, that I never talk of any prior
to him.   He was a day-labourer, and I have heard my father
say that he worked for one farmer from the day of his marriage
to that of his death, upwards of forty years."

This passage is important in the light of some modern
theories about Cobbett.   He has been called "the last

spokesman of the old peasantry"—a statement which is
evidently true in some respects, but not in the meaning that
has often been given it.   His grandfather was not a "peasant"
in the sense of a countryman owning his own bit of land; he
was in the class of hired labourer which is often thought to be
solely the product of the agricultural revolution.   The truth
is that there were peasants and hired labourers existing side
by side in the late seventeenth and early eighteenth centuries.
The new methods of farming and the renewed policy of
enclosing land and taking in commons—what we call for
brevity "the agricultural revolution" of the mid-eighteenth
century onwards—led to a gradual decline in the number of
peasants and a corresponding increase in the number of hired
labourers and in the number of countrymen who left the land
altogether to work in the new centres of industrial development.   It was a complicated process, not easily dealt with in
a brief discussion.   Some people, such as the Cobbett family,
went against the general current, becoming small independent
farmers, like Cobbett's father and eventually himself, where
the grandfather had been a labourer, working for someone
else.   But the general current, particularly as the eighteenth
century gave way to the nineteenth, was certainly in the
other direction.

   What Cobbett goes on to say about his happy, though hard,
life on his father's farm—"I do not remember the time when
I did not earn my living . . ."—is also very important in our
understanding of these complex issues.   Goldsmith, we saw,
put back the time of rural prosperity to the period of his
childhood, and maintained that the time of rural decline was
about mid-century onwards—the very time that Cobbett
looked back upon as the ideal state from which the country
had since fallen!   How do we account for this discrepancy,
other than by saying that conditions varied in different parts
of the countryside?   Something must be laid at the door of
the simplifying memory.   It is common for people of middle-
age and over to look back upon their childhood as a period of
prosperity; and, indeed, a most instructive anthology could
be compiled from English literature of writers lamenting the

vanished glories of the past, all through the ages. The anthology would be best done backwards, each writer glorifying the time of his predecessor's despair.

But this, of course, is not the whole story. There was as certainly an agricultural revolution as an industrial; and both the increase of population, which worried Malthus, and the development of mechanical invention, which worried Cobbett, were essential features of each. The growing propulation had to be fed, and the new methods of farming increased the total yield. The development of mechanical invention was only part of the scientific progress which halted the death-rate, increased the chances of maturity, and made possible both the agricultural revolution, which was dependent on the new scientific methods, and the industrial revolution, which was dependent on the rapid growth of labour. Thus, all these developments were bound up with one another, and it was natural that the total social change should wear a different aspect according to the point of view taken up.

It is only the first part of Cobbett's life that concerns us here, for the time of his greatest work, when he became the spokesmen of the industrial workers as well as the villagers, was after 1815. He as truly spans the two centuries as he is in himself the link between the two domestic revolutions and between the domestic revolution as a whole and the political revolution. He is as representative a figure as Johnson, though compared with his predecessor his place in literature is not high.

He spent much of his early life in America, after enlisting in the army in 1784. He saw service in Canada, and rose to the rank of sergeant-major. Characteristically, he obtained his discharge in order to expose financial corruption among his superior officers, and had to escape to France from the consequences of his interference with what were then regarded as the legitimate spoils of the army. Thence he emigrated to the newly-born United States, where he settled—like Paine— in Philadelphia, and took up Paine's trade of pamphleteering, though on the other side. For Cobbett at this time was violently Tory, and was being encouraged by the English government to defend their cause against the ideas of the French republicans as these showed themselves in America. Philadelphia was then the capital of the States, and it was strongly pro-French. Cobbett did not soothe the feelings of the inhabitants by writing pamphlets, under the name of "Peter Porcupine", defending the English and abusing the Francophiles. Philadelphia soon became too hot to hold him, and he returned to England in 1800 to be welcomed with open arms by the government as a stick to beat the Radicals.

How that stick broke in the government's hands—or descended upon the government's head—is one of the strangest ironies in political history. *Cobbett's Weekly Political Register* started in 1802 with government backing, but as early as 1804 it began to change its tune, as the editor gradually changed from the Tory position to the Radical. For the next thirty years, Cobbett was proclaiming, with as much fearlessness as he had shown in America, that the English nation was being ruined by the politicians and the profiteers. He became converted to some of the ideas of Paine, whom he had formerly abused, and till the Reform Government came into office in 1832—he was elected member for Oldham—was the leading Radical journalist in the country. He died in 1835, carrying on his *Register* to the end.

He acknowledged Swift as the first master of his style; and though he has little of the irony of *Gulliver*, the "proper words in proper places", which was Swift's description of the Augustan plain style, is as accurate a description of the style of *Rural Rides* and the *Register*. It was not the only style practised during the eighteenth century, but it was the most prominent, and it is fitting that we should conclude our discussion of the last prose writer in this book by a reminder of one of the first. Cobbett's views would have seemed strange to Swift, but there is a link between the two writers deeper than politics. Both were men of mixed motives, but equally both were fearless in their denunciation of social abuses. *Gulliver* would have been beyond Cobbett's powers, in Swift's position, but we can well imagine him writing *The Conduct of the Allies* or the *Drapier's Letters*.

CHAPTER XI

BURNS AND BLAKE

1783-1810

> "Lest my works should be thought below criticism; or meet with a critic who, perhaps, will not look on them with so candid and favourable an eye; I am determined to criticise them myself."
>
> BURNS: *Scrap Book.*

> "I am more famed in Heaven for my works than I could well conceive. In my brain are studies and chambers filled with books and pictures of old, which I wrote and painted in ages of eternity before my mortal life; and those works are the delight and study of archangels. Why, then, should I be anxious about the riches or fame of mortality?"
>
> BLAKE: *Letter to Flaxman.*

The End of the Eighteenth Century

The relation of Cobbett to Swift, which we observed at the close of the last chapter, gives an impression of a distinct eighteenth-century form of prose, lasting from the time of the Augustans to what we have called here the Age of Revolution. The impression is not, of course, completely accurate: the Johnsonian style, to take an obvious case, is not the plain style of Swift, Defoe, Fielding, and Cobbett; and the style of Gibbon seems a mixture of the two. But if we were asked for a specimen of "typical eighteenth-century prose", we should probably choose an example from *Gulliver* or *Tom Jones* rather than from *Rasselas* or the *Decline and Fall*. We should certainly not choose an eccentric style, like that of Sterne; and this aversion from eccentricity—however much we may admire the famous eccentric characters of the eighteenth century—is a pointer to what we normally consider the prose virtues of the time. So far as centuries can be said to have typical styles at all, the plain style, from

Swift to Cobbett, seems to be the central line of prose in the century covered by this book.

The position in regard to poetry is far more complicated. There is not the relation between Pope and Blake that there is between Swift and Cobbett; the two poets seem as different from each other as it is possible for poets writing in the same language. There can be said to be an "eighteenth-century style" in poetry; but, significantly, when we use the phrase, we think of the poetic vices of the age rather than the poetic virtues, we think of "the feather'd tribe" and "the terraqueous globe" rather than the *Moral Essays*, *The Vanity of Human Wishes*, the *Elegy*, or the *Songs of Experience*. We are merely, in fact, repeating the criticisms of Wordsworth, expressed in the famous Preface to the *Lyrical Ballads*—the volume which divides the two centuries as accurately as any such division is possible.

There is much interest, however, in the very difference between Pope and Blake. Some of Blake's prophetic pieces are extremely difficult to get through, and he never achieved the organisation of such a poem as the *Dunciad*; on the other hand, some of his lyrics, and some phrases in some of them, are overwhelming experiences, expressing more in a word or two than Pope in a page. Pope, again, can be always paraphrased in prose, however much he loses by the transcription; he has always, that is to say, a clear meaning. Blake, like Shakespeare, is often unparaphraseable; the following familiar passage from *The Tiger*, for instance:

> When the stars threw down their spears,
> And water'd heaven with their tears . . .

is, strictly speaking, meaningless; and we can be sure that it would have been regarded as meaningless by Walsh or Johnson. We can imagine how it would have been discussed in the *Lives of the Poets*:

> The representation [we can imagine Johnson writing] may, perhaps, be defended as allegorical; but where there is no nature, there can be little truth. The reader knows that the celestial bodies have no hands or arms, and the abandonment of what they could never

possess is therefore a figure so fanciful as to appear disgusting. The wisdom of the ancients peopled the firmament with terrestrial fauna, but it is a nebulous mythology that gives armament to Ursus or provides Sirius with a collar. Tradition allows us to speak of the heavens watering the earth, but to represent the stars as watering the heavens is so unreasonable as to provoke risibility rather than consent. The poet who thus indulges his fancy without censure may conceive himself without blame, and proceed in a future effusion to dazzle us with lions of flaming fire or marriages between Heaven and Hell.

The common-sense approach, parodied above, is not, however, completely irrelevant. We have only to read through one of the Prophetic Books to realise that Blake's fancy could get out of control, that his language could degenerate into an extraordinary poetic diction, as false as that of Ossian, which it resembles. But for most of the songs and lyrics, the Johnsonian censure is beside the point. None of us knows the precise meaning of the two lines quoted;* but there are passages in Shakespeare which are equally imprecise (from the point of view of prose statement) but equally powerful in their context. The reference to Shakespeare is justified, for many of the best poems of Blake are highly dramatic, as are some of those of Burns. The repetition of the word "red", for instance, in the famous lines,

My Luve is like a red, red rose,
That's newly sprung in June . . .

---

* The imagery, of course, comes from the Bible, like most of Smart's and some of Cowper's. Defending some passages in his translation of Homer from the common-sense criticism of Thomas Hayley—son of the minor poet William Hayley, friend of both Cowper and Blake—Cowper wrote: "Where the word *reel* suggests to you the idea of a drunken mountain, it performs the service to which I destined it. It is a bold metaphor; but justified by one of the sublimest passages in Scripture, compared with the sublimity of which even that of Homer suffers humiliation. It is God himself, who, speaking, I think, by the prophet Isaiah, says,
The earth shall reel to and fro like a drunkard.
With equal boldness in the same Scripture, the poetry of which was never equalled, mountains are said to skip, to break out into singing, and the fields to clap their hands. I intend, therefore, that my Olympus shall be still tipsy".

is not at all necessary, from the standpoint of strict meaning. The second "red" does not add anything to the first—in Basic Poetry, if we can imagine such a thing, the one adjective would be considered sufficient—nor does the repetition mean "very red" or "extraordinarily red". It is, regarding it technically, a dramatic and rhythmical device; but, to put it less coldly, it is the poet lingering over the word, over the flower's and his mistress's fragrance, so that he seems to be thinking aloud rather than "composing a poem". Only the greatest poets can get such effects by such simple means.

These means were part of the secret of the old ballads' appeal to the later eighteenth century. The Scottish country ballads are as clearly behind Burns as the London street-ballads behind Blake. We could, in fact, have treated of Burns at the close of our chapter on Classic History and Gothic Romance, save that he seems far too important a figure to be considered along with Walpole and Macpherson, even with Percy and Chatterton. The greatest poets naturally stand a little aside from the current of their age, and it would have been as foolish to discuss Blake in the previous chapter, despite his friendship with Paine and Mary Wollstonecraft, his poems on America and on the French Revolution, and the revolutionary nature of his mysticism. There is much to be said, though, for considering Burns and Blake together, for they were almost exact contemporaries, both were largely self-educated, and both were cut off by nature and circumstance from the classical tradition of the majority of their eighteenth-century predecessors.

Treating them thus together, in the final chapter of this book, reminds us of the distance we have travelled from Addison, Swift, Pope, and the Augustan Age. It is a distance, of course, less in time than tradition, for only about forty years separate the last poems of Pope from the first poems of Burns and Blake. They were all "eighteenth-century" poets, but between the *Dunciad* and *Holy Willie's Prayer*, or between the *Epistle to Arbuthnot* and *The Tiger*, stretches a gulf that is partly social, partly literary. We have observed that several poets of mid-century reacted against the "coffee-house" tradition to become meditators among country tombs at twilight. There was a trace of self-consciousness about· this attitude; like the succeeding Gothic and Sensibility movements, it was an attitude taken up by the sophisticated, in this case by scholarly men yearning for simplicity. But Burns and Blake were, so to speak, the real thing: poets of natural simplicity who had no theories whatever about natural simplicity. (It is significant that Burns was no Ossian, that Blake did not admire Rousseau.) They were not, of course, "simple" in any other sense: both were well-read men, the Scotsman in the normal reading of Scotland and England, the Londoner in more eccentric departments of religion and mythology, besides being a most original painter and philosopher of art and life. But neither had, or needed to have, the classical background that unites writers so diverse as Pope and Walpole, as Johnson and Gray.

From the more purely literary point of view, Burns and Blake were together the justification for the ballad-interest of the age. This could so easily have become a mere scholarly idiosyncrasy, or a mere fashion; but when Burns could write songs as masterly as the best of the traditional, and when Blake—almost unknown to the literary world, it is true—could attain a simplicity of genius even superior, the interest became more a contemporary one, if not quite so evidently as the classical interest of the Augustans. Burns greatly admired Pope, and used epigraphs from him for two of his best satirical pieces, and some of Blake's early work (like some of Wordsworth's own) would have received the criticism of the Wordsworth of the *Lyrical Ballads*. Wordsworth could consciously revise his early efforts by the light of his new theories; but when Burns attained his poetic majority, he did so without any theory behind him, making of his Pope-epigraphed satires poems completely different from Pope's but yet not consciously different; while Blake went his own way in all things, in art and mysticism as much as in poetry. He commented in general terms on the enfeebled Augustan tradition—

> The languid strings do scarcely move!
> The sound is forc'd, the notes are few!

—but the poem from which these lines are taken is in his very first volume, *Poetical Sketches*, which contains some of the enfeeblement criticised. He worked his way out of that, not by following a theory, but by finding by trial and error the most effective means to express his original genius. No doubt that is what Wordsworth and Coleridge usually did also, in practice, but in their case the theories they followed were considered important, they had their eye on possible converts to their cause. Blake's feebler poems are just feebler poems; Wordsworth's Goody Blakes and Harry Gills, and the Squire's "little ruddy daughter Bess", were intended to convey "language really used by men"—though they made real men smile.

The theory, the conscious effort to make something new in poetry, is what chiefly differentiates Wordsworth and Coleridge from Burns and Blake. *The Ancient Mariner* has been included in an anthology of eighteenth-century verse, and *Tintern Abbey* is also, of course, an eighteenth-century poem by date. But the usual, convenient watershed, the *Lyrical Ballads* of 1798, has too much to be said for it to be lightly dismissed. To begin the study of nineteenth-century literature with the *Lyrical Ballads* is as accurate a starting-point as any, in view of the theories advanced in Wordsworth's Preface which had so great an influence upon the century's literary development. It is true that Blake lived beyond Keats and Shelley, but he had completed the majority of his best work by 1800. If we regard him as the last great poet of the old century, and Wordsworth and Coleridge as the first great poets of the new, our recognition of the features they have in common will prevent us from attaching to the division any undue importance.

Scottish Poetry before Burns

The overwhelming applause given by posterity to the genius of Burns has tended to obscure his eighteenth-century predecessors in Scotland. We are apt to think of the traditional Scottish ballads, and then of Burns, without bothering ourselves about any poets who may have come in between.

This is not, however, such a great mistake as it might seem at first glance. It was as far back as the fifteenth century that Percy found his English ballads; but throughout the eighteenth century poets and scholars were collecting the traditional literature of Scotland from the oral recollections of the inhabitants. A similar thing was possible in England only on a small scale and in the remotest villages, for most of the old ballads and songs had become hopelessly corrupted by the more professional literature of the street. By the lingering of the old order in the north, poets and scholars were able to take warning from the fate of the English ballads and save their own without serious casualty. The history of eighteenth-century Scottish poetry is largely taken up with these activities.

The first notable figure is Allan Ramsay (1686-1758), a self-educated wig-maker who was influenced partly by the old songs he had himself heard and sung, partly by James Watson's collections, *Comic and Serious Scots Poems both Ancient and Modern*, which came out between 1706 and 1711. He turned from wig-making to bookselling and publishing, and apart from his own poetry—notably the pastoral drama *The Gentle Shepherd* (1725)—he was able to follow Watson in producing collections of Scottish songs, ancient and modern, which had a great effect on his countrymen. The "modern" should be observed; for besides the traditional songs known by heart, the villagers in Scotland still produced new ones till well into the eighteenth century, whereas in England the tradition of composition had almost completely disappeared.

"The excellent Ramsay", as Burns called him, was almost the exact contemporary of Pope, but there would have been little point in considering him as one of our Augustan poets. It is not, after all, with Gay, but with Burns, that *The Gentle Shepherd* can best be compared—as can be seen from the opening of this typical *Sang* from it:

My Peggy is a young thing,
Just enter'd in her teens,
Fair as the day, and sweet as May,
Fair as the day, and always gay.
My Peggy is a young thing,
And I'm not very auld,
Yet well I like to meet her at
The wawking of the fauld . . .

Such things, for all their charm, do not *read* very impressively: we feel we need the tune. Where Burns is so superior is that his best pieces are equally fine as songs or as poems. Only the very best of the traditional ballads, Scots or English, can match him in that; and only rarely do we get a more conscious artist, such as Shakespeare, whose poems meant to be sung— for example, Feste's final song in *Twelfth Night*—are poems able also to be read.

A poet whom Burns placed even higher than Ramsay, and whom modern Scotsmen often place next to Burns, was Robert Fergusson, whose tragic life ended in an asylum in 1774 when he was in his twenty-fifth year. "The still more excellent Fergusson" did not have the material success of Ramsay, though born perhaps in slightly better circumstances, the son of a clerk who took to his father's profession. It was chiefly by his verses on Edinburgh that he became known in his life time; a collected edition of these and other pieces was published in 1773. When Burns arrived in Edinburgh three years afterwards, one of his first acts was to visit the grave of Fergusson, which, however, could not be identified, as the poet had been buried with others by the parish. Had he lived to a mature age, he might have rivalled his mourner or at least filled the gap which seems to exist between Burns and the comparatively second-rate poets of eighteenth-century Scotland.

David Herd was the chief collector of Scottish songs after Ramsay, and his *Ancient and Modern Scottish Poems* (1769) is known to have formed part of the reading of the Burns household. Among the most popular pieces in this collection was a version of the old ballad, *The Flowers of the Forest*, by Jane Elliot. This was the first of several versions of traditional

ballads by women poets, and was followed, among others, by
Auld Robin Gray by Lady Anne Lindsay, and *My Mother
bids me bind my Hair* by Mrs Hunter—a song that had the
honour of being set to music by Haydn.

Robert Burns

It is perhaps the variety of Burns's work that first strikes
us, when we approach him by way of the foothills of minor
Scottish verse—whether versions of the old ballads, or the
lyrics of Bruce and Logan, or the narrative poems of Scott.
When James Ballantyne asked Scott what he thought of his
own poetry "in comparison with that of Burns", Scott
replied: "There is no comparison; we ought not to be named
in the same day". But there is a more valid comparison
between the poetry of Burns and the best of the Waverley
Novels. The characteristic weakness of most of Scott's verse,
as of most other Scottish verse of the late eighteenth and
early nineteenth centuries, is that it is very limited, both in
theme and execution. Generally speaking, it presents a
decided contrast to the range and power of Burns, as to the
dramatic variety of such novels as *The Heart of Mid-Lothian*
and *Old Mortality*.

Burns was born in 1759 at Alloway, in Ayrshire, the son of
a gardener who had become a small farmer. His parents
were pious in the rather narrow tradition of Scotch Calvinism,
but there was nothing particularly narrow about the reading
he acquired at home and at school. He was early acquainted
with the collections of Scottish poetry made by Watson,
Ramsay, and Herd; and he afterwards read the main classics
of English verse, particularly Pope. How far his later reading
extended we do not precisely know, but in his *Scrap Book* we
find him quoting off-hand a line from one of Vanbrugh's
comedies; we know he had read Richardson and Sterne; and
his letters give the impression of a well-informed mind.*

* He was, admittedly, very modest about the degree of his education, but he was probably thinking chiefly of his ignorance of Latin
and Greek and perhaps of philosophy. The critic who seems to have
started the legend of the "Heaven-taught ploughman" in "his humble
and unlettered station" was Henry Mackenzie, in his review of Burns's

To Englishmen who are inclined to look on Scotland as a single "province", Burns's ambition to be the poet of Ayrshire —as he records in his *Scrap Book*—may seem curious. But Scotland in his time was not all of a piece, if indeed it has ever quite become so. Even Southern Scotsmen did not all understand Burns easily; Mackenzie, born in Edinburgh, deplored his "provincial dialect", and Alexander Somerville, brought up in East Lothian, records in his autobiography that he delighted in *Tam o' Shanter*, etc., "in spite of the unfamiliarity of the West Scots dialect". By becoming, after his death, the National Poet, Burns, however, did almost as much as Scott to wield Scotland into one.

When he was twenty-seven, his country almost lost him for ever; for being in personal and domestic trouble he decided to emigrate to Jamaica, and was only restrained by a letter from his friend the blind poet Blacklock and by the unexpected success of his first volume, *Poems, chiefly in the Scottish Dialect*, which was published at Kilmarnock in 1786. A second enlarged edition (1787) proved profitable; he was able to marry and settle down to farming near Dumfries; and he contributed about three hundred songs and adaptations to various Scottish collections during the decade 1787-96. In 1789 he obtained a part-time post as district excise-officer, and when his farm failed in 1791 was able to transfer to a full-time post. He died five years later, after a mishap on the way home from a drinking party.

Much of his verse is a record of personal experience. As he said himself: "For my own part, I never had the least thought or inclination of turning poet till I got heartily in love". His love-songs must be among the best that any country has produced, and certainly the best known in Great Britain and America. *My Luve is like a red, red rose*; *The Rigs o' Barley*; *Of a' the airts the wind can blaw*; *The Banks o' Doon*: these, and many others, are known wherever the

Kilmarnock collection in the *Lounger*. Burns, like Blake, was only comparatively "unlettered", and he seems to have known what was necessary for his purpose. We are entitled to wonder whether Mackenzie had such an intimate acquaintance as Burns with both Pope and traditional Scottish literature.

Scots have penetrated, throughout a Scottish Empire on which the sun has no earthly chance of setting. We have quoted the opening lines of the "red, red rose", which is one of the songs of successful love; as an example of the songs of love scorned, the last verse of *The Banks o' Doon* is among the most characteristic:

> Aft hae I rov'd by bonie Doon,
>   To see the woodbine twine;
> And ilka bird sang o' its Luve,
>   And sae did I o' mine.
> Wi' lightsome heart I pu'd a rose,
>   Upon a morn in June;
> How like that rose my blooming morn,
>   Sae darkly set ere noon!
> Wi' lightsome heart I pu'd a rose,
>   Upon its thorny tree;
> But my fause Luver staw my rose,
>   And left the thorn wi' me.

The sentiment in these poems is often controlled by a dry humour, a combination which we find again in equally well-known pieces like *To a Mouse, The Twa Dogs*, and *A Man's a Man for a' that*. The long Latinised words, for example, in the second stanza of the *Mouse*—

> I'm truly sorry man's dominion
> Has broken nature's social union,
> An' justifies that ill opinion . . .

—are used as a deliberate foil to the homely "beastie" and "foggage" of the rest of the poem. Such deliberate humour usually prevents Burns from sinking into the sentimentality which he often perilously approaches.

In the closing years of his short life, he professed radical principles, at about the time Wordsworth was thinking second thoughts about them. The famous *A Man's a Man* was published during these years, in 1794, and if it would not have appealed to Rousseau—or to Robespierre—it is none the less a striking expression of that northern independence which has meant so much to our democracy. Scott was to remind his readers of the merits of the vanquished feudalism,

and the reminder was necessary in an age when so many
theories about the ideal society were going the rounds.
Burns's poem was no theory, but practical common sense,
the common sense of a man who, like Cobbett, had no patience
with either servility or arrogance. The foolishness of title
has never been summed up more neatly than in the phrase,
"The rank is but the guinea's stamp", and in the two middle
verses of this poem:

> Ye see yon birkie ca'd "a lord",
>   Wha struts, an' stares, an' a' that;
> Tho' hundreds worship at his word,
>   He's but a coof for a' that:
> For a' that, an' a' that,
>   His ribband, star, an' a' that;
> The man o' independent mind,
>   He looks an' laughs at a' that.
>
> A prince can mak a belted knight,
>   A marquis, duke, an' a' that;
> But an honest man's aboon his might,
>   Gude faith, he mauna fa' that!
> For a' that, an' a' that,
>   Their dignities an' a' that;
> The pith o' sense, an' pride o' worth,
>   Are higher rank than a' that.

A similar attitude of easy, good-humoured contempt is seen in
the satires, which—together with such poems as *Tam o'
Shanter* and *The Jolly Beggars*—are his most original
achievement.

Burns and the Holy Willies

Like the love songs and the other lyrics, the satires came
from personal experience. The older Scotland spoke in Burns
against the Puritanism of the Presbyterian Church. Not
long after his pious father's death, he was publicly rebuked
before the congregation of the local parish church for his
drinking and other bad habits; and he made his first counter-
attack in the *Epistle to John Rankin*, a letter in verse to an
old friend who had enquired the truth of the matter. In
the superb *Address to the Unco Guid*, which followed, he

pressed home the attack by asking whether the holiness of the
"rigidly righteous" might not be due in part to a slow circulation or a lack of opportunity.*   The poem has an epigraph
from the Bible which is not the least original thing about it:

> My son, these maxims make a rule,
>   An' lump them ay thegither;
> The *Rigid Righteous* is a fool,
>   The *Rigid Wise* anither:
> The cleanest corn that e'er was dight
>   May hae some pyles o' caff in;
> So ne'er a fellow-creature slight
>   For random fits o' daffin.
>
> > Solomon, Eccles. ch. VII, verse 16.

The poem proper begins with the kind of good-humoured
contempt that we saw in *A Man's a Man* and that was to
reach the heights of satirical verse in *Holy Willie's Prayer*.
The attack is all the more deadly for that good-humour:

> O ye wha are sae guid yoursel,
>   Sae pious and sae holy,
> Ye've nought to do but mark and tell
>   Your neibours' fauts and folly!
> Whase life is like a weel-gaun mill,
>   Supplied wi' store o' water;
> The heapet happer's ebbing still,
>   An' still the clap plays clatter.
>
> Hear me, ye venerable core,
>   As counsel for poor mortals
> That frequent pass douce Wisdom's door
>   For glaikit Folly's portals:

---

* Compare many of Blake's aphorisms, from *The Marriage of
Heaven and Hell*, *A Song of Liberty*, etc., such as: "Those who
restrain Desire do so because theirs is weak enough to be restrained";
"He who desires but acts not, breeds pestilence"; "Let the Priests of
the Raven of dawn no longer, in deadly black, with hoarse note curse
the sons of joy! . . . Nor pale Religion's lechery call that Virginity
that wishes but acts not!"; "Men are admitted into Heaven not
because they have curbed or governed their passions or have no
passions, but because they have cultivated their understandings . . .
Those who are cast out are all those who, having no passions of their
own because no intellect, have spent their lives in controlling and
governing other people's . . . In Hell all is self-righteousness".

I, for their thoughtless, careless sakes,
    Would here propone defences—
Their donsie tricks, their black mistakes,
    Their failings and mischances.

Ye see your state wi' theirs compared,
    And shudder at the niffer;
But cast a moment's fair regard,
    What maks the mighty differ?
Discount what scant occasion gave,
    That purity ye pride in;
And (what's aft mair than a' the lave)
    Your better art o' hidin.

Think, when your castigated pulse
    Gies now and then a wallop!
What ragings must his veins convulse,
    That still eternal gallop!
Wi' wind and tide fair i' your tail,
    Right on ye scud your sea-way;
But in the teeth o' baith to sail,
    It maks an unco lee-way . . .

Hypocrisy has seldom met with a more vigorous onslaught than in this poem. It is remarkably interesting to see satire as penetrating as Pope's, but yet completely different in spirit and method. Samuel Butler had burlesqued the English Puritans in his *Hudibras* (1678), but he seems merely topical compared with Burns. The genius of such poems is in their fine combination of the particular with the universal, and in the dramatic gusto of the expression. Pope has virtues which Burns lacks, but an invitation like "Hear me, ye venerable core" had rarely been seen in our literature since the Elizabethans.

The Twa Herds, written about the same time, was based on a quarrel between two local pastors. It begins, as most of Burns's poems do—and most of the old ballads—straight off, without any more preliminary than the title, *The Twa Herds; or, The Holy Tulyie: An Unco Mournfu' Tale*, and the apt epigraph from Pope:

Blockheads with reason wicked wits abhor,
But fool with fool is barbarous civil war.

We are at once plunged straight into the catastrophe:

> O a' ye pious godly flocks,
> Weel fed on pastures orthodox,
> Wha now will keep ye frae the fox,
>   Or worrying tykes?
> Or wha will tent the waifs an' crocks,
>   About the dykes?
>
> The twa best herds in a' the wast,
> That e'er gae gospel horn a blast,
> These five-and-twenty simmers past,
>   O, dool to tell!
> Hae had a bitter black out-cast
>   Atween themsel.

The gleeful mock-pathetic opening is followed by an extended comparison between the pastors and the shepherds:

> What flock wi' Moodie's flock could rank,
> Sae hale an' hearty every shank?
> Nae poison'd soor Arminian stank
>   He let them taste;
> Frae Calvin's well, aye clear, they drank—
>   O, sic a feast! . . .

Burns knew that "feast", and in the opening of *Holy Willie's Prayer* he expresses, by means of a parody of an elder's devotions, his own generous contempt for it:

> O Thou that in the Heavens does dwell,
> Wha, as it pleases best Thysel,
> Sends ane to Heaven an' ten to Hell
>   A' for Thy glory,
> And no for onie guid or ill
>   They've done before Thee!
>
> I bless and praise Thy matchless might,
> When thousands Thou hast left in night,
> That I am here before Thy sight,
>   For gifts an' grace
> A burning and a shining light
>   To a' this place. . .

The genesis of *Holy Willie* was the public reprimand by an "Auld Licht" elder—that is, an elder of the extreme Calvinist school—of one of Burns's friends, who had failed, like Burns himself, to go to church regularly.   It is the bitterest of the satires, the burlesque of the elder's devotions making the self-revelations of Dickens's Mr Pecksniff seem comparatively innocuous. It shares with Dickens, of course, that dramatic touch, by which the satirist can do more in a few words than by pages of commentary. Once again Burns chooses an extraordinarily apt epigraph from Pope: "And send the godly in a pet to pray"! Such aptness of quotation is evidence of a deep familiarity with the English satirist's work, and the independence of Burns's own satire is all the more remarkable.

Holy Willie and the former pieces enjoyed a wide manuscript circulation locally before they were printed. They belonged to the counter-offensive that was arising in Burns's time against the strict Calvinism of the established Scottish Church. Scott in *Old Mortality* was to give in perspective the mingled virtues and vices of the seventeenth-century Cameronians, and, though his novel caused controversy among scholars, Burns and his contemporaries had already met and defeated the last great attack of the orthodox in ordinary life. It is significant that Somerville's pious father could read Burns with pleasure, despite his attacks on orthodoxy; and that the same poet could write the account of the Bible-reading in *The Cotter's Saturday Night*. There was more in Scottish Calvinism than Holy Willies, and more in Burns than just a simple reaction from its narrower creeds.

With these satires can be considered, finally, a more genial poem of much the same sort and in the same traditional Scottish metre. *Death and Doctor Hornbook* (1787) is a satire on a local schoolmaster who pretended to medical knowledge. Burns relates that once, while he was coming home after a drink or two—"I was na fou, but just had plenty"—he meets a Something on the road who tells him his name is Death. They sit down and rest together, and Burns politely asks him his news and says he supposes he has been on the job quite a while now:

> "Ay, ay!" quo' he, an' shook his head,
> "It's e'en a lang lang time indeed
> Sin' I began to nick the thread,

> An' choke the breath:
> Folk maun do something for their bread,
> And sae maun Death.

But trade is getting unlawful competition from Dr Hornbook, who kills more people "by drap and pill" than Death himself can "by loss o' blood or want o' breath":

> "But hark! I'll tell you of a plot,
> Tho' dinna ye be speaking o't;
> I'll nail the self-conceited sot
>   As dead's a herrin':
> Neist time we meet, I'll wad a groat,
>   He gets his fairin'!"
>
> But, just as he began to tell,
> The auld kirk-hammer strak the bell
> Some wee short hour ayont the twal,
>   Which rais'd us baith:
> I took the way that pleas'd mysel',
>   And sae did Death.

The familiarity of the conversation here reminds us of the popular drama of the Middle Ages. Burns is speaking in the old tradition which had lingered on into his lifetime, the tradition that could see Death as an honest workman and the Devil as Old Nick. The tradition still exists, here and there, among the older generation; and still exists in literature, for if Burns's poem looks back to Dunbar and to Chaucer's *Pardoner's Tale*, it looks forward to T. F. Powys's *Unclay*.

William Blake

The last great poet of the eighteenth century was largely the discovery of the nineteenth. Blake was even more cut off than Burns from the literary world of his time, and it was left to the mid-Victorians, and particularly to the Pre-Raphaelites, to see him as a great figure in literature and painting alike, though earlier a group of young painters, the chief of whom was Samuel Palmer, had recognised him as their master in art. Since Rossetti and Swinburne, the interest in his poetry has steadily increased, and there has been a corresponding interest in his art and mysticism. He is now regarded in English-speaking countries as one of the greatest men that England has produced, though it is curious to note that, compared not only with Byron but with Burns, he is not at all widely known in Europe.

He was born over a hosier's shop in central London, in a family who were so nonconformist that they had become disciples of the Swedish mystic Swedenborg. The date of his birth, suitably enough, was 1757, "the Year of the New Dispensation" in Swedenborgian terminology. From an early age he saw visions, in fact from the age of four, when God looked in at his bedroom window to see how he was getting on. As soon as he could hold a pencil, he began to draw; and he was still drawing and singing songs on his death-bed more than sixty years afterwards.*

His hosier father seems to have been kindly and shrewd as well as mystical, for he not only bought his son cheap casts and prints but took him away from the ordinary school and sent him to a drawing-school in the Strand. Thence he was apprenticed to Basire, engraver to the Society of Antiquaries, and was set drawing the stone memorials in Westminster Abbey. After the termination of his apprenticeship, he studied for a short time at the newly-founded Royal Academy —most of whose precepts were the exact opposite of his own— but was soon employed as an engraver by the London publishers. This remained his professional occupation for most of his life, his engravings to Young and Blair, Dante and Milton, and the Book of Job—and his woodcuts to Virgil— being among the most impressive works of their kind.

Ideally, his poetry and his art, his literature and his mysticism, should be studied together, for they were parts of a whole that was called William Blake. Here we must limit

* "He was failing fast," records Allan Cunningham, "with only his old wife to tend him. Yet he adds here a little, there a little, to his beloved *Ancient of Days*. He sees his wife's tears. 'Stay, Kate! Keep just as you are—I will draw your portrait—for you have ever been an angel to me' . . . He lays chanting songs, and the verses and the music were both the offspring of the moment." His death took place in 1827. We end the present chapter at the year 1810, when most of his poetry had been written. The final years were mainly devoted to art.

ourselves to the reminder that most of his books were printed and designed by himself, the text and the decoration being planned to make an artistic unity. The method of illuminated printing which he followed was his own invention—or, as he claimed, had been revealed to him in a vision by his dead brother Robert. His mysticism was equally connected with his literature, for he not only claimed that some of his poems were dictated by angels, but his comments on life and art, on religion and society—in a word, his philosophy—were often recorded in that mystical state which lies somewhere between common reality and the visionary universe. There probably never existed for him any hard-and-fast line between the real and the imaginative; for him the two worlds were one, the vision real, the real visionary, the divine natural, the natural divine:

> I assert for myself [he once said] that I do not behold the outward creation and that to me it is hindrance and not action; it is as the dirt upon my feet, no part of me. "What", it will be questioned, "when the sun rises, do you not see a round disk of fire somewhat like a guinea?" O no, no, I see an innumerable company of the heavenly host, crying "Holy, holy, holy is the Lord God Almighty". I question not my corporeal or vegetative eye any more than I would question a window concerning a sight. I look through it and not with it.

The analogy in the last two sentences is, of course, more ingenious than logical; but our consciousness of this, and any other reservations we may privately make, do not detract from our general appreciation of Blake's mysticism, which can often throw light upon obscure reaches of the heart. From the point of view of literature, it is what the poet makes of his mysticism that is important; the literary result interests us more than the philosophical stages. On the other hand, to ignore Blake's mysticism altogether, to treat his poetry entirely from the aesthetic or technical point of view, would be like ignoring Gibbon's history or Johnson's morality or Fielding's social criticism and being in the position of the "tuneful fools" whom Pope dissented from in the *Essay on*

Criticism. Blake's is, admittedly, an exceptionally complicated case; and we have already observed (pp. 267-8 above) that many of his poetical expressions have no precise meaning, that the experience they nevertheless convey is one difficult to comment on in critical terms. Here we shall consider some of the principal works, in roughly chronological order, concentrating first on the *Songs* as being perhaps the best of Blake and certainly the poems in which his mysticism is most clearly grasped.

Songs of Innocence and Experience

Poetical Sketches by W.B., the first volume Blake published, came out privately in 1783, being printed at the expense of his friends John Flaxman, "Dear Sculptor of Eternity", and the Rev. Henry Mathew, whose wife was a patron of his art. Mathew explained in a preface that the author was an untutored youth who had begun writing the work at the age of twelve and whose friends, though conscious of its defects and irregularities, believed it to possess "a poetic originality which merited some respite from oblivion". The recommendation is not particularly enthusiastic, but we should remember the derision which greeted the *Lyrical Ballads*, fifteen years later, among critics who were professionally interested in literature. The Mathews were kindly amateurs who must have been genuinely puzzled by Blake's divergences from eighteenth-century tradition. To us, with a knowledge of the later works, this first volume seems a remarkable mixture of "Blake" and "the eighteenth century"—for instance, in the imitations of Spenser and in the famous *Song* beginning "How sweet I roam'd from field to field", written, it is believed, at the age of twelve. The precocity of Pope seems unremarkable compared with Blake's in this extraordinary poem and in others in the same volume.

The chief difference between the *Sketches* and the *Songs of Innocence and of Experience* is one of concentration. The *Sketches*, naturally enough, were experiments, in which the poet was trying his hand in various styles. The volume contains, for instance, poems on the seasons in a kind of

Biblical blank verse; two imitations of old ballads, *Fair Elenor* and *Gwin King of Norway*; a Shakespearian drama, *King Edward the Third*, complete with comic retainers; and some fragments of poetic prose, Biblical in subject and manner. The *Songs* are more of a piece and have a definite purpose behind them, though they were written at various times, from about 1784 to about 1793. The earliest of the *Songs of Innocence* were included in a satirical drama, left unfinished and without title, but usually known as *An Island in the Moon*.* In 1789 revised versions of these were collected with the others in *Songs of Innocence: the Author and Printer W. Blake*—the first volume of the new "Illuminated Printing", both text and decorations being etched on copper, the pages printed from these plates being then illuminated by hand. Towards the end of 1793 was engraved the companion volume, *Songs of Experience*, one copy containing the date 1794. Some time later, Blake added an undated title-page to both series, which thenceforward were issued by him as a single work: *Songs of Innocence and of Experience, Showing the Two Contrary States of the Human Soul*. Wordsworth, reading them in after years, commented: "There is no doubt this poor man was mad, but there is something in the madness of the man which interests me more than the sanity of Lord Byron and Walter Scott".

Actually, even to the most prejudiced reader, this collection is the least mad, or the least maddening, of all Blake's works. It is true Blake, of course, in that the apparent simplicity covers a deep layer of meaning, meaning furthermore which is often by no means easy to grasp at all. But it is something to have a clue to the general purpose in the sub-title, such

* It begins: "In the moon is a certain island, near by a mighty continent, which small island seems to have some affinity to England, and, what is more extraordinary, the people are so much alike, and their language so much the same, that you would think you was among your friends . . .". The chief characters are three philosophers, Suction the Epicurean, Quid the Cynic, Sipsop the Pythagorean; an antiquarian, Etruscan Column; Steelyard the Lawgiver; and a mathematician, Obtuse Angle. *The Nurse's Song, The Little Boy Lost*, and *Holy Thursday* were the poems in the *Island* afterwards revised for the *Songs of Innocence*.

doubles as *The Lamb* in the *Innocence* series and *The Tiger* in
the *Experience*, and the two poems called *Holy Thursday*, and
the two *Nurse's Songs*, and the *Introduction* to each series—
"Piping down the valleys wild" and "Hear the voice of the
Bard!"—being obvious examples of "the two contrary states
of the human soul". Occasionally, though, we seem to get
in the *Experience* series a poem which sums up both states,
such as *The Clod and the Pebble*:

> "Love seeketh not itself to please,
> Nor for itself hath any care,
> But for another gives its ease,
> And builds a Heaven in Hell's despair."
>
> So sung a little Clod of Clay,
> Trodden with the cattle's feet,
> But a Pebble of the brook
> Warbled out these metres meet:
>
> "Love seeketh only Self to please,
> To bind another to its delight,
> Joys in another's loss of ease,
> And builds a Hell in Heaven's despite."

Though thus intimately connected, there is no doubt that
the two series of poems vary much in strength. It is not only
a more experienced Blake, but a greater poet, whom we find
in the *Songs of Experience*. The promise in the last verse of
the *Innocence* Introduction—

> And I made a rural pen,
> And I stain'd the water clear,
> And I wrote my happy songs
> Every child may joy to hear—

is admirably fulfilled, such songs as *The Lamb* and *The Little
Black Boy* figuring often among children's favourites. Even
where the meaning of the poem is deeper, as in *The Divine
Image*:

> For Mercy has a human heart,
> Pity a human face,
> And Love, the human form divine,
> And Peace, the human dress . . .

compared with most of the *Songs of Experience*, the poem is
crystal clear and was evidently intended to be so. With

experience comes complication, and though *A Little Boy Lost*, for instance, is superficially the same kind of poem as *The Little Boy Lost* and *The Little Boy Found* in the earlier series, it is really very different. And we have new-titled poems, such as *London*, whose counterparts are not in any state of innocence:

> I wander thro' each charter'd street,
> Near where the charter'd Thames does flow,
> And mark in every face I meet
> Marks of weakness, marks of woe.
>
> In every cry of every Man,
> In every Infant's cry of fear,
> In every voice, in every ban,
> The mind-forged manacles I hear.
>
> How the chimney-sweeper's cry
> Every black'ning church appals;
> And the hapless soldier's sigh
> Runs in blood down palace walls.
>
> But most thro' midnight streets I hear
> How the youthful harlot's curse
> Blasts the new-born infant's tear,
> And blights with plagues the marriage hearse.

And with that brief masterpiece, *The Sick Rose*:

> O Rose, thou art sick!
> The invisible worm,
> That flies in the night,
> In the howling storm,
>
> Has found out thy bed
> Of crimson joy;
> And his dark secret love
> Does thy life destroy—

with that *Song of Experience* we are in the mystical region of *The Marriage of Heaven and Hell*, far from the Little Lamb and the "songs of pleasant glee".

With *The Songs of Experience* can be considered the poems Blake wrote in a sketch-book from about 1789 to about 1810, a book that long after his death was sold by Samuel Palmer to the artist-poet D. G. Rossetti and hence is usually called the *Rossetti MS*. One of the *Songs of Experience*, in fact—

Infant Sorrow—is given in this manuscript in a much fuller form; and the book also contains a poem entitled *Motto to the Songs of Innocence and of Experience.*

The most impressive poem here is *The Everlasting Gospel,* as the most impressive poem in the other manuscript book, called the *Pickering MS,* is the *Auguries of Innocence.* The former was written about 1810, the latter between 1800 and 1803, when Blake was staying at Hayley's home in Sussex. (The letter quoted in the epigraph to this chapter was written on his arrival there.) *The Everlasting Gospel,* with its independent version of the New Testament:

> Was Jesus chaste? or did He
> Give any lessons of chastity?
> The Morning blushèd fiery red:
> Mary was found in adulterous bed . . .

has its place in the line of Blake's mysticism, from *The Marriage of Heaven and Hell* to *Jerusalem.* The *Auguries of Innocence* sum up the *Songs* in the opening verse, which may be called Blake's philosophy in a nutshell:

> To see a World in a grain of sand,
> And a Heaven in a wild flower,
> Hold Infinity in the palm of your hand,
> And Eternity in an hour.

It is not precisely known whether the title *Auguries of Innocence* refers just to that stanza or whether it includes the couplets which follow it in the manuscript. But the couplets are so clear an expression of Blake's philosophy at its most acceptable, and so impressive a summing-up of all that is most attractive in the *Songs of Innocence and of Experience,* that the usual sequence can be approved. There is a remarkable sensibility about these proverbs which may well have been an essential ingredient of Blake's "divine insanity":

> A robin redbreast in a cage
> Puts all Heaven in a rage . . .
> A horse misus'd upon the road
> Calls to Heaven for human blood.
> Each outcry of the hunted hare
> A fibre from the brain does tear.
> A skylark wounded in the wing,

A cherubim does cease to sing.
The game-cock clipt and arm'd for fight
Does the rising sun affright . . .
He who shall hurt the little wren
Shall never be belov'd by men.
He who the ox to wrath has mov'd
Shall never be by woman lov'd.
The wanton boy that kills the fly
Shall feel the spider's enmity.
He who torments the chafer's sprite
Weaves a bower in endless night.
The caterpillar on the leaf
Repeats to thee thy mother's grief.
Kill not the moth nor butterfly,
For the Last Judgement draweth nigh . . .

Many readers would give—or forgive—for this one poem half-a-dozen of the Prophetic Books.

The Prophetic Books

If "Songs of Innocence and Experience" can be said to be the generic name for most of Blake's short poems, then perhaps the Prophetic Books—as they are commonly called—can be summed up under the title of the most extraordinary of them: *The Marriage of Heaven and Hell*. This was engraved about 1790, and was preceded by *Tiriel* (*c.* 1788) and *The Book of Thel* (1789) and followed by *Visions of the Daughters of Albion* (1793), *America: A Prophecy* (1793), *Europe: A Prophecy* (1794), *The Book of Urizen* (1794), and by others until *Milton* (1804-9) and *Jerusalem* (begun *c.* 1804). Some of these contain memorable things—the *Milton*, for instance, includes the famous *And did those feet in ancient time*—but in general these Prophetic Books are as difficult as the most enigmatic of the short poems and much less readable. We feel often with the *Songs* that, while we cannot understand them fully, we have gained an experience that we would not have missed; with the Prophetic Books, we often feel that our perplexity is only matched by our boredom, that in fact the poet has not succeeded even partially in getting his message across. What his message *is* is not clear even from *The Marriage of Heaven and Hell*, where admittedly we can pick up comparatively easily some fragments of it. Such works as *The Book of Urizen* are almost completely incomprehensible.

The reasons for this are not all included in Blake's natural mysticism, the characteristic spiritual cast of his mind. His extraordinary education must bear part of the responsibility. The denizens of the Prophetic Books—Urizen, Los, and the rest—were not entirely his own invention; probably he would have made them livelier had he created them all himself. They came partly from his early reading of Gnostic treatises, and from the "Celtic" or "Druidical" revival of the later eighteenth century—which was part of the anti-Augustan revolt that we have noticed. He believed, with these revivalist antiquarians, that the ancient inhabitants of Britain were descended from Noah,* and that the Druids taught Pythagoras, who passed on their knowledge to the Grecian poets. So when he makes Adam and the Greeks "Druids", and the "holy Lamb of God" walk on "England's pleasant pastures", he is not writing so figuratively as a modern reader might imagine. How seriously he took some of these beliefs is uncertain; we can, at any rate, note with relief that he had a nickname, "Nobodaddy", for Urizen, the Father of Jealousy. In some moods, evidently, he could see the humorous side of these strange and windy creations of antiquarian mythology.

His Christianity is equally complex. He admits in *The Everlasting Gospel* that his picture of Jesus is almost the exact reverse of the traditional picture. This was not entirely due to his Swedenborgian upbringing, for by the time he wrote this poem he had renounced Swedenborg. He appears, by many passages in *The Marriage* and elsewhere, to have had a deep dislike of priests and perhaps of all institutional Christianity. His morality was not Church morality, but in his despising of money, worldly success and cruelty to man and beast he came close to the ideal of Jesus which many Christians have held. In some moods he was clearly

* The Flood was one of his chief subjects or symbols. "Painting, Poetry, and Music," he once wrote, "are the three Powers in Man of conversing with Paradise which the Flood did not sweep away."

pantheistic, as when he said of Christ: "He is the only God—and so am I and so are you".

The Marriage of Heaven and Hell is the most impressive of the Prophetic Books, if also in places one of the most difficult to understand. The *Argument* which introduces it must be among the best poems in the English language that are almost completely incomprehensible:

> Rintrah roars, and shakes his fires in the burden'd air;
> Hungry clouds swag on the deep.
>
> Once meek, and in a perilous path,
> The just man kept his course along
> The vale of death.
> Roses are planted where thorns grow,
> And on the barren heath
> Sing the honey bees.
>
> Then the perilous path was planted,
> And a river and a spring
> On every cliff and tomb,
> And on the bleachèd bones
> Red clay brought forth;
>
> Till the villain left the path of ease,
> To walk in perilous paths, and drive
> The just man into barren climes.
>
> Now the sneaking serpent walks
> In mild humility,
> And the just man rages in the wilds
> Where lions roam.
>
> Rintrah roars, and shakes his fires in the burden'd air;
> Hungry clouds swag on the deep.

Such passages have, of course, been explained; but we feel like Byron in regard to Coleridge: "I wish he would explain his explanation". In general, the weakness of Blake's allegory here, as in the rest of the Prophetic Books, is that the difficulty of the terminology gets in the way of the meaning it is supposed to make more clear. Contrast the *Pilgrim's Progress* and *Gulliver*, where the "window" (to use Blake's words against himself) is made to be easily looked through; the window of the Prophetic Books is glazed, and only a dim view of the country of Blake's mind is presented to the reader.

The *Argument* is the only part of *The Marriage* that is actually written in verse. The remainder is in that kind of poetic prose that Blake had experimented with in the *Sketches*. Much of it is in the form of paradox, like the first *Memorable Fancy*:

> As I was walking among the fires of Hell, delighted with the enjoyments of Genius, which to Angels look like torment and insanity, I collected some of their Proverbs . . .
> The road of excess leads to the palace of wisdom. Prudence is a rich, ugly old maid courted by Incapacity . . . No bird soars too high, if he soars with his own wings . . . The most sublime act is to set another before you. If the fool would persist in his folly he would become wise . . . The crow wish'd everything was black, the owl that everything was white . . . Enough! or Too Much.

Other Memorable Fancies follow, in one of which Blake tells us:

> The ancient tradition that the world will be consumed in fire at the end of six thousand years is true, as I have heard from Hell.
> For the cherub with his flaming sword is hereby commanded to leave his guard at tree of life; and when he does, the whole creation will be consumed and appear infinite and holy, whereas it now appears finite and corrupt.
> This will come to pass by an improvement of sensual enjoyment.
> But first the notion that man has a body distinct from his soul is to be expunged . . .

These are rather windy observations, only quoted here as typical of the thoughts that occupied Blake for the greater part of his life. They cannot be said to be literature of the order of the *Songs* or the *Auguries of Innocence*, and as philosophy we feel the need of footnotes to nearly every line. That Blake was sincere, and really believed he had had visits from angels and devils, and from Isaiah and Milton, there can be no doubt; in his characteristic state between the everyday world and the world of his imagination, there was evidently

nothing extraordinary to him in such visions and in the
literature he based upon them. His readers, however, while
always remembering that it was Blake's intention that his
text and his illustrations should be considered together, have
to pick and choose, discarding perhaps the majority of his
prophecies and paradoxes, but being grateful for such truly
memorable fancies as "Eternity is in love with the productions
of time". Only rarely do we find an extended passage which
seems to make sense throughout, as in this passage from *The
Marriage* where Blake expresses more exactly than elsewhere
his belief that religion is based on poetry:

> The ancient Poets animated all sensible objects with
> Gods or Geniuses, calling them by the names and adorn-
> ing them with the properties of woods, rivers, moun-
> tains, lakes, cities, nations, and whatever their enlarged
> and numerous senses could perceive.
>
> And particularly they studied the Genius of each city
> and country, placing it under its Mental Deity;
>
> Till a System was formed, which some took advan-
> tage of, and enslav'd the vulgar by attempting to realise
> or abstract the Mental Deities from their objects—thus
> began Priesthood;
>
> Choosing forms of worship from poetic tales.
>
> And at length they pronounc'd that the Gods had
> order'd such things.
>
> Thus men forgot that All Deities reside in the Human
> breast.

We may be sure that Blake himself saw no fundamental
difference between the *Songs* and the Prophetic Books, some
of which were written at the same time; that he was not
aware that in all but a few passages of the Books he had
ceased to communicate anything to the reader. He was
desirous, throughout his life, of interpreting his visions to the
world, and perhaps the lack of any real public made the
interpretations more and more peculiar. The sum of his
readers in his life-time must have been very small, much
smaller even than Burns's and infinitely smaller than Pope's.
If one aspect of literary history in the eighteenth century is
the gradual passing of public literature into private, then in
Blake it reaches as far as it can go.

BIBLIOGRAPHY

General

CAMPBELL, Kathleen W. (editor). *Poems on Several Occasions: Written in the Eighteenth Century. Percy Reprints.* 1926.

FURLONG, Norman (editor). *English Satire: An Anthology.* 1946.

GEORGE, M. Dorothy. *English Social Life in the Eighteenth Century.* 1923.
London Life in the Eighteenth Century. 1925.

HAZLITT, William. *Lectures on the English Poets. Everyman* edition, 1910.
Selected Essays. Edited by George Sampson. 1917.

JOHNSON, Samuel. *Lives of the Poets.* With the *Preface to Shakespeare.* New edition, n.d.

JONES, Edmund D. (editor). *English Critical Essays: XVI-XVIII Centuries. World's Classics,* 1922.

LEAVIS, F. R. *Revaluation: Tradition and Development in English Poetry.* 1936.

LEAVIS, Q. D. *Fiction and the Reading Public.* 1934.

NEEDHAM, H. A. (editor). *Taste and Criticism in the Eighteenth Century. Life, Literature, and Thought Library,* 1952.

QUENNELL, Peter. *Four Portraits: Studies of the Eighteenth Century.* 1945. Essays on Boswell, Gibbon, Sterne, and Wilkes.

READ, Herbert, and DOBRÉE, Bonamy (editors). *The London Book of English Verse.* Second edition, 1949.
The London Book of English Prose. Revised edition, 1949.

REYNOLDS, Reginald, and ORWELL, George (editors). *British Pamphleteers*. 1948.

RHYS, Ernest (editor). *The Prelude to Poetry: The English Poets in Defence and Praise of their own Art*. Everyman edition, 1927.

SAINTSBURY, George. *The Peace of the Augustans*. World's Classics, 1946.

SAMBROOK, G. A. (editor). *English Life in the Eighteenth Century*. 1944.

SAMPSON, George. *The Concise Cambridge History of English Literature*. 1941. Chapters IX-XI.

SCOTT, Sir Walter. *Lives of the Novelists*. Everyman's Library.

SEGAR, M. G. (editor). *Essays from Eighteenth-Century Periodicals*. 1947.

SMITH, D. Nichol. *Some Observations on Eighteenth-Century Poetry*. 1937.
(Editor). *The Oxford Book of Eighteenth-Century Verse*. 1926.

STEPHEN, Sir Leslie. *Hours in a Library*. Three series, 1874 9.
History of English Thought in the Eighteenth Century. 1876.
English Literature and Society in the Eighteenth Century. New edition, 1947.

STRONG, L. A. G., and REDLICH, Monica. *Life in English Literature*. New edition, 1949. Chapters XVIII-XXVI.

THACKERAY, W. M. *The Four Georges* and *The English Humorists of the Eighteenth Century*. People's Library edition, 1909.

TREVELYAN, G. M. *English Social History*. 1944. Chapters X-XV.

WILLEY, Basil. *The Eighteenth Century Background*. 1940.

Times Literary Supplement. Contributions by the present writer and others. 1943-52.

Chapter I

BRETT, R. L. *The Third Earl of Shaftesbury: A Study in Eighteenth-Century Literary Theory.* 1952.

BUTT, John. *The Augustan Age. Hutchinson's University Library,* 1950.

COURTHOPE, W. J. *Addison. English Men of Letters.*

FISHER, H. A. L. *A History of Europe.* New edition, 1952. Chapter LVII: "The Eighteenth Century in England and France".

KNIGHTS, L. C. *Explorations.* 1946. The opening essay on Shakespearian criticism and the essay on Restoration Comedy.

LEVER, Sir Tresham. *Godolphin: His Life and Times.* 1952.

LUCE, A. A. *The Life of George Berkeley.* 1948.
(Editor.) *The Works of George Berkeley.* 1948 *et seq.*

MORLEY, Henry (editor). *The Spectator.* 1883. Introduction includes a long extract from Gay's *Present State of Wit.*

O'CONNOR, D. J. *John Locke. Pelican* philosophers, 1952.

SMITH, D. Nichol. *Shakespeare in the Eighteenth Century.* 1928.

STEELE, Sir Richard. *Letters.* Edited by Rae Blanchard, 1941.

TREVELYAN, G. M. *England under Queen Anne.* 1930-4. *The English Revolution, 1688. Home University Library,* 1938.

WILLEY, Basil. *The Seventeenth Century Background.* 1934. For the philosophical background of the Augustan Age.

Chapter II

CHURCHILL, R. C. *He Served Human Liberty: An Essay on the Genius of Jonathan Swift. P.E.N. Books,* 1946.

CHURCHILL, Winston S. *Marlborough.* 1933-8. Defence of the author's ancestor against Swift, Bolingbroke, and the Tory Opposition.

FITZGERALD, Brian. *The Anglo-Irish*. 1952. Includes a section on Swift.

GARROD, H. W. Essay on the Phalaris controversy. In *Seventeenth Century Studies: Presented to Sir Herbert Grierson*. 1938.

HUXLEY, Aldous. *Do What You Will. Thinker's Library*. Includes an essay on Swift.

LEAVIS, F. R. *The Common Pursuit*. 1951. Includes an essay on Swift.

ORWELL, George. *Shooting an Elephant, and other Essays*. 1950. Includes "Politics versus Literature: An Examination of *Gulliver's Travels*".

PETRIE, Sir Charles. *Bolingbroke*. 1937.
The Jacobite Movement. New edition, 1949.

QUINTANA, R. *The Mind and Art of Swift*. 1936.

SEDGWICK, Romney (editor). *Lord Hervey's Memoirs*. 1952.

STEIN, Walter. "Swift and Nihilism." *Humanitas*, Summer 1946.

STEPHEN, Sir Leslie. *Swift. English Men of Letters*. 1882.

SWIFT, Jonathan. *A Tale of a Tub*, etc. *Journal to Stella. Gulliver's Travels. Everyman's Library*.
Prose Works. Edited by H. Davis, 1939 *et seq.*

Chapter III

AULT, Norman. *New Light on Pope, with Some Additions to his Poetry Hitherto Unknown*. 1949.

BLOM, Eric. *Music in England*. Revised edition, 1947. Chapter VI.

CHURCHILL, R. C. "The Enduring Element in Pope." *Dublin Review*, October 1944.
(Editor.) Pope's *Epistle to Dr Arbuthnot*. 1950.

EVES, C. K. *Matthew Prior*. 1939.

GAY, John. *The Beggar's Opera*. 1923.
Polly. Adapted by Clifford Bax, 1923.

HERBERT, A. P. *Mr Gay's London*. 1948. With contemporary drawings.

PEARCE, Charles E. *Polly Peachum: The Story of " Polly" and "The Beggar's Opera"*. 1924. Chapter III: "Eighteenth Century Ballad Singing".

PINTO, V. de S. "The Street-Ballad and English Poetry." *Politics and Letters*, Winter-Spring 1947.

POPE, Alexander. *Poetical Works*. Edited by A. W. Ward. *Globe* edition, 1869.
Works. *Twickenham* edition, edited by John Butt, 1939 *et seq*. The most authoritative modern edition.

SITWELL, Edith. *Alexander Pope*. *Penguin* edition, 1948.

STEPHEN, Sir Leslie. *Pope*. *English Men of Letters*. 1880.

THOMSON, James. *Poetical Works*. 1853.

TILLOTSON, Geoffrey. *On the Poetry of Pope*. 1938. *The Moral Poetry of Pope*. 1946.

Chapter IV

COLE, G. D. H. *Persons and Periods*. *Pelican* edition, 1945. The essays on Defoe.
(Editor.) Defoe's *Tour through Great Britain*. 1927.

DEFOE, Daniel. *Robinson Crusoe*. *Moll Flanders*. *Journal of the Plague Year*. *Captain Singleton*. *Everyman's Library*.
The Best of Defoe's Review. Edited by William L. Payne, 1952.

DOWNS, Brian W. *Richardson*. 1928.
(Editor.) Richardson's *Familiar Letters*. 1928.
Shamela: by Henry Fielding? 1930.

HERD, Harold. *The March of Journalism*. 1952. Covers the period from 1660 to the present day.

KEIR, David. *Newspapers*. 1948. Chapters III-IV.

RICHARDSON, Samuel. *Pamela*. *Clarissa*. *Everyman's Library*.

WOOLF, Virginia. *The Common Reader*. *Pelican* edition, 1938. The essay on Defoe.

Chapter V

CHURCHILL, R. C. "Henry Fielding: The Comic and the Burlesque." *Library World*, July 1944.

CIBBER, Colley. *Apology for his Life*. *Everyman's Library*.

CLINTON-BADDELEY, V. C. *The Burlesque Tradition in the English Theatre after 1660*. 1952.

CONGREVE, William. *Complete Plays*. *Mermaid* edition. The Introduction by Macaulay, reprinted from *The Comic Dramatists of the Restoration*, includes an account of Collier's attack upon the stage.
Complete Works. Edited by Bonamy Dobrée. *World's Classics*.

DOBRÉE, Bonamy. *Restoration Comedy*. 1924.

DUDDEN, F. Homes. *Henry Fielding: His Life, Works, and Times*. 1952.

FIELDING, Henry. *Plays*. In *Complete Works*, edited Murphy, 1762.
Joseph Andrews. *Jonathan Wild*, etc. *Tom Jones*. *Amelia*. *Hutchinson's Classic Novels*, 1904-5. Also in *Everyman*. *Journal of a Voyage to Lisbon*, etc. *World's Classics*.

NICOLL, Allardyce. *A History of English Drama*. New edition, 1952.

POPE, W. J. MacQueen. *Theatre Royal, Drury Lane*. 1946.

SMOLLETT, Tobias. *Roderick Random*. *Peregrine Pickle*. *Humphry Clinker*. *Ferdinand, Count Fathom*. *Sir Launcelot Greaves*, etc. *Hutchinson's Classic Novels*, 1904-5. First three also in *Everyman*.
Travels through France and Italy. Introduction by Thomas Seccombe. *World's Classics*.
Letters. Edited by Alfred Noyes, 1926.

VANBRUGH, Sir John. *Plays*. Edited by Bonamy Dobrée. *Nonesuch* edition, 1927.

WILLCOCKS, M. P. *A True Born Englishman: A Life of Henry Fielding*. 1948.

Chapter VI

BAILEY, John, and POWELL, L. F. *Dr Johnson and his Circle*. *Home University Library*.

BOSWELL, James. *Life of Johnson*. *Everyman's Library:* new edition, 1950, with Introduction by S. C. Roberts. *Boswell's London Journal: 1762-3*. Edited by Frederick A. Pottle. Yale Editions of the Private Papers of James Boswell, 1950.
Boswell's Column: Being his Seventy Contributions to The London Magazine, 1777-83. Edited by Margery Bailey, 1951.

BOWEN, Marjorie. *Wrestling Jacob: A Study of the Life of John Wesley and Some Members of the Family*. Abridged edition, *Thinker's Library*, 1948.

BURNEY, Fanny. *Diary*. *Everyman's Library*.

CHURCHILL, Charles. *Works*. Edited by James Laver, 1933.

CHURCHILL, R. C. "Dr Johnson and his Ersatz Successors." *Adelphi*, January-March 1944.

COLLINS, A. S. *Authorship in the Days of Johnson*.

DOBRÉE, Bonamy. *Life and Letters of Lord Chesterfield*. 1932. *John Wesley*. 1933.

DUNCAN-JONES, Austin. *Butler's Moral Philosophy*. *Pelican philosophers*, 1951.

GEORGE, M. Dorothy. *England in Johnson's Day*. 1928.

GODWIN, George. *The Great Revivalists*. *Thinker's Library*, 1951. Chapter VIII: "Wesley and the Methodist Revival".

GREIG, J. Y. T. *David Hume: A Biography*. 1931. (Editor). *The Letters of David Hume*. 1932.

HUME, David. *Essays. World's Classics.*
Treatise of Human Nature. Everyman's Library.

JOHNSON, Samuel. *Rasselas.* With Voltaire's *Candide.*
Edited by Henry Morley, 1884.
Lives of the Poets, etc. (See under **General** above.)
Poems. Edited by D. Nichol Smith and E. L. M'Adam,
1941.
Letters. Edited by R. W. Chapman, 1952.
Selected Writings. Edited by Julian Symons. *Falcon
Classics.* 1951. (A more extensive selection also available
in the *Reynard Library.*)

KLINGENDER, Francis D. (editor). *Hogarth and English
Caricature.* 1944. Relates Hogarth to the life and
literature of the age.

LASCELLES, Mary. "*Rasselas* Reconsidered." *Essays and
Studies of the English Association.* 1951.

LAW, William. *A Serious Call to a Devout and Holy Life.
Everyman's Library.*

LEAVIS, F. R. "Johnson as Critic." *Scrutiny,* Summer
1944.

MACNABB, D. G. C. *David Hume. Hutchinson's University
Library,* 1951.

MORLEY, John. *Walpole. English Statesmen,* 1889.

POSTGATE, Raymond. *That Devil Wilkes.* 1930.

PREVITÉ-ORTON, C. W. *Political Satire in English Poetry.*
1910.

REYNOLDS, Sir Joshua. *Discourses.* With the Letters to
The Idler. World's Classics.

ROBERTS, Michael. *The Modern Mind.* 1937. Chapter V:
"Reason and Imagination in the Eighteenth Century".

TURBERVILLE, G. S. (editor). *Johnson's England.* 1933.

VULLIAMY, C. E. *James Boswell.* 1932.
Mrs Thrale of Streatham. 1936.

WEARMOUTH, Robert F. *Methodism and the Common People of the Eighteenth Century*.

WESLEY, John. *Journal*. *Everyman's Library*.

Chapter VII

ARNOLD, Matthew. *Essays in Criticism*. Second series, 1889. The Essays on Gray and The Study of Poetry.

BLAIR, Robert. *The Grave*. With Life of Blair, etc., n.d.

CECIL, Lord David. *The Stricken Deer: A Life of William Cowper*. 1929.

CHURCHILL, R. C. "Gray and Matthew Arnold." *Criterion*, April 1938.

COLLINS, William. *Poems*. Edited by Edmund Blunden, 1929.

COWPER, William. *Selected Letters*. Edited by E. V. Lucas, 1911.
Selected Poems. Edited by Hugh l'Anson Fausset. *Everyman*, 1931.

FAUSSET, Hugh l'Anson (editor). *Minor Poets of the Eighteenth Century*. *Everyman*, 1930.

GARROD, H. W. *William Collins*. 1928.

GOSSE, Edmund. *Gray*. *English Men of Letters*, 1882.

GRAY, Thomas. *Selected Letters*. Edited by John Beresford. *World's Classics*, 1925.
Poems. Edited by A. J. F. Collins, 1948.

HUMPHREYS, A. R. "A Classical Education and Eighteenth-Century Poetry." *Scrutiny*, September 1939.

MURRY, John Middleton. *Countries of the Mind*. First series, 1922. Includes an essay on Collins.

NICHOLSON, Norman. *William Cowper*. 1951.

SHELLEY, H. C. *Life and Letters of Edward Young*. 1914.

THOMAS, Gilbert. *William Cowper and the Eighteenth Century*. Revised edition, 1949.

WHITE, Gilbert. *The Natural History of Selborne.* Edited by James Fisher. 1947. Includes White's poems.

YOUNG, Edward. *Night Thoughts.* 1821.

Chapter VIII

BURNEY, Fanny. *Evelina. Everyman's Library.*

CRABBE, George. *The Village.* Edited by Arthur Sale. 1950.
Life. By his son, the Reverend George Crabbe. 1901.

CUMBERLAND, Richard. *Memoirs. World's Classics.*

GIBBS, Lewis. *Sheridan.* 1947.

GOLDSMITH, Oliver. *Miscellaneous Works.* Edited by David Masson. *Globe* edition, 1868.
Collected Letters. 1928.
The Traveller and *The Deserted Village.* Edited by M. M. Weale, 1950.

GREENE, Graham. *British Dramatists.* 1942.

JONES, M. G. *Hannah More.* 1952.

LEAVIS, F. R. *The Great Tradition.* 1948. Introduction relates Fanny Burney to Richardson and Jane Austen.

MELVILLE, Lewis. *Life and Letters of Laurence Sterne.* 1911.

NICOLL, Allardyce (editor). *Lesser Comedies of the Eighteenth Century. World's Classics.* Includes Murphy, Colman, etc.

SHERIDAN, R. B. *Plays. World's Classics.* Also in *Everyman.*

STERNE, Laurence. *Tristram Shandy.* Introduction by George Saintsbury. *Everyman,* 1912.
A Sentimental Journey. Introduction by Virginia Woolf. *World's Classics.*

THOMPSON, H. W. *A Scottish Man of Feeling.* 1931.
(Editor). Mackenzie's *Anecdotes and Egotisms.* 1928.

WOODFORDE, James. *The Diary of a Country Parson: 1758-1802.* Edited by John Beresford. *World's Classics,* 1949.

Chapter IX

FEARENSIDE, C. S. (editor). *Classic Tales.* 1906. Includes Walpole's *Castle of Otranto.* (Also in *Shorter Novels of the Eighteenth Century. Everyman.*)

GIBBON, Edward. *Autobiography. World's Classics,* 1907. *The Decline and Fall of the Roman Empire.* Edited by Oliphant Smeaton. *Everyman,* 1910.

HODGART, M. J. C. *The Ballads. Hutchinson's University Library,* 1950.

HOUSMAN, John E. (editor). *British Popular Ballads. Life, Literature, and Thought Library,* 1952.

PENZOLDT, Peter. *The Supernatural in Fiction.* 1952.

PERCY, Bishop. *Reliques of Ancient Poetry. Everyman's Library.*

RADCLIFFE, Mrs Ann. *The Mysteries of Udolpho. Everyman.*

SCOTT, Sir Walter. *Journal.* New edition, 1891. *Narrative of his Life.* Continued by J. G. Lockhart. *Everyman,* 1906.

WALPOLE, Horace. *Selected Letters. Everyman.* (See also under FEARENSIDE above.)

YOUNG, G. M. *Gibbon.* 1951.

Chapter X

ASHTON, T. S. *The Industrial Revolution: 1760-1830. Home University Library,* 1948.

BRAILSFORD, H. N. *Shelley, Godwin, and their Circle. Hutchinson's University Library,* 1913.

BURKE, Edmund. *Letters.* Introduction by H. J. Laski. *World's Classics.* *Reflections on the Revolution in France.* Edited by H. P. Adams, 1951.

CHURCHILL, R. C. "The Utilitarians." *Tribune,* 11 November 1949.

Disagreements: A Polemic on Culture in the English Democracy. 1950. Chapter IV: "Culture and Agriculture".

COBBETT, William. *Autobiography.* Edited by William Reitzel. New edition, 1947.

COLE, G. D. H. *William Cobbett.* 1925.

FAST, Howard. *Citizen Tom Paine.* 1945.
(Editor). *The Selected Work of Tom Paine.*

GODWIN, William. *The Adventures of Caleb Williams.* 1904. *Political Justice.* Abridged edition, 1926.

HALÉVY, Élie. *The Growth of Philosophical Radicalism.* New edition, 1949.

HOLCROFT, Thomas. *Memoirs. World's Classics.*

KLINGENDER, Francis D. *Art and the Industrial Revolution.* 1947.

LASKI, H. J. *Political Thought in England from Locke to Bentham. Hutchinson's University Library,* 1920. For the philosophical background of Burke and Bentham.

MALTHUS, T. R. *Essay on the Principle of Population. Everyman.*

MORLEY, John. *Burke. English Men of Letters.*

PAINE, Thomas. *The Rights of Man. Everyman's Library. The Age of Reason. Thinker's Library.*

PEARSON, Hesketh. *Tom Paine.* 1937.

PETRIE, Sir Charles. *George Canning.* New edition, 1946.

RODWAY, A. E. (editor). *Godwin and the Age of Transition. Life, Literature, and Thought Library,* 1952.

SMITH, Adam. *The Wealth of Nations. World's Classics.*

WOLLSTONECRAFT, Mary. *The Rights of Woman. Everyman's Library.*

WOODCOCK, George. *William Godwin: A Biographical Study.* 1947.

Chapter XI

BLAKE, William. *Poetical Works*. Oxford illustrated edition, 1934.
Poetry and Prose. Edited by Geoffrey Keynes. *Nonesuch* edition.

BRONOWSKI, J. *William Blake: A Man without a Mask.* 1943.

BULLETT, Gerald. *The English Mystics*. 1950. Chapter on Blake.

BURNS, Robert. *Poems. World's Classics.*
Letters. Edited by J. de L. Ferguson, 1931.

CARSWELL, Catherine. *Robert Burns*. 1930.

ELIOT, T. S. *Selected Essays*. Revised edition, 1934. Includes an essay on Blake.

GILCHRIST, William. *Life of Blake. Everyman's Library.*

GODWIN, George. *The Great Mystics. Thinker's Library,* 1945. Chapter VI: "Emanuel Swedenborg and William Blake".

GRIERSON, Sir Herbert. *Lyrical Poetry from Blake to Hardy.* 1928.

MURRY, John Middleton. *William Blake.* 1933.

SHIPP, Horace. *The British Masters*. 1933. Chapter on Blake.

SPEIRS, John. *The Scots Literary Tradition.* 1940.

WILENSKI, R. H. *English Painting*. 1933. Chapter on Blake.

INDEX

PRINTED IN GREAT BRITAIN BY UNIVERSITY TUTORIAL PRESS LTD, FOXTON
NEAR CAMBRIDGE